First Edition 2025
Copyright © 2025 by Anthony Abelaye
All rights reserved
Printed in the United States of America

No portion of this book may be reproduced in any form without written permission from the publisher or author, except as permitted by U.S. copyright law.
Names have been changed to protect the privacy of the individuals.

Thai Dyed

—

Heartbreak and Hedonism in the Land of Smiles

Anthony Abelaye

Part One

Phuket, Thailand

November - December 2021

Hamad International Airport (DOH)
Doha, Qatar

15-hour flight from Dallas to Doha. Spent much of the time trying to sleep while semi-bent like an upright pretzel. Very uncomfortable, and I was expecting it. Many Indians on the flight. Older Arab guy I was sitting next to was on his way to Palestine via Jordan.

"You have to cross the bridge," he said. He assumed that I knew what bridge he was talking about. "You know, the bridge," he repeated.

My stomach was cramping up badly during the flight. Maybe I'd been sitting too long. Or maybe I'm getting too fat. Sitting there quietly writhing in pain as I felt my intestines slowly tying themselves into knots, like a python curling up in my abdomen. I'd made the mistake of bending down to tie my shoe. I think that's what triggered it. I must have squeezed my intestine into a position it didn't like and now it was slowly twisting and constricting.

I took deep breaths. Tried bending forward, then arching my back while in the seated position. Tried tilting my head back and yawning. I wanted to scream in pain. Instead, I sat there and suffered in silence while the flight attendants lugged giant metallic carts down the aisles. The food service portion of the flight was underway. Dinner was being served.

Qatar Airway served us three hot meals during the flight. Not too hungry now. Otherwise, I would get something to eat at one of the few Starbucks-like shops sprinkled around this airport. Most of the kiosks here are selling perfume. Never would have thought that perfume was so high up the list of traveler requirements. I realized later that I was in the shopping mall area of the airport. The food court is located in another section. This place is huge.

My flight to Phuket doesn't board until 1:00am Doha time.

—

Fifteen hours earlier in Dallas while I was waiting to board my flight, I noticed a group of roughnecks sprawled out in the seating area. They were all similarly dressed in worn blue jeans, dusty cowboy boots, baseball caps. I figured them to be American good ol' boys on their way to work out on an oilfield somewhere in the Middle East. But later when we were standing in line at the gate, I asked one of them if I was standing in the correct line. He responded with a distinctly foreign accent. I later overheard him speaking with an older Indian man, who was curious about where he was from, where he was going. The roughneck explained he and his buddies were returning to South Africa. They had been working as farm hands here in the States, but now that the soybean harvest was over, they were returning home. I counted at least ten or twenty of them standing around the boarding area. These guys traveled all this way just to go work on a farm. I don't know if this says more about the U.S. job market or the South African economy.

Day 4 in Phuket. Patong Beach. I think I've seen enough of this place. One week might be four days too long.

I plan to travel further down the Andaman coast to another beach town called Karon. I'll stay there for a week, then cut over to the eastern side of the island. My original plan to fly out to Chiang Mai and then fly to Bangkok might have been overly optimistic. Too many plane rides and sitting around in airports. I'd be wasting money. There was mention on one of the Thailand travel forums on the Internet that Chiang Mai might be going into another Covid lockdown. I wouldn't want to fly out there only to get trapped in a 14-day forced quarantine. I think I'll stick around Phuket, instead.

Been doing a lot of walking these past two days. 7.55 miles on the 20th, and 11.6 miles on the 21st. My knees have been hurting, so today I'll take it a little easy.

I've been eating at this burger stand across the street from the beach. Place is called "Five Loaves." I met the owner yesterday, a chubby thirty-something Millennial-looking guy. Big guy, a little taller than me with a full beard that poked around the edges of his Covid face mask. He was hovering around the customer side of the counter. We got to talking, and he mentioned that he's got a few other stores open now. He rattled off the cities in Phuket where he's opened up shop. One is a full sit-down restaurant in old Phuket Town. He showed me pictures of the place on his cell phone.

I asked, mistakenly, if Five Loaves was a play on the Five Brothers name.

He corrected me. "You mean, Five Guys," he said.

But no, he got the name Five Loaves from a story in the Bible. He is also a pastor, he explained, and has even hired a few people in his congregation to work in his restaurants.

He asked if I was visiting Thailand by myself. Yes, I said. This wouldn't be the last time someone asked if I was visiting by myself. I later surmised it was a way to judge if a guy was here for sex tourism. Bangla Road was just around the corner, and at night the neon-lighted bars are lined with half-naked Thai girls waiting for customers to buy them drinks. Or other things that might be up for sale.

When my order was ready, I wished him luck and ate my burger across the street near the beach.

—

Thirty years ago I fell in love with a blonde-haired girl from Colorado. Thirty years later, to the month, the pattern appears to be repeating itself.

My mind is consumed with fretful anticipation. Nervous expectation. Heart flutters and palpitations. I find myself filled with sudden bouts of doubt and uncertainty. Is she using me? A deep sigh. A quickness of the breath when I think of her. This was unexpected. Completely out of the fuckin' blue. Does she feel the same way?

Try to play it cool.

Force yourself to focus on other things — writing, traveling. Traveling, remember??

Go for a walk. Get something to eat.

Goddamnit. Why are you always so obsessive? You're setting yourself up for bitter disappointment. It will never work out. And then she texts me, asks what I'm doing, and — BOOM — all that pep talk self-talk gets thrown right out the fucking window.

We went to dinner — pizza and pasta. Then we went for 90-minute massages at one of the spas down the street. Not one of those filthy jerk-off parlors where the girls and ladyboys try to grab your crotch when you're passing by. I took her to one of the genuine spas, where many Western tourists go, who come hobbling up the storefront steps, clumsy and plodding like large farm animals compared to the svelte gracefulness of Thai women. Afterward we sat on the beach, holding hands and chatting. Romantic teeny-bopper stuff.

I walked her back to her room later. She's renting a tiny room at the K&K Guesthouse, a run-down motel on the other side of Bangla Road. No air-conditioning, she said. Just a fan. But she is acclimated to the heat. She grew up in the Thai countryside in the Songkhla province in far southern Thailand.

Her name is Chaiya. She has a thirteen-year-old son, and her elderly mother works on a rubber tree plantation.

Heartsick. Obsessed. I'm unable to think about anything except her. My vacation doesn't even matter anymore. Where am I going to sleep? What am I going to eat? It doesn't matter. I don't care. I feel like I've been sent to this seemingly random spot on the other side of the world specifically to meet her.

I'm fifty fuckin' years old (fifty-one, to be exact). What the hell am I doing?

Listening to Current Joys' "A Different Age" and Cigarettes After Sex over and over again.

Trying to come off like some sophisticated international man of mystery when I'm just like every other douche-bag flying into Phuket with a few measly thousand dollars to spend on whores, food, and drinking. Company-approved vacation.

Has your vacation been approved?

Yes, sir. I submitted my vacation request last month.

Well, make sure your tasks are covered by the rest of the team and update them on all the project statuses before you leave.

Yes, sir. Right away, sir. Go fuck yourself, sir. I might never come back from this trip, sir. So fuck you and fuck your goddamned company approvals. From this point on, I shall endeavor to do whatever the fuck I want.

Okay. Enjoy your vacation.

Thank you very much, sir.

Cell phones, text messaging, WhatsApp.

Interesting how modern technology allows us to remain in contact with the muses of our dreams. Long after the dream has faded and the facade has fallen away.

I've been here a week. Checking out of the Hotel Clover and making my way a few miles south to Kata. I didn't come all this way just to get my heart broken by some bar girl.

Onward.

Spending a few days in Kata. Later, I'll walk to Karon Beach and see what the water is like.

I have this room booked till Monday, November 29th. Today is the 27th. Might not be another two day's worth of stuff to see or do out here. I see many empty shops and many empty bars. The streets are vacant. No traffic. No people. The Covid pandemic has wreaked havoc on the place.

Fine with me.

Need to clear my head of all that bar girl bullshit.

Weak instant coffee in the room. Better than nothing. The A/C blows cold, and the balcony is nice and roomy with enough space to hang my clothes out to dry. I could live in a place like this. This won't be the last time such thoughts cross my mind as I travel through the region.

I'll take another walk to the supermarket this afternoon and pick up more supplies — beer, cheese, bread, mustard.

Save money. Got to start sticking to some kind of budget. Most importantly — no more wasting money in nightclubs and bars.

Use this time to hole up in broken down hotel rooms and get some writing done.

The place I'm at now is called *Phuket Racha at Kata Homestay*. It sits at the end of a quiet street. The entire town is too quiet. I can tell in better times this place must have been crowded with beach-goers and tourists. Now, most of the hotels and motels sit vacant. At night, the buildings across the street and across the alleyway sit eerily darkened. One lone lamp post illuminates the street with a dull orange glow. No traffic on the street, and no people. The place is devoid of life. Eerie.

The cab ride down here from Patong cost $400 Thai baht (about $12USD).

More teen romance shenanigans.

Walking around Patong's crooked sidewalks at night and holding hands. Feeling lighter than air and in love, love, love.

Rainy Thai evening. Late-night dinner, late-night conversation at a busy Thai restaurant. I accidentally make eye contact with the older farang men sitting at tables with their Thai dates. I glance around. Many of these couples aren't talking or even looking at each other. They seem ashamed to be seen with one another. Older gentlemen with their older women. Heads down. Quietly eating in silence. Embarrassed.

Boy meets girl. Boy loses girl. Boy reunites with girl. It's all happening in his mind. The girl has ten other "customers" that she's hustling on the side.

But no, not my girl.

She tells me two Korean men tried to "buy" her last night and take her back to their room. I see tears welling up in her eyes. Her voice is trembling. They behaved disgusting and offensive toward her, and she asked Mamasan if she could move to another table. The rule is you're not supposed to abandon a customer if he bought you a drink, but she asked Mamasan to make an exception. They were trying to grope her under the table.

She tells me she had a boyfriend in Malaysia, and that her mother forbade her from working in the bars. One of her friends convinced her it was easy money. Same old story told over and over again across who knows how many tiny plastic tables in crowded Thai restaurants.

Her biggest fear is that she will be kidnapped and sold into sexual slavery. Or going back with a customer to his room and discovering five other guys waiting there for her.

We have plans to eat at Maru Korean BBQ for lunch tomorrow.

She's flying to Bangkok on Monday. She has an appointment to get a tattoo for good luck.

—

In Rawai at *The Title KR Beach Condotel*. Arrived yesterday afternoon. Checking out tomorrow.

I returned to Patong and spent another night at the *Hotel Clover.*

She spent the night and was planning to come with me to Rawai, but first she had a few errands to run that rainy morning. She had to go to the bank and get something squared away with the mortgage on her apartment in Hat Yai, and then she had to stop by the clinic and get a Covid swab test for her job at the bar. Her test came back positive, which was unfortunate. Which meant that I also had to get tested. We brought her back to her hotel, and then I asked our taxi driver to take me back to the clinic for testing. My test came back negative. Luckily, we're both fully vaccinated. She'll need to get a PCR test at the hospital to confirm the results of the swab test. If that also comes back positive, she'll need to quarantine for 14 days, which means I probably won't be seeing her again.

This has all the tell-tale markings of a doomed relationship where you can sense the ending before it ever began.

I instructed our taxi driver to take me to Rawai, leaving Chaiya behind in her room.

"Your friend look like she crying," he said.

"Yeah," I replied.

"You don't mind dating bar girl?"

"She's just a friend," I say.

Looking at me through the rearview mirror, he nods his head.

Making my way up to Phuket Town today.

Two more weeks to go, and then the dream is over.

Was thinking to fly over to Bangkok for a quick trip, but I don't feel like dealing with airports.

Is it real?

She's a bar girl. They all have their tricks.

But it feels real to me.

They are experts at building and maintaining the illusion. They have had hundreds of men to practice upon. Prey upon. You are merely a single line amongst many that she has placed in the water. Hook, line, and sinker.

She texts me every night before she goes to sleep and again first thing in the morning when she awakes.

How do you know she hasn't been sending similar text messages to other guys? Ten other guys? Twenty other guys?

When we're in my hotel room laying amongst the soft pillows and blankets, I snuggle into her and feel her sleeping in her silk pajamas. Her breathing is soft and slow. She's like a kitten. There are no other guys in the room with us. I have her all to myself. All is fine in the world. This is where I belong.

Careful.

The years spent working in bars have turned those purring kittens into feral cats. Quite adept at surviving in the wild and seizing prey. That pussy has claws.

We had our first argument the other night. I accused her of sneaking out with other customers. (She had only been gone for half an hour. She went back to her room to retrieve a clean shirt to sleep in.) I was filled with such jealousy and rage. My heart was breaking.

She shot back, saying "I'm a bar girl, not a restaurant worker. You knew who I was when you met me."

—

I've been here in Phuket for two weeks. Twelve more days to go before the dream ends and I fly back to reality.

After Rawai, I caught a taxi to Phuket Town and spent a couple of days wandering around downtown, an area densely packed with old-school architecture and low-rise buildings, its streets an endless stream of motor-scooters and small trucks. It has a Main Street, USA feel to it, with old-timey shops. But unlike businesses in Main Street, USA, which are nowadays primarily the domain of overpriced consignment shops, boutique cafes, and places catering to niche hobbyists, the small businesses in Phuket Town aren't just there for nostalgia and reminiscing about the good ol' days with "historical landmarks." The businesses here still provide real, practical services — watch/jewelry repair, tailoring, hole-in-the-wall shops selling kitchen or household appliances, coffee shops, Thai cafes. Most of this place looks like it was built in the 1940s or 1950s.

I caught a taxi back to Patong late yesterday morning.

I miss her. She was my lunch and dinner partner. She tells me she might be able to take another Covid re-test in a few days and get a negative result, but the sad reality is that I probably won't get to see her again before I leave for good on December 15th. But this is likely more significant to me than it is to her. For her, there will always be more customers. For me, there was only her.

Back in Patong, I bought some Indian food for her and left it at the front desk of her hotel. It's a seedy rundown place located halfway down a dank alley with massage parlors and questionable looking Thai restaurants. No air-conditioning, she told me. Just a room with a toilet and bath down the hall. A few of the other girls from the bar stay there as well.

I brought a loaf of bread, some ginger tea, and a few oranges to her room. She said she also needed money to buy food, so I slipped $3,000 baht into the grocery bag and left it at the front desk of the guest house where she's staying.

She still has a fever, off and on.

Spent some time with another girl I'd met my first night here. I met her for another short-time session at a place called the *Gemma Hotel* on the edge of the city, going toward the hills on the southeastern side of town.

Her name is Mei, and she is a hustler. She's young, in her late-twenties. Tight, smooth body, tight little ass. Almost looks Korean with a short bobbed haircut. She says she was born and raised here in Thailand.

She wastes no time with the "I miss you" messages on WhatsApp. It's clear she makes most of her money outside of the bar. She is tactical in her approach and uses military time when setting appointments. "Meet me at 18:00, okay baby?"

I paid the front desk clerk for the room — $450 Thai baht. Mei met me in the room a few minutes later and asked me to shower first. When I came out of the bathroom, she was wearing red lingerie and kneeling doggy-style on the edge of the bed, looking back at me over her shoulder, smiling. Like I said, the girl doesn't waste any time. I paid her $3,000 baht for her time.

She shares a room upstairs at the Gemma Hotel with two other girls. Rent and electricity, she says, is around $6,000 Thai baht per month ($177USD as of this writing), split between the three of them. Two girls share the double-bed. The third sleeps on a mattress on the floor.

Later, she met me downstairs and had changed into a conservative looking Thai-style dress, frilly white and draped down to her ankles. I assumed she was done working for the night. One of her roommates also joined us while we waited for a taxi to take us back to Bangla Road.

"Do you have any friends for me?" her friend asked, smiling flirtatiously. She looked older than Mei by about ten years. She was a little thick and not as graceful or alluring as Mei, who was at my side, holding hands and smiling.

Mei asked me to join them for dinner at a Thai restaurant, which I agreed to at first, but after waiting over twenty minutes for the taxi standing out in the muggy heat (we were farther from the downtown area than I realized), I became tired and wanted to go back to my hotel room to rest. When I explained as much to Mei, a brief look of disappointment flashed across her face, but then I think she remembered the nature of our relationship and wrote me off with a sayonara smile. And then I realized she was probably disappointed that I wouldn't be there to foot the bill. I gave her another $1,000 baht and told the girls to enjoy themselves.

—

Time is running out. Ten days left on this 26-day trip. Longest vacation I've ever taken, but also the fastest. I have been working full-time jobs since I was 21. Now at 51, I think I need more than measly two-week vacations. Six-week vacations seem more reasonable to me, if I am to continue holding down a steady job.

Thirty years a working schlep.

Time in the blink of an eye — GONE.

Catching a flight out to Bangkok later this afternoon.

When I told her of my plans yesterday, she asked why I didn't wait for her since she thought we had made plans to travel to Bangkok together. I've got little more than a week left, I explained. Time is running out. She might not get that negative Covid test until the day I'm scheduled to fly back to the States.

All dreams must come to an end, even the ones you had thought long since forgotten.

I never got a chance to say farewell to my Indian friend who owns that T-shirt and trinket shop down a side alley and across the street from Karon Beach. Located in what appeared to have been a once-busy outdoor touristy shopping mall, his little shop, along with the Thai restaurant across the way, where I ate a few times after my morning swim, were the few places which remained open in a city that had evidently been devastated by the Covid pandemic these past two years.

Each morning, I'd walk from my hotel in Kata down to Karon Beach. After my morning swim, I'd walk along the long stretch of beach road leading back to my room. The streets were mostly empty of traffic or people. Across the beach, numerous store fronts were boarded up with "For Rent/Sale" signs.

Along this seemingly desolate stretch of vacant shops, I noticed a man waving a restaurant menu at me from across the street. I crossed over and followed him a short ways down an alley where there was a lone restaurant open for business. Both times I ate there, I was the only customer, and I sat at my table eating my breakfast while an Indian guy sat a few yards away in front of his shop of t-shirts and trinkets. It was just me and him in that long, empty shopping corridor. He kept looking my way as if he was eager to engage in conversation, and when I finally removed the headphones from my ears and nodded "hi" to him, he pounced and began peppering me with all the usual questions.

Where was I from?

Was I married?

How long was I staying?

What did I do for a living?

What did I think of the food? The beach? The weather? Thailand in general?

Was I traveling alone?

He spoke fluent English and reminded me of many of my Indian co-workers back home. I assumed he possessed some kind of advanced education. Perhaps a degree in engineering or one of the sciences. This is usually the case with Indian transplants in the U.S. But no, he arrived in Phuket 17 years ago with a friend to enjoy some of the partying and nightlife. He didn't know what he wanted to do with his life. He just wanted to have a little fun, he explained. He grinned slyly, then quickly glanced around to see if his wife was still within earshot.

"It all changes when you get married," he said.

He met his wife, a Thai native, a few years after his arrival. They've been running their little T-shirt and trinket shop for the past 15 years and live in a two-room apartment above their store. They have two boys, one in grade school and the other just entering his teens.

"The schools here are not very good," says my friend. "They need to learn English."

Since they live in Thailand, I reasoned, isn't it better that they learn to speak Thai?

"Yes, of course," he says, "They teach the Thai language in school, but if they want to succeed in the world, they will need to learn English."

I notice him speaking Thai to the restaurant staff while I leisurely finish off my breakfast — two sausages, a slice of ham, a fried egg with toast, coffee and orange juice.

"How long have you been speaking Thai?" I ask.

He couldn't speak a word of Thai when he first got here 17 years ago, he says, but he had no choice but to learn if he wanted to live here.

"You eat a lot," he comments, eyeing my empty plate.

"I'm American," I say, patting my stomach. "Can't help it."

"You're not that big. Swedes are fatter."

"Really?"

"Yes. Germans, too," he says, holding his arms out around his midriff. "Much fatter than Americans."

"You get a lot of Swedish and German tourists out here?"

"Before the Covid," he says, "but not now. Last two years, very difficult."

I tell him about my plans to travel further south to Rawai, and he offers to drive me.

"What about your shop?" I say. "Don't you need to watch it?"

He waves me off. "It's okay. My wife will watch. I can drive you. I get bored sitting around all day. When are you going? You want to go today? I charge you a fair price."

I tell him I plan to leave the next day, and we make plans to meet at his shop, but Chaiya texts me later that afternoon and wants to meet for dinner later that evening. I check out of my room in Kata and catch a taxi back to Patong.

I never see my Indian friend again.

What can I say? I was in love.

—

Bangkok.

Spending the next few nights at the *Arawana Regency* in Bangkok, on Soi Sainamthip just off Sukhumvit Road. Got in earlier this evening.

Feeling a little adventurous and brave, I decided to catch the subway from the airport into the city. I rode a series of escalators down into the bowels of the airport and was hopelessly confused. I couldn't tell which was what as every sign was in Thai with no English translation. I wandered around aimless until I found a large corridor and followed it until I came upon what appeared to be a set of turnstiles. Nearby I spotted uniformed employees sitting in a glass booth. I bent my head toward the little hole in the glass window and asked if any of them spoke English. They looked at me, confused and slightly annoyed. One of the women waved dismissively with a swiping motion, and I couldn't tell if she was telling me to go in a certain direction or was telling me to fuck off. But I spotted more signs further down the corridor and saw what appeared to be a row of ticketing machines. There was a map of Bangkok (presumably) and near each stop was a tiny button you had to select. When you pushed one of the buttons, the price of the fare to that destination would be displayed on a tiny screen above the payment area where you either slipped in bills or coins. This was hardly evident to me at first, and I stood off to the side and observed a few people purchasing their tickets so I could see how it was done.

It's about a 30-minute trip into the heart of the city on the subway. A pleasant enough experience. The trains are clean and modern. People, Thais mostly, are quiet and reserved. Unlike public transportation in the U.S., there were no homeless people, no drunken lunatics or people blasting loud music from portable electronic devices. No loud-mouthed teenagers. When people spoke, it was in hushed tones. And strangely (to me, anyway) — no garbage or litter anywhere.

—

I had dinner at an Indian restaurant a few doors down from my hotel — chicken tikka masala, garlic naan, and two bottles of Singha beer. $750 Thai baht. The evening's entertainment was a very large cockroach which crept up from the underside of my table and popped up between my elbows as I was tearing off a piece of naan. It quickly scurried sideways along the edge of the table and disappeared down the side of the wall. I said nothing and continued eating. What would be the point of voicing my complaint? There were probably a million of those things crawling behind the walls. But I suppose seeing one crawling around my table did speak to the overall cleanliness of the place, and over the next few days I would be plagued with watery diarrhea, which I attributed directly to the meal I ate in that establishment.

I didn't wander too far that first night. Feeling burned out and drained. Mildly heartbroken. The timing is always a little off. What is the lesson to be learned here? Do not become so easily attached to the unattainable. The damaged ones, the calloused ones, the ones who were forced to grow up in a world of deprivation and desperation. Those who have not had the same choices in life. They're doing what they can to survive.

From their perches atop barstools, the girls gaze out upon the slow, steady stream of farang (foreign men) with money in pocket and an itch in their pants. Easy pickings. These poor, lonely individuals, soon to be parted from their measly funds.

The younger, more attractive girls can pick and choose from the more attractive ones, the ones seeming to possess greater virility, with muscles and tattoos. The guys with the toned physiques and confident postures. Well-dressed and put together. No matter how handsome or drippingly virile, he is no match for the cunning bar girl. She spends much more time playing the game than your typical run-of-the-mill whore-mongering vacationer. These so-called "two-week millionaires."

I recognize the dynamics, and yet why do I become so filled with jealousy and insecurity? This is the lesson which must be learned. I am again given an opportunity to learn how to move beyond infantile emotional attachment.

———

Not far from my hotel, I happened upon an alleyway filled with girls in skimpy outfits standing outside a number of neon-lighted massage parlors. One spotted me and began shouting and waving me over. Then, like a chorus of birds the other girls erupted in unison, shouting and calling for me to join them. It was a cacophony of "Handsome man! Handsome man! Massage! Massage!"

I ventured into the crowd and a few of them latched onto my arm, trying to pull me towards their shop. One girl grabbed hold of me and clung tight with both arms around my arm, her face buried in my shoulder, while the others pulled me this way and that, but the girl on my arm refused to let go and I eventually went with her. When it was clear that I had made my choice, the shouting and groping stopped and the girls went back to chatting amongst themselves and ignored me as if I had become invisible.

—

These are some of the memories I will take with me.

Walking from my hotel in Kata down to Karon Beach with the song, "A Different Age" by Current Joys, playing over and over again. The town is vacant. A mere handful of tourists in sight. The beach wide and beautiful. I spend some time in the warm water with just the right amount of wave action.

I walk the entire length of the beach, and on the way back I stop by the little Thai restaurant and spend some time chatting with my Indian friend sitting in a plastic chair at his T-shirt and trinket shop across the way.

Late-night dinners with her at hole-in-the-wall restaurants all over Patong — Thai, Korean, Indian. (Crappy pizza at a crappy Italian restaurant that first night.)

Walking her back to her room at the K&K Guesthouse and then walking along the Paton beachwalk back to my hotel at the Baan Boa Resort on the southern end of the beach. It's just after midnight, and a breeze comes in off the Andaman sea. I've got a nice buzz on from all the drinks we had earlier that evening.

Laying next to her in bed at the Hotel Clover. Buried beneath a pile of white pillows and blankets. Feeling the warmth of her body against mine, snuggling next to her and listening to her slow and steady breath while she sleeps.

―

Today I walked from my hotel to Wat Pho and the Reclining Buddha. A two-hour walk. On my return, I walked half-way back before I decided to catch the BTS lightrail back to Asoke station on Sukhumvit Road. My feet were aching, and I was exhausted. It was a total of 14 miles that I had walked, according to my Samsung Health App.

I'm drinking alone in my hotel room now, feeling heartbroken and drained. This isn't love. Love doesn't make you feel this way.

What the hell is this feeling?

This is the lesson which must be learned.

Love is not doubt.

Love is not mistrust.

Love is not suspicion.

Feeling such things is evidence that suggests what stands before me is an illusion. A lie.

There is no substance. There is nothing.

(As I write these words, she texts me on WhatsApp: "What R U doing?")

―

Standing outside a flower garden across the street from Wat Pho temple, I stopped to catch my breath and change my socks. They were completely soaked through with sweat from the nearly two-hour walk from Sukhumvit Soi 22. (Anticipating this, I'd brought along a few extra pairs.)

I watched tourists and worshippers leaving the temple complex. There was very little traffic on the street. The sun was shining. Butterflies floated amongst the flowers in the garden. It was as if that tiny little section of the city had been paint-brushed with colors I'd only ever seen in dreams. Filled with such serenity and feeling suddenly uplifted, as if I had become weightless and at risk of floating away across the Chao Phraya River, I broke into tears and uncontrolled sobbing. I am not sure why. Perhaps feelings of unworthiness and the guilt associated with it? Was I merely some undeserving hack?

I'd been waiting a lifetime to experience this very moment in this particular space and time, and here it was. And here I was, and I realized I was utterly lost and hopelessly unprepared.

Drenched in sweat from that two-hour walk in the Bangkok heat and feeling like an out-of-place loser, I felt as if I had been cleansed. I wandered into the garden and found a bench just off the little paved walkway and removed my shoes to air out my feet and rest a bit before heading over to the temple.

—

Wat Pho was the first and only temple I visited in Thailand. If you've seen one shining golden Buddha, you've seen them all. I took a few pictures and wandered around the complex in the heat of the noonday sun amongst the crowds of Chinese tourists in frilly, flowery dresses posing for Instagram photos. A young, dreadlocked white woman, her arm around her Rastafarian boyfriend, had brought along her yoga mat, rolled up and slung over her shoulder. Get thee back to Khao San Road, hippie poseurs!

—

It's a weekday morning, and I passed throngs of office workers heading into work. I stopped at a food cart, one of many that had lined up along the sidewalk, and purchased a plastic container of rice and chicken. Breakfast. I walked a few blocks down and ate it sitting on the steps of a closed shop.

My goal for today was to walk down Sukhumvit Road and see how far I could go. I didn't have anything else to do. Perfect opportunity to go wandering about. A plaque along the way mentioned something about Sukhumvit being the longest road in Thailand. I made it as far as the Phra Khanong River.

I happened upon the river by accident. Sukhumvit Road appeared to dead-end where the off-ramp of the freeway came over the river. I couldn't go any further on foot, so I followed some broken concrete steps leading down to the riverfront and found myself wandering through a little neighborhood of derelict shacks lining the narrow pathway. I was surprised to find people living here. Mere blocks from the highrise buildings along Sukhumvit and right next to the freeway, here was a quiet reprieve from all the noise and traffic, a meditative solitude of poverty here on the outskirts of town.

The path along the riverfront led me through what was essentially people's backyards. I could see them going about their daily routine — an elderly woman hanging clothes out to dry; an old man napping in a plastic chair; someone watching TV in a gloomy unlit room; small children riding little plastic tricycles and wandering dangerously close to the water's edge. I was intruding on their privacy. None of them made eye contact or acknowledged me when I passed. Perhaps they had grown accustomed to strangers wandering through their backyards?

—

2pm flight back to Phuket. I miss the beach.
And so begins my final week in the Land of Smiles.

—

Back in Texas.

After two days of sitting around in airports and on airplanes, I'm finally home.

Traveling from Phuket and arriving in Qatar is a psychological and cultural jolt. Imagine experiencing the sweetest, most exquisite dream and then awakening into a depressing gray land of frowning faces and looming shadows. It is four in the morning, and your flight has arrived at Hamad International Airport.

Just a few hours earlier, you were in the Land of Smiles, enjoying the company of friendly and beautiful Thai women, eating the best food, living the best life, and then you have to board a long-haul flight packed with boorish Indians, getting bumped and jostled, watching them nit-pick and argue with the flight attendants. They always seem unnecessarily confrontational and rude, mistrusting and irritable.

Exiting the plane, you see the trash littering the floor. They've thrown everything on the floor — soiled napkins, empty wrappers, plastic cups, empty water bottles. Piles of trash everywhere. It's like the polluted banks of the River Ganges. What a mess.

You stumble off of the plane and into an airport terminal crowded with women dressed in burkas; Somali refugees sleeping on the floor — the stench of their collective body odor is like a wall surrounding and shielding them; Afghan youths affecting hip-hop, thug life attitudes with their sideways baseball caps and shiny new sneakers. All seemingly unfriendly and unsmiling, oppressed. All the world's Third World countries have converged into this one spot — Hamad International.

Saudi princes, tall and proud, dressed in immaculate white robes, cut through the crowds with the confident authority of wealth and status.

Filipino women scurry along in tiny groups, probably on their way to work as cleaning ladies or hotel/restaurant staff in some wealthy Arab nation — Dubai, Qatar, Saudi Arabia.

At the food court, there is a long line of people waiting to place their orders at the McDonald's counter, and I am one of them. A small, rotund Indian man shoves his way to the front of the line and asks the smiling Filipino girl working behind the counter if he could order a cheeseburger. She happily obliges. Perhaps because the place is so busy and chaotic, or that there are so many people coming to retrieve their orders as their numbers are called, that no one except me seems to notice that this dude just cut to the front of the line and ordered himself a cheeseburger, much to my annoyance.

I've got an eight-hour layover, so I settle in and make myself comfortable in this depressing gray purgatory. I am nobody with nowhere to go.

—

I spent my last week in Phuket with her. She never spent the night in my hotel after that second night, but we would spend the entire day together and late into the evening. She would send me a text message as soon as she awoke (some time between noon and 4pm), and then I would walk over and meet her at the guesthouse where she was staying. We'd go for lunch or dinner, then end the evening with drinks at some beach-side restaurant bar.

Nearing the end of my stay, I took her shopping at Central Market in Phuket Town. Bought her a purse, some dresses, and perfume. Simple things. Not more than a few hundred dollars on my American Express.

Later, we went to Airport Beach and missed getting any decent photos of the planes taking off directly over the beach, zooming out into the sky over the Andaman Sea. We sat on the sand and watched the sunset, eating coconut ice cream over sticky rice. This was one of the happiest moments I'd had in a very long time.

On the way back to Patong, we stopped for dinner at Three Monkeys, a supposedly popular and highly-rated restaurant tucked in the jungle hills overlooking Phuket Town. Over-rated by both our assessments. She ordered pork chops, which were dry and hard as a rock, she later confessed. The braised pork I had was just okay.

—

Each morning at the Hotel Clover, like every other hotel in the area, old white men file into the restaurant for breakfast with the bar girls they picked up the night before, the girls looking a little rough for the wear in the harsh morning light. Some, who had the foresight to bring along a change of clothes, arrive dressed in sweatpants or modest dresses. Others are still in their bar girl outfits from the night before — short shorts; leather mini-skirts and platform heels; frilly lingerie tops. Here, I use "girls" generously. Some of these women, without the disguise of makeup, appear old and haggard. Grandmotherly. While others still look as if they were yanked right out of some Third World shack and shipped on a bus straight to Bangla Road. They have that monkey flesh-eating indigenous look to them, haggled for a bargain at the lowest Thai baht and scooped up by drunken Aussies or American perverts. These old white men with lust on their minds and Viagra in their veins. Grasping, groping with wrinkly old fingers. Poking and prodding with wrinkly, pink misshapen penises. The harsh morning light reveals the guilt and shame on a few faces. And regret, for the ones that ended up with the grandmothers. While they wait patiently in line at the breakfast buffet.

I opt for breakfast at the cafe across the alley from the Hotel Clover. The clientele is more digital nomad than pervy grandpa.

I see two older white men in their sixties come out of the hotel lobby accompanied by a dark-skinned Thai girl. She's got that typical bar girl look — long black hair to her waist, tiny and thin, tattooed, wearing short cutoff jeans and a flimsy tank-top. Each of the old men have got their arms around her, and they're smiling and joking as they walk her to her scooter parked on the side. I watch them through the cafe window as they each give her a big hug, then hop into a taxi and drive off. The girl is left standing there next to her scooter. She straddles the thing and for a few minutes struggles to get it started. One of the taxi touts, a frail looking old man, thin and wrinkled, comes over to see if he can help. Together they try to start the thing. Still no luck. Then, after about five minutes, one of the bellhops comes over and tries to kickstart it manually. He's a big guy and moves the tiny scooter around like a toy. The tiny girl could barely move it off its kickstand earlier. Between the three of them, they finally get the bike started. The girl thanks them and drives off.

Just one example of locals helping each other in this very strange economy.

—

She came to my hotel to see me off. My last day in Thailand. It was early for her — just before 11am. The night before we'd gone for drinks, then caught a tuk-tuk back to my hotel. She wrapped her arms around me, gave me a big hug and left. I wasn't expecting to see or hear from her again.

I had already gone for my morning swim and had eaten breakfast at the cafe across the alley. I was in the middle of packing when she texted and met me a few minutes later in the lobby. She squealed excitedly and greeted me with a tight hug, the same way she squealed and hugged me tight when I picked her up that night I returned from Bangkok.

"Where do you want to go?" I asked.

"Let's just go for coffee at your place," she said, her arm in mine, pointing to the cafe across the street where I'd just eaten breakfast.

She ordered some Thai noodles, and then we shared a chocolate cake, which she decided was her favorite when we ate there a few days before. She let me have the cherry.

Afterward, we went up to my room and laid in bed watching TV until it was time to catch a taxi to the airport.

—

I traveled half-way around the world and fell in love. Or did I just hallucinate the whole thing? Was it all just an illusion?

Nothing there. No substance to any of it. Just fleeting moments of lovey-dovey emotion.

Her eyes. Her smile. Her lips. The enchanting, graceful ease with which she carries herself. Absolutely mesmerizing. But so fragile. Brittle. The slightest misstep, one careless misspoken work or misunderstanding, and it all disappears in a puff of smoke.

Poof — she's gone.

—

This was supposed to be a simple travelogue recounting my vacation in Thailand. All of that got blown out of the water when I met her my second day here. From then on, my days were spent waiting to be in her company. Time passes like a dream. Those short trips I took to Kata, Karon, Rawai, and Bangkok — just ways to pass the time and keep myself distracted until I could see her again.

Such a pleasant feeling — that feeling of giddy anticipation and butterflies in the belly.

—

I did not sleep well. Thinking about her all the time.

Memories of my stay at the Baan Boa Resort along Patong Beach. Memories now slowly fading into the distance.

I wait for the sunrise before heating water in the electric kettle for my morning cup of instant coffee. Most hotels come equipped with an electric kettle and packets of instant coffee, sugar, and powdered cream. These kettles are so much more efficient than the crappy Mr. Coffee mini-coffee makers found in American hotels.

I go for my morning swim, then get breakfast at one of the hotel restaurants. I return to my room, shower, and hang my swimming trunks and shirt on the balcony to dry. I stretch out on the bed and take a nap with my phone beside me, waiting for her next text message.

—

I have lived half a century and had to wander halfway around the world to find the love of my life.

—

Stuck in lovesick purgatory. I've been back a week, but it doesn't feel like home anymore. Is this what long-term travel does to you? Can a single month-long trip even be considered "long-term?" Is this what happens when you travel halfway around the world and fall in love completely by accident? There are no real accidents, are there?

It's the Christmas season, but I'm not feeling it this year. The wife has bought a ton of gifts and placed them under the Christmas tree. I made sure to hang the Christmas lights around the outside of the house before I left for Thailand, but that was the extent of my involvement this year. The wife and granddaughter put up the tree and ornaments.

On Christmas Eve, I remained holed up in my room, fantasizing about the life I could be living on the other side of the world.

The wife kept bugging me to open my presents, but I didn't feel like it. Our daughter and granddaughter weren't going to arrive until tomorrow, Christmas Day. I would rather wait for them, I explained.

She came into the room when I was in one of my brooding, irritable moods.

"C'mon, just open one!" she says. "There's one present you're really going to like!"

"Why did you buy me all those gifts? I don't need anything."

"Just open one!"

"When we get divorced, you can keep the house," I said. "I just want to keep traveling."

She stops for a moment, sniffs and wipes something from her eye.

"There's something in my eye," she says quickly and leaves the room.

Why do I always have to be such an asshole? We've been married since 1998 and probably should have gotten divorced ten years ago. We've discussed it often. But why did I have to be such an asshole and bring it up right now, during Christmas, which has always been a special time for our family? We don't celebrate any other holidays. I've always found it ironic that my wife gets more excited about the Christmas holiday than I do. And she's Muslim.

—

It's the day after Christmas. I just barely returned from Phuket, and I booked another three-week trip back to Thailand, from the end of March to the middle of April next year. I plan to celebrate my 52nd birthday out there. I don't even have any vacation time. I'm planning to take it without pay, if my managers even let me go at all. I haven't yet put in the request. And I somehow got it in my head that I'll be able to extend my stay to a month by bringing along my work laptop and working remotely from whatever hotel room I happen to be staying at.

How the hell did I allow myself to get so easily knocked off balance?

This isn't love. This is obsession. This is desperation.

This is madness.

—

All she has to do is send me a single text on WhatsApp, and I am once again pulled into her orbit, like a yo-yo on a string.

My defense systems blown hither and tither, like a shoddy house of cards in a tornado. My alarm systems dismantled. I am rendered completely vulnerable and exposed.

Once again I find myself going down that delusional road and thinking that anything is possible. Mind is creator!

Sure, my job will allow me to work remotely — from Thailand.

We'll get married. It will have to be a Thai marriage because I haven't yet divorced my current wife back in the States.

I'll buy a condo on Phuket and begin a new life with my new wife.

All of it completely doable.

And completely batshit insane.

What the fuck am I thinking?

—

Our relationship is on-again, off-again. But only in my mind. She doesn't know how many times I've deleted her number from my cell phone and cleared out our WhatsApp chat history.

And yet, I am unable to completely purge her from my life. All she has to do is send me another text message, and I end up adding her right back to my contacts list.

But something doesn't feel…..right. Something has changed. Maybe she's got another customer on the line. Maybe her feelings have simply changed. Time and distance has an eroding effect on relationships.

I suspect some other guy is paying her bar fine and taking her out.

I understood this from the beginning. Knew it was bound to happen sooner or later. My mind tells me to simply let her go. No hard feelings. This is the nature of her work, how she needs to survive and support her son and her mother — she's just a bar girl doing bar girl things in Thailand. If she enjoys a good fuck now and again, even if it is just for money, who am I to whine and complain about it? I'm 8,000 miles away. What am I going to do?

But the heart refuses. It behaves selfishly. Desperately.

I need to let her go.

She still texts me when she awakes each morning and again when her shift is over and she reaches her room at the K&K Guesthouse. There will come a time when she stops texting me regularly, and I will feel the pang of rejection at that seeming non-event. It is inevitable that some customer will come along, pay her bar fine, and take her out for a day or two, maybe even a week. This is the nature of the business. This is how bar girls survive.

I recall her warning to me on one of the first nights she stayed with me: "I'm a bar girl, not some restaurant worker."

Do you fault the tiger for its stripes? Or the leopard for its spots? Or a bird that flies from — you get the picture….

Her energy is hers, and my energy is mine.

Enjoy it for what it was and let it go. The connection is no longer there. Time and distance made quick work of that.

Aside from the hassles of having to provide proof of Covid vaccinations and negative PCR test results at nearly every checkpoint entering and leaving Phuket airport, leaving the airport in Bangkok, or catching my connecting flight out of Hamad International in Qatar — these checks were merely minor annoyances with whatever airport official waving you through after a quick glance at your documents. The only time I actually got stopped by immigration was when I landed back on American soil and was trying to get through immigration at Dallas-Fort Worth International. It was mostly my fault, I think. I should have kept my fucking mouth shut.

The first immigration officer I met once we got off the plane asked how long I'd been in Thailand. When I said a month, he raised an eyebrow.

Then he asked if I was bringing back any fruits or vegetables, and I blurted out, "No, just t-shirts and gifts for the wife and kid."

He leaned back in his chair and looked at me incredulously. "You took a month-long vacation to Thailand? Without your family? How did you get away with that?" He shook his head, chuckling, and slipped my passport into a clear plastic box before handing it back to me. Still smiling and shaking his head, he said I'd need to go through a secondary inspection to check my luggage for fruits or vegetables.

So I make my way through a cordoned-off section and downstairs to the secondary screening area. An agent wearing blue surgical gloves asks me to place my backpack and suitcase on a narrow examination table.

He begins looking through my belongings, pulling out one item at a time and holding it up at eye level. He asks me the same questions as the previous guy and expresses the same incredulity when I tell him I spent a month in Thailand.

"You spent a month in Thailand without your family?"

He finds an opened box of condoms in one of the side pockets of my Tumi satchel. "I see you had some company," he says.

I laugh nervously. He tells me I'm good to go and sends me on my way.

My stomach is turning the entire cab ride back to the house, and my Egyptian driver is taking his sweet time moseying down the George Bush Turnpike, driving five, ten miles under the speed limit. It must have been those crappy tuna salad and chicken salad sandwiches I purchased from one of the kiosks back at Hamad International.

When I get home, I barely say a word to the wife as I barge through the front door, throw my luggage down, and sprint for the bathroom to avoid a potentially explosive situation in my pants there in the hallway.

We chat every day on WhatsApp. Still on the usual schedule. She'll text when she awakes in the morning and again when she's home from the bar.

We talk about meeting again in March, but I doubt this long-distance relationship will make it that far. It's bullshit. An illusion. These Thai bar girls are expert scammers, and I allow her to string me along. I know what I'm in for: heartache and madness. Heartache and madness.

Yet, I go along willingly. Phuket is where I must return. There is where I wish to live my life now.

2022.

2 + 0 + 2 + 2 = 6.

Is 6 the money number in numerological terms? Will 2022 be a money year? What are the tarot card readers and astrologers saying?

Why do I fixate on such things when I am in a state of uncertain love? This bewildered state of confusion?

I trust her, and I believe her. She has been nothing but honest and upfront with me. She is innocent in so many ways.

I don't know if I can wait until March. I need to see her RIGHT NOW.

But — my Youtube astrologer says for Aries to wait until February before making any definite plans. What may seem like a sure thing in January might not be so certain come February.

I will heed that astrological warning that I randomly came across on the Internet and wait.

—

I find myself watching tarot card readings on Youtube. Libra readings for her. Aries readings for me. They all say the same thing — twin flames, powerful attraction, long-distance separation. Soul mates. Mirror energies.

What they describe is how I feel. But is it how she feels?

The tarot card readings also say that things are in a holding pattern. There is no movement. Which is true. I won't be able to travel back to Phuket until March. Taxes. Work. Vacation days. Money.

It's a whole lot of bullshit. But it gives me something to hope for. Some vague idea of which way the wind is blowing. Does it matter if the wind blows at all? Or in which direction? Aren't I the sailor on my own seas of fate?

Need to make it to March. Just hold on until March.

—

She gets too drunk most nights. In fact, it is very likely that she is an alcoholic.

I have started writing so many break-up text messages in my mind, but I always stop myself from sending them. She is in such a fragile state right now that telling her yet another bit of bad news might wreck her completely. Or not. But I wouldn't want to take that risk and be the one responsible for sending her over the edge. I do still love her.

Sounds toxic and manipulative, doesn't it?

(As I pen these very words, I receive a text from her, and all that stuff I just wrote, once again, goes right out the fucking window.)

—

I sent her $50,000 Thai baht via Western Union to buy a new iPhone. She says her old phone was no longer detecting the SIM card. Calls were dropping. Sometimes she'd get a "No Signal" alert.

On a video call with me, she was crying as she was walking home and saying how everything in her life seems to be falling apart. She stopped by 7-Eleven to see if she could buy a new SIM, but they didn't sell one that was compatible with her cell service. The next day she took it to the cell phone repair shop at the Big C in the Jungceylon shopping mall. The tech told her they'd need to ship her phone back to Apple to be repaired, and it could take 14 to 21 days before she got it back. So I just gave her the money. She didn't ask for it. I just sent it to her and told her to buy a new phone.

Am I trying to buy her love, or am I doing this because I love her?

I'm a goddamn fool.

I still haven't requested that time off from my job for when I travel back to Phuket at the end of March. Mercury is in retrograde until February 4th. Until then, communications will be hit or miss, according to the Youtube tarot card readers. Why take a chance?

She usually texts me in the morning when I wake up. Often she'll send me a few texts in the middle of the night, just to let me know that she's thinking of me.

So far, not a peep from her since she received that $50,000 Thai baht I sent her a few days ago.

Maybe this was all she'd been waiting for? The big payday?

Is this how our relationship ends?

Whatever.

I will refrain from reaching out to her until I hear from her.

This could be the "TRUE INTENTIONS REVEALED!!" that the Youtube tarot card readers have been warning about.

Whatever happens, it was a good feeling while it lasted. That hopeful love, soulmate, twin-flame connection.

Whatever.

—

Many Youtube tarot card readings for Aries are indicating some kind of financial windfall coming my way. No sign of anything so far. Maybe they're talking about my yearly HCL bonus? I should be getting something at the end of this month.

—

She texts me every day. She moved back to her apartment in Hat Yai for a few weeks, and now she's complaining about the dust in her place. From what I can tell from the short video clips she sends me on WhatsApp, it looks like she lives in a converted storefront, what is known as a Thai shop house. Her "front door" entrance is a huge sliding accordion-style gate, like the sort you see at the front of your typical storefront. This metal gate makes up the entire front side of her apartment, and the roof over her kitchen is sheets of corrugated aluminum.

—

My job won't allow me to work overseas, but at least they approved my two-week vacation at the end of March. I asked her to plan an itinerary for all the things she wants to see and do while I'm out there. I still have reservations if this will work out, if this will progress beyond anything more than a short-term long-distance relationship. For now, perhaps it's best if I just see her as my own personal tour guide whenever I'm in Thailand.

—

Part Two

—

Phuket / Hat Yai / Bangkok

March - April 2022

Got home last night. I'd just spent the past three weeks in Thailand.

Budget and finances blown out of the water. Credit cards maxed out. Checking account balance in the negative. (Thank you, IRS.)

I lost my Charles Schwab debit card the first night I was there, and an ATM machine ate my Wells Fargo card the day before I was scheduled to return home.

I was supposed to fly home on April 14th, but I neglected to read the updated travel requirements for people traveling into the U.S., which requires a negative Covid PCR test not older than one day prior to the day of travel. I thought it was still 72 hours, like the last time. I wasn't allowed on the flight and had to catch a taxi back to Patong and scramble to find another hotel and book another flight. All of this going on with my credit cards maxed out and zero cash left in any of my accounts.

This was the overall vibe of this trip: Broke-ass broken down junk heap.

Heartbroken. Used and abused. Left out in the cold.

And yet I still found time to enjoy myself. This was Thailand, after all. The Land of Smiles. I grew more familiar with Bangkok and learned to ride the BTS lightrail everywhere. I explored all the back alleys and seedy clubs along Nana Plaza and Soi Cowboy. Patong Beach was like visiting an old friend, although I'd only traveled there for the first time not more than four months previous.

That first evening in Patong was really the only time I spent alone with her. We agreed to meet on Bangla Road, and when I spotted her, she was wearing a curve-hugging yellow cotton dress and a white baseball cap. Here was my Thai beauty again in the flesh. Skin so white, lips pouty and red, long black hair down the length of her back, her breasts looking plump and ripe. And her eyes. Her eyes are the first thing you notice about her. I get lost in them, and she can see right through me.

I'd brought along a $300 bottle of perfume from the States. Something she'd asked for. We dropped it off at her room, then went for drinks at a hotel bar along the beach.
Then she tells me she's getting plastic surgery.

I said I didn't think she needed it. I say to her, "Don't you notice all the guys that just stop and stare at you when we're walking by?"

She doesn't like her nose, she says. It isn't straight enough.

She doesn't like her eyes. They aren't slanted enough. She wanted to look more Asian.

"You are beautiful," I say. "You don't need plastic surgery!"

She smiles. "I'll think about it," she says, dismissively.

I walked her to a spa around the corner, where she had an appointment for a two-hour massage. Then we went for a late-night dinner at the Thai shop we frequented previously on my first trip out there. I walked her back to her room at around two in the morning.

—

She got her period and for the next few days she stayed holed up in her room at the K&K Guesthouse. She gets really bad cramps those first few days. I didn't realize how bad until she texted me to bring her some pads and pain medicine. I buy the stuff and take it up a gloomy flight of stairs to her room on the second floor. In the dark, narrow hallway I didn't see her laying on the floor in the doorway to her room. I jumped at first, thinking it was a ghost or an overdosed crackhead. She crawled back into her room and dragged her way to the side of her bed, writhing and twisting in pain.

I asked her why she wasn't in bed. She prefers to be on the floor when she has these cramping episodes, she explained, huffing and puffing. She pulled herself up to a sitting position against the bed. From where I was standing in the doorway, I could see her stomach churning and writhing, like one of those automatic massage recliners at that mall, or like that scene from 'Alien' when the baby alien bursts from that guy's stomach. I went down to the pharmacy across the street and bought her some stomach cramp medicine, but she later told me it didn't help.

Quick note about pharmacies in Patong: When I tried to buy the entire box of medication, the tiny woman behind the counter shook her head and waved me off.

"Too much!" she said. Then she opened the box, peeled off a strip of the sealed pills, and handed it to me. "Use little bit first. Come back if you need more."

This would never happen in the States.

She took me out to dinner the next night to celebrate my 52nd birthday. I told her we could wait until she felt better, but she insisted on seeing me. She was still suffering from cramps and couldn't walk very far, so went to this steakhouse right across the street from Bangla Road. She was wearing a bright red short dress and, for some reason, a plastic tiara on her head. I paid for everything, of course. A Thai bar girl never pays. An unspoken rule of the trade.

After dinner, I walked her back to her room and called it a night.

We didn't have any real conversations this time or any time afterward over the course of the three weeks I was there. She always seemed distant and unavailable, rarely making eye contact when I spoke to her. Where was that same cozy, loving feeling from the last time, last November when we first met? And yet....she continued texting me sweet-nothings in the morning when she awoke and at night before she went to sleep.

(We never once spent the night in the same bed the entire time I was there.)

We flew to Hat Yai that following weekend. She wanted me to see her house and the repairs she'd made to the leaky roof and the kitchen ceiling. I'd sent her $25,000 Thai baht a few months prior to pay for these repairs. (She didn't ask. I just offered.)

She also wanted me to meet her mom, who lived in the country a few hours to the south. She was catching a bus up to Hat Yai to meet me.

I got a room at the Leevana Hotel, a short distance away. It was an older hotel. A bit dated. But I like these older places because the rooms tend to be a lot larger with more walking space and room to spread out, unlike newer "boutique" hotels, where the rooms seem to be designed with more thought given to maximizing space efficiency and not so much to guest comfort.

Her mom took a liking to me. She was much friendlier in person and nowhere near as serious as she looked in the few photos Chaiya shared with me. Her mom was always laughing and cracking jokes, which Chaiya had to translate for me since her mom didn't speak any English, and I of course spoke no Thai. She's an older woman — looks to be in her 70s or 80s. She gave off a cozy, grandmotherly energy. Very animated and affectionate. Smiling and joking around with her two grandkids and Chaiya's brother. One of the grandkids was Chaiya's son, a 13-year-old boy with big, droopy eyes and thick eyelashes.

None of them spoke any English, and we communicated mostly using hand gestures and smiles with Chaiya providing the necessary translation.

I've often wondered how she came to speak English so well. She claims she learned it mostly by watching Youtube videos. I've accepted this explanation and have been unwilling to delve any deeper since this would very likely lead into an uncomfortable discussion about her past experiences with foreign men.

Her past is none of my business. And anyway, I've probably been with just as many women and still can only speak my native English, like the dumb American I am. The few foreign words and phrases I know, I learned in massage parlors and whorehouses. (My wife never had the patience to teach me any Arabic.)

The day after her family's arrival in Hat Yai, we took them for lunch at a halal restaurant near the airport. Chaiya's mother is a strict Muslim, so she could only eat at Halal places. Often, Chaiya would prepare her mother's meals at the house.

Afterward, we took them shopping at one of the local malls, with Chaiya driving the rental car we picked up near the airport. All four of her relatives crammed into the backseat — mom, brother, son, and niece.

I continued paying for everything, a practice that I would soon come to regret — looking back now with my credit cards maxed out and over the limit, my checking and savings accounts hovering near zero.

Why did I allow this to happen? Was I desperate? Stupid? Blinded by love?

All of the above, perhaps. Mostly, I think, it was just plain burn-out. Burned-out from working. Burned-out from living. Burned-out from being in a dead marriage. Burned-out from living day to day in the suburbs. The same old goddamned thing day after day, every fucking day. Just fucking burned-out, man. Thirty years of working full-time. Thirty years of being a full-time schlep. Two-week paid vacations sprinkled here and there. What amounts to little more than breadcrumbs at the chicken factory.

For once I just wanted to fuck off and not give a shit about anything. Just go out there and enjoy myself. Really cut loose. Do the things that I feel like doing. Not worry about agendas, itineraries, guilt trips, or even Time itself.

My to-do list was this: NOTHING. I had nothing to do. Nothing left to prove. The mortgage on our house was finally paid-off after fifteen years — fifteen years earlier than we had originally anticipated. Our daughter was grown and making a decent salary at her job in the oil and gas industry. Granddaughter is chubby and happy.

It was time for me to fuck off. Go do the things that I felt like doing.

Yeah, sure. I knew I'd be spending a pretty hefty wad of cash, but I didn't care. I could always make more when I got back. Money is energy — it comes and goes. I wanted to relax and enjoy myself, and spend time with the person I thought I was in love with.

The whole time I'm paying for everything, but since it was for her family, I didn't mind. I didn't care.

Three kids and her mom. Poor people from the country spending a few days in the big city of Hat Yai. I bought them t-shirts and new shoes. Makeup for her mom. Paid for their mango ice creams. I wanted them to have fun and enjoy themselves. I am the wealthy stranger in their strange land backed by the mighty U.S. dollar.

Sometimes it feels like she's not even there. I am sitting right beside her, and she becomes distant. She checks out, like her soul or her mind has floated off somewhere, and I'm left there feeling alone. And it's more than just that feeling of being alone — I feel a pang of loneliness wash over me. It is a sad feeling of distance and abandonment.

Is she ignoring me? Is she purposely trying to make me feel this way? Purposely trying to shut me out? Push me away? It seems as if she doesn't want me physically there beside her.

Lost little girl who imprisons herself in her own little world.

My time and money are running out, and I must return to reality. No time for these mind-games.

The language barrier makes it difficult to discuss the emotional nuances of childhood abandonment, betrayal, and loneliness. What might otherwise be discussed intelligently between two people who speak the same language fluently instead becomes a strained silence, a windswept chasm of non-communication.

If you were only looking at my social media posts — on Youtube, Instagram, and Twitter, where I was posting on a daily basis photos and videos of food, the beach, city street scenes — you would never guess that the sole reason for my traveling back to Thailand was to see her again.

After spending time with her mom in Hat Yai, we planned to fly to Bangkok. Chaiya had been compiling a bucket list of places she wanted to visit and saving it to her phone — rooftop bars, Chinatown eateries, night markets. Activities that I, too, was eagerly anticipating. For months, I had envisaged romantic evenings as we rode in the back of a taxi or strolled down Sukhumvit, holding hands like we did just a few months prior along Patong Beach.

For the first few nights, I booked us a room at a 5-star hotel across the street from the Wat Pho temple. I thought it would be romantic and set the mood for the remainder of our time there. I ended up sleeping alone in that place the entire time I was there. About a week later, still sleeping alone, I relocated to a cheaper room at the Red Planet Hotel just off Sukhumvit near the BTS Asoke station, where I really decided to cut loose and let the monger in me take over.

Whatever notions I had of spending romantic evenings alone with her went right out the fucking window.

Hah! What horseshit.

She failed to mention the real reason she wanted to go to Bangkok was because she had scheduled the surgery for her nose-job later that week, which was to take place at some hospital in the far northern part of the city.

And, oh, she would need me to pay the $10,000 baht down payment the day of the surgery, which was scheduled to take place that following morning. We were sitting outside a night market when she told me.

"Why didn't you tell me sooner?" I said.

"I'm telling you now," she replied.

I had some trouble withdrawing the money from the row of ATMs outside the crowded night market where we were planning to have dinner. I told her the bad news.

"My American Express card isn't working here," I said. "I'm not sure why. I'll call them when I get back to my hotel."

She stopped talking to me for the rest of the evening, and refused to even look me in the eye. I'd been having problems with my American Express card earlier in Hat Yai trying to buy her a gold necklace. None of the jewelry shops could get the card to accept the charge.

When Chaiya and her friend, Kanthip, who was acting as our chauffeur and tour guide, dropped me off at my hotel, I found another ATM around the corner from Wat Pho and was able to withdraw the $10,000. I texted Chaiya, telling her the good news. She texted back, saying that Kanthip would be there in the morning to retrieve the money. We texted each other good night with the usual kissy-kissy, lovey-dovey emojis.

Then I caught a tuk-tuk to Nana Plaza. No sense pretending that our relationship was anything more than a financial one at this point, one where I stood to get little out of it other than being shown around town on my own dime.

—

I went to Nana Plaza to see if I could find Oum, a woman I'd met there a few nights earlier. She didn't look like the other bar girls working in those clubs when I spotted her that first evening, sitting out on the patio outside one of the downstairs clubs. She looked about a decade older than the other girls and, considering the environment, was dressed rather conservatively in a thin, peach-colored knit sweater and matching knit mini-skirt, in sharp contrast to the other girls, who were dressed in French maid outfits or flight attendant uniforms or were just walking around in skimpy bikinis. She had long black hair, dark skin, and big dark eyes. Your typical Thai beauty from one of the northern provinces. (As if I knew the difference.)

She latched onto my arm as I was passing by and refused to let go of me until I bought her a drink. She ordered drinks for the both of us, and we sat at one of the small tables. She possessed a self-confident air about her — and she was, I noticed as we were chatting, quite voluptuous beneath that knit sweater. I was explaining something to her when she held her hand up. "Slow down," she said smiling, "I don't speak English very good. Speak slowly, please."

A few drinks later, she asked if I wanted to get a room. I was too tired and had been drinking prior to my arrival, I explained, and probably wouldn't be able to perform.

"I just want to have a few drinks then head back to my hotel," I said.

She smiled gently and said okay, then she took me into the club to watch the go-go dancers onstage. We had a few more drinks, and at some point over the course of the next hour or so, she had me up against the stage, gyrating her ass into my crotch while I massaged her shoulders and cupped her breasts. Then she spun around and leaned into me, running her tongue around my ear before jamming it into my mouth. There was another, younger girl off to my side, short and pixie-like with dyed silver hair and dressed in a skimpy outfit. She was dancing along with us and massaging my shoulders. I'd been buying her drinks as well.

I realized Oum had made herself wet. I could feel the dampness on my leg as she grinded her crotch against my thigh. I howled with excitement and slapped her ass. The pixie girl cracked up laughing, then threw her head back and mimicked my howling. I noticed an Indian couple sitting at one of the tables directly in front of us. The Indian woman was watching us with a look of shock and disgust on her face.

I changed my mind and got us a room.

"Oum no work tonight!" said one of the mamasans, recognizing me as I came walking up to the patio the following evening. "You come back tomorrow!"

"That's fine," I said. "I'll just have a drink."

I should have kept my mouth shut. Two old mamasans swooped toward my table like pigeons descending upon food tossed into the street and began hustling me for drinks. I ducked inside the club and sat at one of the bleacher seats off to the side of the stage and towards the rear. I was looking for that younger girl from the previous night, the pixie girl that was massaging my shoulders and howling along with me. She was a little firecracker, short and cute. I spotted her sitting near the front next to an older gentleman who looked to be in his seventies. Another girl sat on the other side of him. Both girls had their arms around him, playing with what little gray hair remained on his head. The old man sat there stone-faced, not saying a word to either of them.

I spent more time watching the girls interact with customers in their seats than paying any attention to the ten or so girls dancing onstage. If you could call it dancing. Most were just swaying back and forth in a lackluster fashion, like fish swimming about restlessly in a crowded fish tank.

Then someone sat next to me. I looked over and it was Oum.

"I THOUGHT YOU SAID YOU NOT SEE ME TONIGHT?" she said, yelling loudly into my ear so I could hear her over the thumping music blasting throughout the club.

"MY PLANS CHANGE," I yelled back.

"I BUSY TONIGHT," she said. "I HAVE TO MEET SOMEONE. NOT CUSTOMER."

"OKAY."

"YOU COME BACK TOMORROW NIGHT?"

"OKAY."

"YOU PROMISE?"

"YES."

I noticed her looking at me sideways in the darkened club, her eyes narrowing. "WHY YOU NO TEXT ME SAY YOU COMING TONIGHT?"

"MY PLANS CHANGE. I JUST COME SEE IF YOU HERE."

"WHAT YOU DOING BY YOURSELF?"

"I DRINK BEER THEN I GO."

Seemingly satisfied with my response, she pecked me on the cheek and ducked out of the club. I noticed she was wearing that same peach-colored knit sweater from the night before but with a pair of jeans.

I didn't feel like waiting around for that other girl and left before the mamasans could hustle me into buying them more drinks. The old bats were aggressive. And annoying.

I texted Oum the next morning, and we made plans to meet for dinner later that evening.

After Chaiya's surgery, she spent a few days recuperating at her friend Kanthip's apartment. She sent me a selfie with her nose all bandaged up and her eyes nearly swollen shut. It looked like she'd met the business end of a baseball bat down a dark alley somewhere.

Once again, I found myself with a lot of free time on my hands. And waiting for her. Just as I had waited for her to get over her Covid illness last December. Just as I had waited for a text message from her each day telling me that she'd just woken up. "Is the princess ready to begin her day?" I would usually ask. "Ya," came her usual reply. Then we'd meet for lunch or dinner somewhere.

"I'm probably not going to see you again the rest of this trip," I said to her, shortly before her surgery.

"I'll only need three days to recover," she said. "Then we can fly back to Phuket together.

This would turn out not to be the case, and even as I write these words nearly four months later, she is still struggling with the impact of that botched surgery and hasn't been able to work at all.

But at the time, I just shrugged and decided to make the most of my time in Bangkok while I waited for her to recover.

Chaiya wouldn't be able to work at the bar while she recovered, which meant she would have no income. She was going to need financial assistance. Surprise.

And, oh, she would need me to put her up in a hotel near the hospital for ten days, so she could have a place to rest and recuperate while she waited for her follow-up appointments at the clinic.

And, oh, she would need me to pay for her airfare back to Phuket.

And by the way, she was also planning to fly back to Hat Yai. She wanted to celebrate the end of Ramadan, known as Eid in the Muslim community, with her mom and the rest of her family. So if I could pick up the tab for that as well as the bus fare from Hat Yai to her mom's house four hours to the south, it would be greatly appreciated. Thank you very much.

Whatever naive and idiotic notions I was still clinging to at this point of spending romantic evenings with her in Bangkok was thoroughly, decidedly flushed down a Sukhumvit sewer. I was like some feral animal that had been released back to its whorehouse keepers.

I felt free again. Sort of. But heartbroken and over ten grand in debt. This was the real surprise. How did I spend so much fucking money in such a short amount of time?

Don't bother answering that. I already knew the answer.

—

Chaiya stayed with her friend Kanthip the entire time we were in Bangkok and up until the day I flew back to Phuket. She was our unofficial taxi driver, tour guide and chaperone. Everywhere we went, she also came along.

Kanthip was an animated, excitable woman in her forties, diminutive and lively. And she loved to talk. She never stopped talking. Born and raised in Bangkok, she was like an electrically-charged offshoot of the city itself. Barely able to see over the steering wheel of her Honda mini-SUV, she deftly maneuvered us through the insanity that was Bangkok's infamous city traffic, zipping between cars and motor scooters with a seeming sixth-sense awareness of where every other vehicle was located physically in relation to her own at any given moment and at any given speed.

On a few occasions, she noticed me discreetly slipping on my seatbelt in the backseat, and she would laugh. "Are you scared?" she'd say, smiling at me through the rear-view mirror and keeping her foot on the accelerator.

I must have paid her a total of around ten to fifteen thousand Thai baht for all the days she drove us around Bangkok and down to Pattaya. I also picked up the tab for all of her meals.

I would sit quietly in the backseat, staring out the window, while Kanthip sped us to wherever we were going. And I sat quietly, still, while we ate at restaurants, while Chaiya and Kanthip conversed in Thai. Perhaps they were talking about old times. Perhaps they were discussing the food. I would never know. Chaiya made no effort to include me in any of those conversations. I was a stranger and an outsider. A farang. And so I sat quietly, eating in silence.

It was during these times — driving in the car or having a meal — that Chaiya seemed to consciously ignore me or pretend I wasn't there. It was as if she were angry with me for an argument I wasn't aware we'd had. Maybe she was ashamed that she had become so dependent on this wealthy (in her mind) American? Maybe she had changed her mind and decided that she was not attracted to me after all?

She would stare straight ahead and not even look at me if I spoke to her or made any attempt at conversation. She would respond in Thai to Kanthip, who then had to translate her response to me in English. But Chaiya spoke much better English than Kanthip, and I knew she understood whatever it was I was saying.

I failed to understand why she behaved this way.

Of course, the bill always came to me, and I always paid.

—

Chaiya's behavior puzzled me. I struggled to understand it then and am still now trying to figure it out months later as I write these words. The coldness and far-away distance I feel when I'm with her has to be more than just some personality quirk. She continues to text me each morning when she awakes and again in the evening before she goes to sleep, always warm-hearted and lovey-dovey, peppered with heart emojis. And yet — when I'm with her in real life, face to face, sitting right there next to her, I feel more alone than if I'd been sitting by myself in a dull gray, empty landscape. I feel this sensation of loneliness, sadness, and abandonment slowly creeping over me. Then I realized that maybe these energies were emanating from her? Perhaps I'd been picking up on her vibes? How long has she been this way? What traumatic events had she experienced in her past that caused her to become so withdrawn?

It couldn't have been anything that I had caused. We had only recently met last November, three months hence, and we hardly knew each other.

But what the hell do I know? I'm no psychiatrist or psychic Youtube tarot card reader. This was supposed to be a travel journal detailing my first trip to Thailand.

Yes, I realize that I am the classic definition of a "simp" — Internet slang for "men who are seen as too attentive and submissive to women, especially out of a failed hope of winning some entitled sexual attention or activity from them." (Dictionary.com - September 1, 2020).

Those days I spent in Bangkok, waiting around to see her — always waiting to see her — I figured I might as well spend some time exploring the city.

I thought I could catch the BTS Skytrain from Sukhumvit out to Khao San Road, but the closest it could take me was Victory Monument, which was about 3 miles away (or around 5 kilometers). An easy hour-long stroll, I figured.

I failed to take into account the Bangkok heat and the fact that I was wearing a brand-new pair of sandals that hadn't yet been properly broken in. And then I got lost trying to find the correct road leading away from Victory Monument and had to backtrack a couple of times because I was too lazy to pull out my phone and check Google Maps.

But I think that's all part of the fun in using modern technology, especially when you find yourself walking around large, densely-packed cities, like Bangkok or Mexico City. I refrain from checking my phone and instead allow myself to wander about aimlessly, following one curious looking street to another, breadcrumbing from one distraction to the next, following the crowds of people or trying to escape them. I'll have a general idea of where I'd like to end up — a particular restaurant, a cafe, a bar or nightclub — but more often than not, I'll check Google Maps on my phone an hour or two later and realize that my sense of direction is shit and that I had wandered way off the mark.

I eventually made my way to Khao San Road, after walking through what appeared to be a civic section of the city, with official-looking buildings and wide streets circling roundabouts displaying large flags and statues. Large posters of what I assumed were paintings of the royal family adorned various buildings. The area was giving off a very Communist China or North Korea vibe. Excellent place to hold a military parade. If I had been a good little travel writer, I would have made note of the street and building names. But does it matter? Probably not. Mere trivialities that anyone could look up on Google Maps. Yet another benefit of modern technology.

It was still a little early, around 11am. Most of the shops and restaurants along Khao San Road were still closed. I could tell from the billboards and unlit neon signs that during busier hours, this place must look a lot like Bangla Road in Phuket, choked with tourists and loud music blaring from every club. Nothing much to see at this hour of the day except a few backpackers loaded down with 90-liter backpacks towering over their shoulders. (Why do kids still do this? Have they not heard of the ultralight, one-bag travel movement? All you need is a single pair of underwear and your passport stuffed into a plastic sandwich baggie.)

I continued south…or was it north? Maybe it was east…? I couldn't tell. Earlier, I had noticed a river in the distance, and so I made my way toward that. It wasn't clear how to get to the riverfront, but I wandered down some side streets and alleyways, then found a concrete ramp leading to the water's edge, where I spotted a few tourists boarding a longboat. It was a sunny, clear day, and I could see that this river was quite wide. Boats, ships, and barges made their way across the surface. This was the Chao Phraya River, the source of which begins in Nakhon Sawan, 231 miles to the north, and runs south through Bangkok before emptying into the Gulf of Thailand.

But something else captured my attention. I took out my phone and recorded a video clip of garbage floating along a side-channel — discarded candy wrappers, plastic shopping bags, paper cups, assorted trash — trash which clogs our oceans and waterways and washes up on beaches. I have no Ph.D. in sanitation services or any formal training in the science of garbage collection, but I would argue that the source of 95% of the litter around the world is from packaging and containers of some sort. This convenience of mass consumerism has wreaked havoc upon the planet.

But I would not solve any of the world's problems standing here on the river's edge, baking beneath the Bangkok sun. It was hot and my feet were aching. I could feel blisters forming on the soles of my feet.

I wondered if I could catch one of those river taxis back to Sukhumvit Road. I glanced at a map on a board that was posted especially for tourists, but it was written in Thai and being largely ignorant of the geographical layout of the city and unable to recognize any of its landmarks, I had no way of finding Sukhumvit Road on that thing, so I walked until I found another passageway leading back to the city streets. I caught a tuk-tuk back to Victory Monument then hopped on the BTS Skytrain back to Asok Station.

Checking the Samsung Health app on my phone, I had walked just over 14 miles that day.

That was about the extent of my exploration of the city. I was only going to be in town for eight days. Nowhere near enough time to explore much of anything beyond the go-go clubs and Chinatown noodle joints. I would need eight months or ten years to really get a feel for the place.

I visited Bangkok for the very first time last December and spent a scant three days feeling my way along Sukhumvit Road. I didn't wander very far. The traffic and the heat, even in December, held me in check.

The heat and humidity were slightly worse when I returned four months later, and here I was once again, distracted by the pungent scent of pussy and whatever emotions that entailed. I was here to travel and see the world, goddamnit. I couldn't allow myself to get sidetracked again. This has been the story of my life.

In my early twenties, my first love and subsequent first heartbreak resulted in putting our firstborn up for adoption. Grist for another story which likely will never be told, but that one-two punch and body-slam of an early life lesson launched me into a downward spiral of depression and feelings of worthlessness which lasted years. I had resigned myself to the notion that I would never amount to anything more than a minimum-wage file clerk eking out a lonely existence in a cramped ten-by-twelve-foot efficiency studio apartment in San Francisco's Tenderloin district.

By my late-twenties, I somehow found myself working in the booming tech industry. The Internet was a thing now. Computer programming and working with computers was suddenly seen as something cool. And with a sudden boost in income, I began fantasizing about travel. I was going to fit what I could into a backpack and get the hell outta the States. Round-the-world travel. I was going to go big and see it all, man — India, Nepal, Tibet, Vietnam, Morocco.

I told myself that I was only working to save up enough money to travel the world for a year. I started buying up travel guidebooks for all the places I was planning to visit (this was before Youtube). I read blog sites on the Internet on what to pack, how to pack it, and what to pack it in. This triggered within me a mania for all things related to backpacks and luggage. Soon I had a closet full of the stuff, in various carrying capacities and styles.

I packed and repacked and organized gear lists before I got anywhere near an airport terminal. On the weekends, I would load up my backpack and go traipsing about the city, then return to my apartment and put the stuff back in my closet. I was a world travel poseur.

That was twenty-five years ago.

Those backpacks sat in my closet, mostly unused except for a few week-long trips to Hawaii. My passport expired without receiving a single stamp.

More than a decade had passed before I did any real traveling.

In 2009.

To Mexico.

Cancun, Mexico.

A short, two-hour flight from where we were now living in the Dallas/Fort Worth metroplex.

It wasn't exactly round-the-world adventure travel, but we fell in love with the place. Who knew that in less time it took to drive from Dallas to Austin, you could be in a place as beautiful and mesmerizing as the Yucatan Peninsula? We returned each year for our family vacation, but as our daughter grew older and our marriage faded, I began returning by myself.

Nearly twenty years had passed. The mortgage on the house was paid. I was still working in the tech industry and making a decent six-figure salary. Traveling around the world again began to occupy my thoughts.

Now fifty years old, I made plans to travel to Thailand. The Covid pandemic delayed these plans for a year, but in November 2021 I at last found myself in the Land of Smiles. Like the millions of others that have traveled to Thailand, I fell in love with the place.

I had only been there two days when I met Chaiya. Within a week, I was a goopy mound of puppy-love mush. I'd made that often fatal newbie mistake of falling in love with a Thai bar girl.

Big deal. What else is new?

EVERYTHING was new!

It was like I had been revitalized. Recharged. And I realized that for years I had been trudging through life on a sort of low-battery energy, living in a gloomy shadow of something that I no longer recognized — my own life.

But this feeling, too, proved to be an illusion. It was a feeling based on an idea, a preconceived notion in my mind, that had the barest grasp on any kind of reality.

I didn't know this girl other than what little scraps of information she decided to tell me. There was nothing concrete, no real understanding that can only come from having lived with a person for years. We'd only met last November.

Yet when I returned last March, she took me to meet her mother and 13-year-old son. She took me to the condo she owned in Hat Yai. In the back of my mind I kept asking myself: Is this really just another bar girl trying to scam me out of my money? Or did she want something more? Something more meaningful and lasting, something more than spending every night waiting around for strange men to buy you drinks and getting so wasted that you end up puking your guts out the next morning?

I don't know. Should I even care? Perhaps I was putting too much thought into it. Overthinking the whole goddamn situation.

—

It was during that week in Bangkok when I decided that she would be nothing more to me than a passing acquaintance.

Why was I pretending we were married? I was already married. Still married, in fact.

Here I was in this sprawling ancient, alien city on the other side of the world. New adventures. New experiences. All of it was waiting for me. Staring me straight in the face. All I had to do was shift my perspective ever so slightly — look past this girl that brought me so much disappointment and heartbreak in such a short amount of time — and find the new life that awaited me.

I spent my nights drinking and hanging around Nana Plaza and Soi Cowboy, smiling at the half-naked girls in the bars and go-go clubs. They descended upon me like serpents on a vine.

The girls onstage danced and wiggled. Sadly, disturbingly, many looked underaged and malnourished. I had to look away. Some were barely dancing, hardly moving at all, and spent most of their time glancing about with bewildered looks on their faces, perhaps not so much out of any fear as confusion and disbelief. Could very well be that just a day or week before, some of these girls might have been eking out a life on their family's farm in the Thai countryside, and a three-hour bus ride later, they find themselves in the middle of

Bangkok and its grand cacophony of traffic, pollution, and neon signs. Narrow, gritty streets. Honking horns and beeping motor scooters. The heat, humidity, and the stench of sweaty farang, pawing and groping at them in the darkened clubs of Nana Plaza. And the Indian men, too, with their curry breath and body odor. An unfair if not common sentiment expressed by a handful of girls I spoke with.

"They're cheap and they smell."

Massage parlor girls in Dallas have expressed similar sentiments. Indian men haggle over everything and are known for making insultingly low-ball offers.

"$45 for half-hour massage? How about $20? C'mon, it's almost closing time. Don't you want to make an easy twenty dollars before you go home?"

What's a simple girl from the Thai countryside expected to do? Surely, they've known older sisters or cousins who went venturing into the big city and returned with the latest model iPhone or two-baht gold necklaces, and surely they would have asked how they scored such treasure?

But expectation never hits quite like reality, and that might explain the confused and bewildered looks I see on their faces when they realize the filthy things they have to do with these wrinkled old men in order to earn those new iPhones and gold necklaces. The experience must be like having a bucket of cold hotdogs dumped over their heads. A real fuckin' sausage fest.

The ones you have to be on guard for are the ones who possess a good command of the English language and are seemingly at ease around farangs (white men), the ones who welcome you with a languid smile and a relaxed, easy grace. And if they are swimsuit model attractive, you need to be on particularly high alert — you are in the presence of a seasoned professional. She may or may not already have a stable of men overseas sending her a monthly allowance, and by the time you have exchanged pleasantries — your name, your length of stay, your purpose for visiting Thailand, your occupation — she will have already gauged your financial worth and whether or not you're worth her time. She might let you buy her a drink or two, but after that she'll ignore you and move on to bigger game.

The really successful ones only need to work a few days a month and might spend the rest of the time getting bar-fined and serving as arm candy for wealthier mongers who might take her for a week or two out to one of the islands or on a sightseeing trip to Bangkok. I had seen a number of these couples on flights between Phuket and Bangkok and have to admit that I did look upon them with a tinge of jealousy. They looked happy and successful, enjoying the best of their lives. Why couldn't I feel the same? A dour, 52-year-old Filipino man, sitting on the floor in that crowded airport terminal with smelly feet and running dangerously low on cash.

A bar-fine is the term used to describe the amount of money a customer must pay to the bar in order to take the girl away from that bar for a certain amount of time, usually paid on a per-night basis and typically costing anywhere from $500 to $2000 Thai baht. This money goes directly to the bar and does not include the cost of "services rendered," which is negotiated separately between you and the girl.

This is where a bar girl stands to make most of her money — by getting bar-fined by customers. And if they happen to like the guy or find him remotely attractive, even better.

Some girls refuse to be bar-fined, maybe out of loyalty to boyfriends or sponsors. Or are simply not too particularly hard-up for cash and can afford to be picky with who they decide to go with. They'll gladly allow you to buy them a drink, but the relationship will go no further than that.

I had yet to ascertain where Chaiya fit within this spectrum of bar girl behavior. Having only been twice to Thailand within a span of the past six months, my exposure to bar girl protocol was limited to a handful of places along Bangla Road in Phuket and around Sukhumvit in Bangkok.

Chaiya was the second bar girl I met. She appeared like an angel of light late one afternoon. I had been in Phuket for two days when she crossed my field of vision as I gnawed on a plate of barbecue spare ribs at the food market on Bangla Road. She wore a long white smock all buttoned up as if she were a sales clerk working the cosmetics counter in a department store. Maybe it was the glare of the setting sun shining down the length of Bangla Road, but she was literally glowing in a golden light. She passed by as if floating on air and in slow motion. The first thing I noticed about her were her eyes. She didn't look at me. She wasn't looking at anyone. She kept her head straight and stared straight ahead with those big, black eyes. She was like a goddess that had come down to earth, mildly annoyed that she once again had to interact with this stinking mass of humanity, mere mortals.

The hustle and bustle of the evening crowd was just starting to pick up. Loud, blaring, bass-driven music began blasting from a few bars. Soon the street would be shut to motor traffic, and Bangla Road would come alive. But all of it became silent and faded to the background, while she came into sharp focus, made visible for me and only me to see. It was as if the Universe was calling out to me in that very moment: "HERE. LOOK!"

I remember saying out loud to myself, "Wow." Then I turned back to my plate of ribs. A woman like that was meant for greater men.

Thinking back now, I thought it peculiar that I had decided to go out for something to eat at that particular time of day. I had already eaten breakfast and lunch earlier in the day. Dinner time would be in a few short hours. What prompted me to leave my hotel room and go searching for a bite to eat at that precise moment? Was it some cosmic force, some guardian angel, some spirit guide from beyond spurring me to get out there and meet my soulmate?

I finished my plate of ribs and made my way down Bangla Road, heading back to my hotel. I came up on two large white guys, obese good ol' boys who looked like they'd been drinking for a better part of the day. They were standing in the street pointing and cat-calling one of the girls in a bar. I drew closer and saw that it was her. She was unbuttoning her white smock, revealing a skimpy outfit underneath, which set the two guys off with more hooting and hollering. She looked past them and saw me standing there. She beckoned me in with a flick of her hand, and I joined her for a drink.

—

She didn't seem like the other girls. Not that I'd met many other girls working the bars along Bangla Road. (Farang mongers will laugh and say what a naive simp I'm being, about to be taken for a ride and relieved of all my money.)

What I mean is that she wasn't overly friendly or too familiar with customers. She didn't drape herself over random guys, rubbing their backs or caressing their knees. She had an air about her of decency and self-respect. Almost reserved.

That first day I met her and bought her that drink, she seemed outright irritable and non-communicative. She just sat there staring down at her phone. Then, like a fool, I asked her if she wanted to go "boom-boom." We'd barely been chatting for ten minutes.

She chuckled. "Wow, you're fast." she said, smirking. "Maybe next time."

We exchanged numbers, and I asked her to call me the next day if she was still interested. "Sure," she said, giving me a sidelong glance.

I waited.

She didn't call the next day.

After my morning swim, I lounged around my hotel room watching Youtube videos.

Hmm. I was over-thinking. Over-analyzing.

Maybe I'd misread her. Maybe her noncommittal and unemotional responses the night before were exactly that — she wasn't interested.

That didn't make any sense. What bar girl isn't interested in making a little extra money?

Maybe she had a boyfriend?

Maybe she'd been bar-fined by another guy who was better-looking and offered more money?

I waited until late in the afternoon the following day to text her.

"Hi, I'm sorry but I fell asleep," I wrote, hoping that I wasn't sounding too desperate or pathetic. "Did you still want to meet me at my hotel?"

She responded with a laughing emoji and said she wasn't the type of bar girl that went with men back to their rooms.

I apologized and left it at that. After three days in Patong, I was growing bored of the place and began making plans to wander further south to Karon/Kata and Rawai.

She texted me back a few seconds later, "What R U doing?"

I responded that I was just laying around in my hotel room watching Youtube videos.

She replied with another laughing emoji and said she was doing the same.

I asked her if she'd be interested in meeting me for dinner later. I added, "No boom-boom."

She responded with another laughing emoji, and we made plans to meet later that evening.

—

I ended up staying in Patong another week. We were inseparable from the beginning, but it seemed the Universe had other plans.

When she came down with Covid last December and had to quarantine for ten days, and I ventured alone to Rawai, it was at that point, I think, that the Universe seemed to be working to separate us.

She became like a ghost in my phone. Our cell phones were our sole means of communication. Simple text messages on a tiny screen. It was about as abstract of a relationship as you could get. I might just as well have been corresponding with a robot for all I knew. Ghost in the machine, indeed.

When that first trip ended, and I had to make my sad, lonely way back to the States, we exchanged text messages like teenagers in the throes of puppy love. But unlike two teens — like the two kids I once saw dry-humping each other on a patch of grass outside my old junior high school one sunny afternoon — I knew the feelings would fade and the intensity would subside. I knew where this road ended. I'd been down this way many times. Exchanging lovey-dovey text messages each day would not be enough to sustain the long-distance relationship.

But I was a fool in love. I was the Fool in the tarot card deck. I made plans to fly back to Phuket barely three months later. I didn't care what my wife or my job thought.

I came up with some bullshit reason, something based on a sliver of half-truth, one that stemmed from a misunderstanding I had with the travel website I had used to book my trips.

Because I had rescheduled my flight a few times since the original booking back in 2019, the cost of the ticket fluctuated each time. And by the time I settled on my flight in November 2021, I had earned an $800 flight credit. I thought I had already used my credit, but after I had returned from that first trip, I checked my account and saw that the credit was still listed. This was due to some lag in the website's system, which was soon corrected. But I didn't tell my manager that. Instead, I informed him in an email that I was going to take another three-week vacation at the end of March. I worded the message in such a way that it was a statement of fact and not a request. Maybe they would decide to fire me before I returned, but what did I care? I was in love.

—

I hadn't quite thought it through. Yes, Thailand is an extremely affordable country to live in, especially if you're making the sort of tech salary that I was being paid back in the States. But it was still just a salary. I had to work to get paid. And if I was fucking around overseas in Thailand, it probably meant that I wasn't doing any work. No work, no money. Once my cash was gone, that was it. The party is over. Time to go home and make more money. I was no expat retiree with a pension. I was no wealthy investor living off a steady stream of passive income. At the end of the day, I was still just another working schlep.

I succumbed to delusion that first trip to Thailand and fooled myself into believing all sorts of fantasies of buying an apartment on Phuket and spending the rest of my days along the beach, when in reality I had only saved up enough cash and vacation time to survive for a few scant weeks. But I lived like a king in that short period of time. I was what expats refer to as a "two-week millionaire." Short-time vacationers. Short-time johns.

I returned in late March with big dreams. I'll buy a condo near Kata. Or maybe something along the hillside in Patong. Don't want to buy anything too far inland. I wanted to be close to the beach.

Hah! What horseshit.

Anything within a mile or two of the Andaman coast will run at least $3 million Thai baht (around $80k USD) for some halfway decent place that wasn't a one-room, roach-infested shit-hole. And here I was, talking like a millionaire with barely $3 grand in the bank and dwindling quickly by the day.

If that first trip to Phuket had me feeling like a two-week millionaire, that second trip a few months later brought me to the other end of the spectrum. Within three weeks I had racked up ten grand in credit card debt and was so low on cash toward the end, I had to ask my wife to wire $300 to my bank account just so I could afford a taxi to the airport and buy some food.

I was wiped out. Cleaned out. Dare I say — taken for a ride.

What did I care? I was in love. And anyway, the tarot card readers on Youtube said that I would soon be enjoying a great abundance of wealth and love.

But when? When??

I needed the cash now.

I lost my Charles Schwab debit card the first night I was there, and an ATM machine ate my Wells Fargo card two days before I was scheduled to fly out. Both of my credit cards were maxed out.

I had become something I had not expected, something I had managed to avoid in all my years of traveling and taking beach vacations — I had become a broke-ass tourist in a foreign land. This two-week millionaire was now utterly bankrupt.

I was a drunk Russian staggering confused down Bangla Road with an icepick-in-the-forehead hangover after having been relieved of his wallet, his passport, and all of his money the previous night by an enterprising team of ladyboys.

I was a pseudo-hippie backpacker who forgot his backpack and all of his belongings in the back of a tuk-tuk before hopping out and disappearing down Khao San Road.

I was the soft-spoken accountant from the English countryside who came to Bangkok on holiday and quietly spent all of his savings on bar girls and a perverse need to satiate a number of very detailed sexual appetites.

I was a sunburned soccer mom with too many kids and an overstuffed wallet stuffed into an overstuffed beach bag, everything tumbling out across the sand as she chased her kids down the shoreline.

I had to make that $300 USD last. I remembered I had about $5,000 Thai baht stashed in my luggage. I'd be okay as long as I paid close attention to where my money was going.

Gone were $750 baht breakfasts at the hotel restaurant across the street from the beach. I'd have to content myself with a croissant and a cup of coffee at Starbuck's.

No more $1,500 baht teriyaki steak dinners at that hip Japanese bistro. I'd have to content myself with eating street food. Half-rack of ribs and a bottle of Singha or a plate of fried pork intestines over rice with an egg on top. $450 baht.

I set aside $1,000 baht for the taxi ride to the airport.

When I got back to Texas, I spent two weeks waiting for that next paycheck. Until then, my lunches were cans of pork 'n beans or sardines with potato chips or steamed rice. Thank God I had that prepper mentality of stocking up on canned goods a few years back. The disaster I was dealing with now was not a natural one but one stemming from credit card debt spiraling out of control, like a mile-wide tornado slowly making its way across my financial landscape.

But what did I care? I was in love.

—

I didn't see her at all during that last week I was in Phuket. She was recuperating at a hotel in Bangkok, near the clinic where she had her nose-job done.

I checked in at the Baan Boa Resort on the southern end of Patong Beach. I fell in love with this place when I stayed here last December. It was far enough away from the hordes of drunken tourists on Bangla Road that there was very little foot traffic and it was relatively quiet, yet it was right across the street from the beach.

The rooms are large and spacious with room enough to move about freely without bumping your knees into the bed or the wall or the desk.

This is what I love about older hotels like the Baan Boa or the place I stayed at in Kata — they feel like an actual living space, a place you can live in, and with room to breathe and move around. You have to walk way over there to get to the bathroom and shower. You have to walk way over there to get to the writing desk/dining table. There was room to spread out.

Yes, I could live here for months at a time, perhaps writing that great American Thai novel. Like I'd mentioned in a video that I posted on Youtube, this is the place to stay to get over a broken heart or to kick a drug habit. The staff weren't nosy and stayed out of your way. And I encountered so few guests that I sometimes had the feeling I was the only one there.

My daily routine went something like this:

Awake around seven or eight in the morning.

Heat some water in the electric kettle and drink two cups worth of instant coffee. The stuff is weak but enough to get me going.

I'll write anywhere from 30 minutes to an hour, take a shit, then head to the beach for my morning swim. Waiting for that first bowel movement is key. I don't like to be stuck out in public somewhere with no guaranteed access to decent toilet facilities.

Then onto the second stage of my daily routine: my morning swim. I'm trying to recall when I first began this beach vacation ritual. It may have started during that first trip to Maui we took back in 2010. I'd be wide awake at five or six in the morning, and nothing would be open for another few hours. Where we were staying in Lahaina, an historical landmark and touristy town, there were no 7-

Elevens or early morning coffee shops. Nothing to do but go for a swim in that cool water, calm and still in the early morning, like glass across the surface, the sun just barely peeking over the hills to the east.

I would continue this morning ritual on later trips — Mexico, Costa Rica, and now in Thailand. I no longer spend entire days sitting on the beach with the wife and kid. Nowadays I'm content to just go for a dip in the morning and then maybe again in the afternoon, depending on the heat and the crowds. There sre too many other things to do, like napping or eating.

Maui, 2010. This period of my life also marked the beginning of the end of my marriage, although I failed to recognize it at the time.

Or maybe it was Cabo San Lucas, 2011?

Or that second trip we took to Maui in 2013?

Somewhere at some point during this time, our family unit unraveled and collapsed, and I realized that my marriage was one of convenience and on keeping up appearances. I started taking these vacations by myself. Although we were still married, there was little need to pretend anymore. Too much shit had happened.

When we emerged on the other side, scarred and bruised, it felt as if we'd been through a war. But that's another story, one that I'm not quite ready to tell, or if I should even be the one to tell it. There are other points of view — namely, the wife's and daughter's — that also have some bearing on the events.

Of course, I still wanted to travel and didn't feel like waiting around. Might as well go it alone and enjoy myself while I still could.

After my morning swim, the third step of my daily ritual is finding breakfast or brunch. While I was in Phuket, this typically meant eating at one of the hotel restaurants near the beach. I frequented one place in particular, which had outdoor seating, received a good amount of sunlight, and had good distance between the tables such that patrons weren't sitting on top of each other and you didn't have to worry about knees bumping into tables. The place was well-maintained and clean, and the food wasn't bad. I forget the name of the place, but it was a good spot for people-watching. The hotel had a varied clientele of vacationing European families, digital nomads with their laptop computers, and the usual lot of creepy old guys with their feral looking bar girls from the night before.

Breakfast was my usual "American" breakfast — eggs, toast, sausage, bacon. Coffee and orange juice. Around $500 or $600 Thai baht, if I remember right.

It's always fun watching the old white men (they're almost always white) with their companions in the morning. The look of regret and shame on some of their faces. Funny to see it on the men. Somewhat depressing when you see it on the faces of the girls.

One girl in particular stands out in my mind.

It was early afternoon, and I was having lunch at another restaurant down the street along Beach Road. (I don't know if that's the actual name of the road, but it's the main road that follows the beach. So "Beach Road.")

This guy comes into the dining area with this waifish thing in tow. She's thin and very young looking — young like thirteen or fourteen, very likely underaged. The guy is in his thirties or forties, fit and muscular, wearing a crisp white button-down, short-sleeve shirt and khaki shorts. Your typical Phuket whore-monger. Very Aryan looking.

They take a seat at a table directly in front of me. The man is at ease and confident, leaning back in his chair, casually inspecting the menu. The body language of the girl gives off a completely opposite demeanor. She's sitting with her head down, shoulders slouched, hands tucked into her lap. It almost looks like she's praying. Or trying to make herself as small and as unseen as possible. There is an unmistakable look of sadness and distress on her face.

Throughout their meal, they don't speak a single word to each other. The girl eats with her head bent over her plate, one hand shielding her face. She's trying to hide. She doesn't want to be seen. The shame and embarrassment she feels might as well be a neon sign flashing over her head. Who knows what sort of sexual perversions were forced upon this girl in the secrecy of that guy's hotel room? It might very well have been her very first time with a man, and a farang no less. And she's like every other girl out there, working those bars and hustling those men every night, with the hope of making just enough money to survive and maybe send a little extra to their families back home. Her family is depending on her. She isn't like the more experienced girls, who have grown accustomed to farang with their pungent "white man" stench and wrinkled cocks — half-flaccid penises shoved in their faces or old man fingers stuffed all up in their nether regions. There is an animal-like desperation to these farang and how they come at these equally desperate, cash-starved girls. It is an urgency of lust and perversion. Farang mating season on a 30-day tourist visa.

The other girls can tell her what to expect, but it won't prepare her for the shock of that first experience, especially if she has the poor luck of finding herself alone in a room with a particularly aggressive guy wanting to toss her around like a ragdoll or satiate some sick fetish which may or may not involve strangling the girl to the point of unconsciousness or requiring her to do the same to him with the aid of a leather belt with her sitting in his lap while he slowly jerks himself off.

She may soon realize that the experience itself has very little to do with the act of sexual intercourse and everything to do with the psychological mind-fuck stemming from some perverse bloodlust for domination, punishment, or thinly-veiled violence. The poor girl ought to consider herself lucky if she doesn't find herself tossed from a 14th floor balcony. Such accidents are known to happen here in the Land of Smiles, with disturbing regularity.

The same accidents can happen to seasoned professionals, I suppose. Or even to your hapless run-of-the-mill farang, who may have gotten in over his head with the bar tab or drugs or angered the wrong girl and her vengeful Thai boyfriend, himself in the throes of methamphetamine hallucinations and cold sweats.

I delve too far into perverse fantasy. I can't help it, seeing what I've seen, especially when I see the look on a girl's face or notice her body language, like the young girl eating with her much older date that one sunny afternoon or on the many other occasions as I sat people-watching in hotel restaurants or in Thai noodle shops, and I spot a hot young Thai dish sitting across the table from a decrepit old geezer.

Most of the time it's just a harmless transaction involving a bit of sexual release in exchange for a few thousand baht.

Most of the time and more than likely, it's the other way around — it's the girls preying on the men, and often the ones who get taken are the rookies, the first-timers, the newbie two-week millionaires. Those poor, hapless farang who have no fucking clue what they're getting into. One such as myself.

"He was thinking with his little head and not his big one."

"He didn't stick to the three-day rule. Never stay with the same girl three days in a row. Now look at him. He's got his emotions all mixed up into it. Wanker!"

"Never fall in love with the first bar girl you meet. You need to fuck at least ten or more before you make up your mind!"

Just a bunch of blokes at the local expat bar having a laugh at the expense of one of their mates who just arrived from Sydney. Or London. Or Mumbai. Or Texas.

The guy awakes in the morning a few thousand-baht notes lighter. ("Keep your cash hidden or tucked away in the hotel safe, ya wanker!")

One of the girls he brought home the night before made off with a gold necklace. ("What the hell are you doing flashing your jewelry, anyway, pretty boy? Damn simp!")

Another girl's got him on the line, and he's sending her $15,000 Thai baht every month, wired directly from his bank account to hers. ("Worse case scenario, mate. Worst case scenario.")

This is what lures the girls from their tiny villages in the countryside.

Hope.

Dreams.

The need to survive.

The need to support their families.

Some will lie, cheat, steal. Some of the farang will do the same.

"Yer preaching to the choir, mate! Get off your high horse and come have a drink!"

—

I'd been reading about the Songkran celebration online but didn't know what it was really about until someone blasted me in the face with a Super-Soaker water gun. I was coming down Bangla Road and passed people laughing and screaming all around me. They were soaking wet and shooting each other with colorful plastic water pistols. Phalanxes of young men dressed only in swimming trunks marched down the center of the street taking aim at bar girls and tourists alike. Some of the bar girls fought back by hurling buckets of ice water over the entire crowd.

I found myself caught in a crossfire. Someone dumped a bucket of ice water down my back, and as I stood there in frozen shock, I got blasted in the face with a water gun and again in the back of the head. It was like the Kennedy assassination, Songkran style.

Someone grabbed my arm and pulled me into the nearest bar. It was Mei, the girl I'd met the very first night I was here back in November. Her hair was drenched and hanging in wet strands over her face. She was laughing with a huge smile on her face.

"How are you?" she yelled into my ear over the blaring music in the club and the crowds of people howling at each other in the street, buckets of ice water defending against Super-Soaker water guns.

"I'm soaking wet!" I yelled back, wiping my glasses on the end of my shirt. I was surprised she remembered me. I bought her a few drinks and we made plans to meet for dinner the following night.

"We go seafood restaurant," she said with a big smile.

"Okay," I replied. I slipped her a thousand-baht note and left before she could ask me to buy more drinks for her bar girl friends.

Mei asked if I wanted to bring her back to my hotel room, but I told her that I didn't think the place I was staying at allowed guests. This two-week millionaire was going broke. I was hemorrhaging cash and my credit cards were nearly maxed. Mei, I knew, would not be a cheap date. I had started paying more attention to what I was spending my money on, and although I didn't have a specific budget, taking bar girls back to my hotel definitely wasn't on the list.

"Why you have to leave so soon?" she frowned.

"I have to meet someone," I said. Which was true. Chaiya's friend, Koy, was expecting me. I had texted Chaiya a few minutes earlier, letting her know that I was on the way to drop off the $3,000 baht to Koy as she had requested. Koy would need to pay the month's rent on Chaiya's room since Chaiya would be laid up in Bangkok for another week recuperating from her surgery. Once again, I was the chump that footed that bill. What could I do? I couldn't just leave her hanging. I couldn't just abandon her like that.

Mei looked at me, then she looked down at the drink in front of her. "Did you come here with your wife?"

"What? No," I said. "I just have to drop off some money really quick, but I'll be right back."

"You promise?"

"Sure," I said.

Mei's bar girl manipulations were not as honed as Chaiya's. Where Chaiya made it seem effortless, almost sleight of hand, in the way she hustled every last baht from customers' pockets, Mei by comparison was somewhat clumsy and heavy-handed.

Where Chaiya would drop seemingly innocuous comments about being a little short on cash to pay her cell phone bill this month, Mei would just ask me point-blank, "Honey, can you give me $5,000?"

Or during the Songkran celebration when Mei pulled me into her bar — I had barely finished my first drink when three older-looking women crowded around us.

"Can you buy drinks for them, too?" Mei asked. "Pleeeeease…?"

Here again, Chaiya's approach was more like a seasoned professional. She would introduce me to her friends one at a time over the course of a few drinks. "This is my friend, Koy," she would say. "Would you like to buy her a drink?"

I suppose from another perspective, one could argue that Mei was a simpler girl. Guileless and naive. She hadn't yet become jaded and cynical from working in bars every night.

Days later, as I was making my way back to Texas and waiting for my connecting flight in Qatar, Mei texted me: "Honey, I need $15,000. Can? Me tired of going with men all the time."

She wanted $15,000USD to open a karaoke bar with a friend. I politely told her "No" and haven't heard from her since.

Chaiya was subtle in her approach and more disciplined in how she plied her trade. You could spot hints of her financial success if you were paying close enough attention.

When I first met her, I noticed she was using an iPhone 10 when many of the other bar girls, I later realized, were using cheap Android phones, like the ones you can buy at 7-Eleven.

She wore expensive-looking jewelry — a silver wristwatch on her wrist and a fine gold necklace around her neck.

She mentioned in passing that she had once owned a car but had to give it up when Thailand went into lockdown from Covid, and she couldn't work to make the payments on the note.

She owns a two-bedroom shophouse in Hat Yai that she says she bought on her own for $3.2 million baht.

All of this on a bar girl's earnings from drinks alone plus a monthly commission? Hmm.

My last day on Phuket — or what I thought was going to be my last day — I went for a swim and loitered around the beach most of the morning before having a late breakfast at one of the food carts lining the sidewalk. $120 Thai baht for a plate of pad krapow (fried egg and chicken or pork over steamed rice, with slices of cucumbers and tomatoes on the side). The old women working those carts are always asking me if I'm from Malaysia.

Later that afternoon, I went for lunch at the hotel restaurant where I normally go for breakfast. The waiter who serves me breakfast was also working the afternoon shift.

"Don't you ever go home?" I said, joking.

He smiled and patted me on the back. "Pretty soon," he said.

He's a dark-skinned and muscular guy in his thirties or early forties. I never got his name, but I can tell from his posture and the way he stands that he either spends his free time lifting weights or practicing muay thai kickboxing. He's no slouch and can probably kick the shit out of most us pot-bellied tourists lounging around the dining area. He is polite and respectful, even as he waits on the white men with their bar girl companions. I watch him closely to see if his countenance or demeanor changes in the slightest, but he remains the utmost professional.

A cloud of disillusionment drifts over me. This isn't the real Thailand. This is an illusion. These people are living in a tourist's dream, a fantasy. An economy propped up by foreign investment and foreign men. How quickly, I wondered, would this beach resort turn into something much more sinister if the locals, especially the local men, decided one day that they would no longer be so obedient or servile? If these men were not so dependent on foreign dollars, holding their hands together and bowing their heads to the white man sitting at a table with his Thai woman?

The man-servant and bar girl have a common understanding. Both are doing what they do to survive. The white man is the water buffalo in a rice paddy — it has the potential to feed their families and bring prosperity. The man-servant and bar girl share a quick look which no one else notices. The white man, this hapless farang, pays for everything.

I had been paying for everything. Was this how Chaiya felt toward me?

Obviously. Perhaps.

Yes.

I had played the fool and paid the price. She was now sitting in a hotel in Bangkok that I had paid for, recovering from a nose job, the down payment for which I had also paid. And here I was about to leave Thailand with a few measly baht in my pocket.

Things were about to get a lot worse.

I had spent all my time focusing on the travel requirements in and out of Thailand and failed to look up the updated requirements that the United States had put into place. I had assumed that the entry requirements would be the same as last November — proof of a negative Covid test within 72 hours of your departure time. At some point within the past three months, they shortened that time to 24 hours prior to departure time. I would learn this the hard way.

I checked out of my room at the Baan Boa Resort. It was late afternoon and the sun had begun its slow descent toward the Andaman Sea, casting a golden light across Patong Beach and silhouetting beachgoers lounging on the sand and splashing about in the water. I was leaving Thailand now for a second time within three months, feeling beaten and downtrodden. This latest trip would have to be marked as a loss. A failure. And yet — I felt as if I was leaving my new home and returning to my old one. My old life patiently waiting in the background.

I caught a taxi to the airport, my mind already pondering what I was going to do when I got back to Texas. I couldn't wait to get home. I needed to get home. I had to get back to my job and start making money. Whatever dreams I'd been fantasizing about three weeks earlier had been curb-stomped into a million pieces and flushed down a Bangkok gutter.

"You will gain sudden clarity," said one of my Youtube tarot card readings.

"Keep an eye on your finances," warned another. "Pay close attention to how you are spending your money."

"You will be disappointed in something for which you had high hopes."

I stared out the backseat window and watched the tourists and Thai locals and the little storefronts pass by as the taxi worked its way down the main beach road, through town and onto the winding road through the hillside leading toward the highway. This might not be the "authentic" Thailand — with its nightclubs, go-go bars and tourist shit-holes – but it was real enough for me, and I had fallen in love with the place. I came here alone and I was leaving alone. What the hell had happened?

—

There is a certain uniqueness to beachbum culture in towns like Patong that you will almost always encounter in some form or another in beach towns all over the world. It doesn't matter if it's Waikiki, Hawaii…..South Beach, Miami….Cabo San Lucas or Playa del Carmen in Mexico….or Jaco in Costa Rica. There's a certain vacationing "type" that is drawn to these places specifically for the beach lifestyle. A certain laidback attitude, lazy and languid. The dress code is simple: t-shirt, flip-flops, and board shorts. Maybe you want to go surfing. Maybe you want to do some fishing. Or maybe just a little eating, drinking, and fucking.

Manana.

Pura vida.

Sabai sabai.

Hakuna matata.

Don't worry, be happy.

The beachbum will be at home anywhere where it's warm and sunny, has a good beach, and where the locals are friendly and the local women not half-bad to look at.

In the beginning, this might have been a small fishing community that only a VW bus full of blonde-haired, blue-eyed surfers knew about. Or a small village where GIs came ashore to sample the local food and local women.

And so it goes.

Fast-forward twenty, thirty years — and the landscape has transformed considerably.

Here come the newlyweds venturing out into the world as husband and wife for the first time. Hailing from a cooler clime, they are as pale and white as the sand on the beach. In a day's time, both will be horribly sunburned and red as lobsters. Sex will be awkward and uncomfortable. His new wife will break down in tears as he takes the bottle of baby lotion into the bathroom and fantasizes about one of the local girls he spied at the beach earlier that day. So tan and brown. Her bikini bottom could barely contain that fat pussy.

Here come the soccer moms with their pot-bellied husbands and children in tow, trying to make the most of that company-paid two-week vacation. They will book connecting rooms — one for mom and dad, the other for the kids. It will look like a bomb went off — clothes and old food containers everywhere; empty bags of chips on the floor; the waste bin overflowing with empty beer cans; the bathroom counter littered with makeup and lotion and toothpaste and mouthwash and prescription medication. One of the kids still wets the bed, and housekeeping is always having to bring up extra towels. The older kid streamed a few rolls of toilet paper off their hotel balcony, six stories up. Dad shakes his head, chuckling. Kids will be kids.

Here come the upwardly mobile Indian couples — engineers, doctors, project managers — petty and mistrustful, fearful and constantly on the lookout for being ripped off by locals, haggling over the price of two-dollar veggie omelettes. The frizzy-haired Indian woman becomes irate, her eyes bulging and bulbous nose expanding and contracting as if they are about to blow completely out of her head. How dare this establishment charge an automatic 10% gratuity fee! The husband idly picks his nose, forgetting he's in public.

The Chinese arrive by the busload, four or five buses at a time. They descend like ravenous locusts, consuming everything in their path. Nothing is safe. There is a palpable buzz in the hotel lobby when they arrive, and you can see the fear and panic in the eyes of the desk clerks at the counter. Much blood will be shed before that 2pm check-in time.

Nobody speaks a word of the local language. There is no need. Foreign money communicates effectively enough. Foreign money is what keeps the local economy moving along. The U.S. dollar reigns supreme. This is common knowledge. Local politicians and real estate developers will pocket what they can. What remains will be reinvested into infrastructure — building airports, paving roads, improving city-wide sewage and drainage systems. Gone are the days of backpacking hippies and pot-smoking surfer dudes. Nobody wants to sleep in non-air-conditioned school buses, at least not anyone with money to spend.

As for the flora and fauna? Certain species of birds and small mammals may go extinct. Some collateral damage must be expected. Sensitive ecosystems might be completely eradicated. Merely the cost of doing business.

This tropical Garden of Eden has been transformed into a beach vacation paradise, with flights arriving daily from every major city around the world.

Shops will sprout up along the main beach road selling flip-flops, tie-dye t-shirts, bumper stickers, and artwork created by local indigenous people — carved wooden statues, straw hats, handwoven blankets — all authentic, of course. Convenience stores with automatic sliding doors will blast ice-cold air-conditioning from every street corner, the same corners where prostitutes will loiter later that night hoping to snare pot-bellied German tourists. Bar selling $1 margaritas will blast Bob Marley songs — the only kind of reggae they know, evidently — while the pub across the street will be playing The Eagles's "Hotel California."

There will be street performers and busking musicians. Touts selling tour packages and restaurant staff handing out flyers for burgers and fries or pepperoni pizzas.

All of this exists solely for the benefit of the tourists. And because of these tourists, these non-natives, these haoles, these farang, these white devils — an artificial environment is created. Much like a man-made aquarium. Like Disneyland or Sea World.

It may not be authentic, but it's real enough. It may not be how it was five hundred years ago when indigenous tribes lived in harmony with their environment, innocently bashing each other's skulls in with stone hand-axes or cannibalizing neighboring families. This can be forgiven; they hadn't yet been introduced to the teachings of the Church. At least the air was clean, and plastic trash nonexistent. Who's to say which culture is better or which era was preferred? The Arrow of Time moves in one direction: Outward. Human consciousness is ever-expanding, and those kids living in the jungle have grown weary of being eaten alive by mosquitoes and biting flies every night. They, too, want the latest Nike sneakers or Sony Playstations or iPhones. They have developed a taste for cheeseburgers and white women in string bikinis.

This is beachbum culture. Good, bad, but always laidback and not a care in the goddamn world. This is my Sunday church. This is my religion. Free for anyone to join. Free for anyone to enjoy. Bring your own flip-flops, t-shirt, and board shorts.

On the beach, we cannot hide beneath layers of clothing. The sun's warmth encourages us to release our inhibitions and insecurities. When at last, we succumb to the heat and disrobe, revealing ourselves in the daylight — flabby and pale; varicose veins and cellulite; cottage cheese asses and sunburned beer-bellies. Leave the false eyelashes and wigs at home, children. The only makeup you'll need is a dab of sunscreen. Get your knobby knees in the water and grow accustomed to getting sand in your ass-crack.

Come as you are. Beachbum culture accepts you all.

—

Once I watched as an older gentleman waded out into the surf. He looked to be in his sixties. Tall, fit, and tan. Distinguished looking with coiffed gray hair and sporting designer sunglasses and designer board shorts, he stood knee-deep in the water with his hands on his hips, like some captain of industry surveying his latest conquest. A large wave crept up behind him and knocked him over. He tumbled into the surf on hands and knees, feeling around for his sunglasses.

Dispense with any affectations of wealth or status. The ocean is unimpressed. She knocks us to our knees and tumbles us around in the surf, goading us to become as children once again, laughing and playing in the waves.

These acolytes of beachbum culture will learn the way. Their attachment to 9-to-5 office life will lose all meaning or purpose. Their attachment to time itself will revert to a primordial, innate awareness rather than something riddled with schedules, deadlines, or appointments. Their need to be fully clothed will be stripped away. The sound of the surf gently lapping the shore on a calm empty morning will be as their morning prayer.

—

My beachbum days were drawing to a close for the foreseeable future, as would messing around with bar girls or Thai women in general. No longer would I worship so fervently upon that altar of languid hedonism. Beat down and stung, I would be flinching all the way back to Texas. My next foray would require a little more planning and a lot more hardening of the mind and soul.

Thailand is a sensuous yet unforgiving god, arousing your emotions and playing tricks with your mind. She is multi-faceted and many-tentacled and hails from an age long since forgotten by the white man and their hollow currencies. Her voice comes gently across the surface of the Andaman Sea, whispering a song like the wind in a soothing language you cannot understand but can feel in your heart, lulling you into a trance before she cuts you open and splays your guts about like a street market vendor selling chunks of durian fruit to hungry tourists clamoring for a piece of that sweet, sweet flesh.

I didn't know what to expect that first trip, and I wasn't adequately prepared that second time around. I had returned too soon to Thailand. I was overcome with an urgency to see her again so convinced was I that I had met the love of my life. I should have waited, put more planning into it, saved more money. I hadn't put much thought into budgeting or what I was going to be doing for money if I decided to stay out there. At some point, I actually believed that I would just start living there and never have to come back. I had assumed it would all just sort of fall into place. Instead, everything fell apart.

When the two attractive Thai girls in Qatar Airways uniforms informed me at the check-in counter that my Covid PCR test was no longer valid, I knew the Universe had another lesson in store for me. The Universe tends to introduce new lessons when you least expect it.

Now was not a good time, goddamnit. I was critically low on cash, and I was ready to get the hell out of Thailand, far away from the heartbreak and disappointment I was feeling.

I ended up staying in Phuket for another three days while I got another Covid PCR test done.

On the way back from the airport, I texted my wife and explained the situation in short three- to five-word bursts. I was agitated and panicky. My taxi driver kept glancing back at me through the rearview mirror, a concerned look on his face.

"No worry," I said. "I pay you."

He nodded, "Okay!"

I was explaining my situation to him while I was texting the wife. "They not let me on plane. Covid test no good. Go back Patong."

He was the same guy that dropped me off. Now he was driving me back. He was making an easy $1,400 baht that day.

"Go back Baan Boa?" he asked.

"No, no, no," I said. "I find new hotel."

I received a notification on my phone. The wife had just wired $300US into my bank account. It was five or six in the morning back in Texas. She would be getting ready for work right about now.

Then I switched over to the travel app on my phone and searched for a room.

"Best Western," I said a few moments later. "Patong. You know where that is?"

The taxi driver nodded. "I know. I take many customer there."

We were still working our way through rush-hour traffic somewhere around the Kathu district.

In the span of a few panicky minutes sitting in the back of that taxi, I was able to re-book my flight, get money wired to my account, and find a hotel room — all of it done on my cell phone, this little electronic device hardly bigger than a candybar. Such an amazing piece of technology. If this were thirty years ago, or even fifteen years ago — what would I have done? Kids born after the year 2000 take this stuff for granted, but me, I'm still amazed. And I've been working in the tech industry for over 25 years.

Another downside to this unexpected turn of events and not having any cash meant that I would be putting those additional costs on my credit card, which was beginning to creak beneath the weight of all the debt I was piling onto it. How much longer could it hold? I was afraid to check. I only had to survive three more days.

Chaiya's recovery hadn't gone as planned. Her nose wasn't healing properly. Weeks after her surgery, there was still pus oozing from the incision where the doctor had inserted a strip of silicone to make her nose straighter.

She tried to go back to work, but she wasn't making any money. Nobody wanted to buy drinks for a girl with a bandaged nose.

She was ashamed and humiliated. Further adding to her misery, she texted, "Too many Indians."

The Thai tourism board had been advertising heavily in India, and their efforts were beginning to show results. Bangla Road was crowded now with groups of young Indian men, gaping at the young Thai bar girls standing outside the bars or sitting perched on stools. But Indians were not heavy drinkers, and they were known for being cheap. "One beer, three straws," joked one farang.

Chaiya was having a hard time of it. Her wound became infected, and I sent her money to fly back to Bangkok to see her doctor, who prescribed stronger doses of antibiotics and anti-inflammatory medication. It didn't help. Weeks turned into months, and the wound in her nose was still oozing pus.

During this period, she would sometimes go for a week without texting me. Once, I initiated a video call with her, but she declined it. I blocked her for a week. When I finally unblocked her, she immediately texted me, "Why did you block me? I thought you block me forever."

"I tried to call you at 3am your time, and you declined the call."

"You know the bars stay open till 2am now, right?"

Petty arguments. Petty jealousies, Petty insecurities.

There wasn't enough substance to our relationship to justify these petty annoyances. There wasn't even a relationship. We were just words on a cell phone screen to each other. A mere handful of WhatsApp text messages. It had been three months since my return from Thailand. Why was I still struggling with these feelings for her?

Cut it loose. Forget it. Let it go.

It's Thailand, I told myself. There's always more where that came from, where making new friends is as simple as strolling down one of the many Walking Streets. Meet a girl, buy her a drink, take her back to your room. Rinse, repeat. The formula couldn't be simpler.

I shake my head violently. Why am I even thinking about this shit? I have the money and the time now to travel anywhere in the world. Why get tripped up over some bar girl and her struggles with poverty? If she's got to down ten or twenty shots a night or go down on just as many men to pay her family's bills, then so be it. As harsh and cynical as it sounds, that world existed long before I happened upon the scene.

In July, the infection in her nose became worse, three months after her initial surgery. Her doctor advised her to return to Bangkok and have that silicone implant removed from her nose.

Chaiya texted me, crying. Her nose was going to look worse than it did before the surgery. She was going to look ugly. And could I send her money for plane fare and taxi to and from the airport to the clinic? Then she would need money again to return to have the stitches removed.

I scraped together some cash and wired it to her. This was getting old. And pointless. But I felt responsible for her. I felt this way the first day I met her. I was filled with a powerful urge to take care of her and make sure she was okay. I don't know why. There's nothing my rational mind can offer up that would justify my behavior this past year, but there you have it.

A month later, she moved out of her room at the K&K Guesthouse and caught a bus back to Hat Yai. She started working at one of the clubs out there. She didn't tell me the name of the place, and I didn't ask. Most of those clubs maintain a Facebook page and often post photos of the bar girls drinking and mingling with customers. Chaiya was sly and secretive. She wouldn't want me seeing such photos if they existed. I searched and couldn't find anything. When did I become such a jealous, insecure person? Have I always been this way?

Maybe it was because of the distance between us and the fact that I couldn't see her every day. And the fact that her "job" was sitting around in a bar every night, trying to get as many men as possible to buy her drinks?

I simply had no way of knowing for sure what she was up to, and this alone was teaching me something about myself, something that I have yet to appreciate or fully understand.

Why do I even care? I don't need these kinds of headaches in my life anymore.

I'll make new friends. Bar girls are a dime a dozen. No need to over-think the bullshit. Shove it to the side and keep going.

I hadn't met many bar girls, but I knew Chaiya was different. I know, I know — famous last words of a lonely farang about to get fleeced. Another walking ATM. But she really did seem different. It felt different with her. There was no put on, no come on. No false flattery or superficial flirtation. Rarely smiling and not one for making small talk, she maintained an aloofness about her, keeping an emotional distance.

Long after I left Thailand and had given any hint that I would ever be returning, she continued texting me every day, sometimes sending photos of what she was eating or sending short videos of her and her friends. I noticed none of her friends were of the dark-skinned or heavily-tattooed variety of bar girls you typically find in Nana Plaza or along Bangla Road, dressed in skimpy bikinis or lingerie, grinding their asses in the crotches of old white men perched on barstools. Chaiya and her friends tended to dress on the more conservative side — long-sleeved blouses, silk slacks — classier looking. Chaiya, I know, prided herself on her light skin. She and her friends could have been mistaken for Chinese tourists on holiday.

If you scanned through the photos they posted to their social media accounts — Facebook, Instagram, etc. — you would have no idea that any of them worked in a bar, getting as drunk as possible from the shots of vodka customers were buying them every night. Some of them had Thai boyfriends. Most of them had kids.

But what do they think? How do they feel?

Some clues might be gleaned from the captions they include with the photos they post online.

"Tired. Exhausted. Must keep working to make that money."

"Someday I will be able to rest. Someday I will find peace."

"I want to belong to myself. Not to others."

"No matter what you go through, it is important to realize your true worth."

"Ignore the haters and keep going!"

Most of the comments are written in Thai, obviously, and I used the Google Translate app to discover the usual pithy aphorisms and rather incongruous comments, given the stylized and sometimes provocative poses of the young women in the photos themselves. Dinner dresses and fancy restaurants. Poses with champagne or glasses of red wine. Sexy shots on one of the many beautiful beaches of Thailand. Here is another shot standing near a wall of flowers. Or on this bench overlooking the ocean.

The overall feel was one of exhaustion and never having enough money. Such was the life of a working bar girl.

But was it real? Or was it just pretending and play-acting, some sort of game in which their friends are all in on the charade?

At the end of their shifts in the early morning hours of another long evening of drinking and pretending to be interested in the clumsy flirtations of drunken farang men, the young women will return to their rented rooms in rundown guesthouses and sleep it off, only to wake a few hours later to do it all over again.

Some might land a guy for the night. Make an extra $3,000 to $6,000 baht depending on the looks of the girl and the gullibility and desperation of her john. Everything is negotiable.

But what the hell do I know? I had only vacationed in Thailand for a total of seven weeks. Hardly a subject matter expert, I was barely a tourist.

Perhaps this is what drove my confusion over my relationship with Chaiya. I had no idea how to approach a relationship with a bar girl. Was there some cultural protocol I could follow? Was there a list of frequently asked questions I could reference to gauge my own situation?

I believed she had genuine feelings for me and wanted to bring this relationship forward. Why else would she go out of her way to have me meet her mom and her son? And then make plans for me to return and visit her mom's place and meet her extended family later in the year? Would a bar girl do this for some random farang she's turning tricks on? Maybe it was. Maybe this was all some complicated ruse that her family was in on to milk yet another lonely foreigner for all his worth? I was mentally exhausted thinking about it.

Was I the only one? Were there other guys? I looked for hits and clues in the text messages she sent me, noting the time of day and the tone she used. Friendly? Irritable? Was she in a hurry to get me off the line? Was it just my insecurity or was she no longer so forthcoming with information — her comings and goings, who she was meeting for lunch or dinner, what was she doing at three in the morning after the bars had closed?

I made a point never to ask her anything. I didn't want to seem nosy or insecure. I didn't want to come across as controlling. I always waited for her to text first, and then I would respond, almost always immediately. She had me on the line, and she knew it.

Meanwhile back at home, the wife and I were getting along like never before. We would never be intimate again — those days were long gone. In fact, we had been sleeping in separate beds in separate rooms for the better part of the last decade. Despite the sleeping arrangement, we were friends again. We could talk again. We could speak to each other without raising our voices and having things escalate to a point where our daughter would have to call 911 for police intervention. (I hate to admit this happened on more than a few occasions.)

But we moved past those difficult times and found a way to make it work. Our daughter was grown now and out of the house. She was working in the oil and gas industry, making three times my salary. There was a time when the wife and I worried that she would end up locked away in a mental hospital. Thankfully, those fears proved unwarranted. Instead, she gave us a granddaughter who comes to visit every weekend and brings chaos and life into our otherwise quiet household. It's a good kind of chaos — the chaos of toys scattered all over the livingroom floor; chasing the ice cream man down the street, waving dollar bills in hand; the constant laughter and playful yelling; juice spilled on the floor and potato chip crumbs all over the couch; setting up outside Halloween decorations inside the house, in the middle of summer. And then at last, when the granddaughter is tired and begins with the whining and crying: nap time. Peace and quiet in the house once again.

Our granddaughter keeps the wife busy. Gives the wife something to look forward to on the weekends and holidays. Her mother passed away last year after struggling with lung cancer for years. Wife was taking her to all of her doctor and chemo appointments. Stayed with her on the weekends to cook and clean for her. Wife would bring the granddaughter there to help cheer her mom up. She'd text me photos with her mom looking frail but still smiling with her great-granddaughter in her lap. But near the end, the photos the wife texted showed a distinct change. Her mom was no longer smiling and she looked increasingly fragile, shriveled. Gone was her smile, and she would be staring off into the distance, not bothering to look into the camera. I'd ask the wife how her mom was doing, and she remained upbeat. She's fine, was her reply. She's getting better. We're making plans to go to Florida. She wants to go to Turkey next summer.

A few months before I was scheduled to fly out to Thailand, her mom fell and broke her hip trying to open her front door. At the hospital, doctors said she needed a hip replacement, but they couldn't operate right away — her lungs were filling with fluid because the cancer had returned. They had to drain her lungs before performing the surgery. She never left the hospital.

One of the nurses pulled the wife aside to inform her that her mother was dying, her response was not a surprising one. I rushed to be at her side and to wait with her as we watched her mother slowly fade to the other side. I didn't know until later, when the wife told me, that her mom had been sleeping in the recliner we gave her for the past few years because she could no longer sleep laying down. Her lungs would fill with fluid and cause too much pain. I was saddened to hear this. She suffered alone for so long. Finally, she knew peace.

—

The wife doesn't care to travel anymore. Her passport expired years ago, and she has neglected to renew it, despite my constant nagging. I wanted her to come with me to Thailand, but she isn't interested. She prefers to stay close to home nowadays. She doesn't want to be too far from our granddaughter.

There was a time when she loved going to the beach. She still does. But too many things have changed. She has changed. It would be selfish of me to expect her to be the same person she used to be.

I told her I couldn't wait any longer. I wanted to keep going. There were too many places I wanted to see. She waves me on, go ahead. Have fun. She will stay close to home.

The house is finally paid off, I explain. We could rent it out and live overseas.

She shrugs. She likes our cozy house and would prefer to live in it. She doesn't want to move to another country and have to learn yet another language. She's already fluent in Arabic, French, and English. She would have an easier time of it than I would, I imagine, when it came to learning Thai. Or Spanish. (I had also tried convincing her to move to Mexico.) But to no avail. She is content to stay right here in Plano, Texas.

We've been having this same conversation for years. Finally, I decided to go it alone. We simply drifted with neither of us paying much attention to how far apart we had grown, and yet the gravity of our shared life kept us tethered together. We were still comfortable living under the same roof, even after those years of struggling with drug addiction, mental illness, court orders, and accusations of domestic violence. The 911 calls I've already mentioned, and you might begin to understand why when this story is finally told, but it is not my place to tell it. I'll leave it at that.

Things have settled down and have been quiet for a few years now. I marked my fiftieth turn around the sun with a quiet reticence. I sold some acreage I owned in Hunt County and used the proceeds to pay off the mortgage on our house.

"You and Sara will never have to worry about being homeless again," I tell the wife.

In the evenings, after she had prepared my dinner, which I would eat sitting alone at the kitchen table, we retreated to our respective rooms — she to her Playstation to play the latest survival horror game (her favorite genre), and I to my Youtube videos and books. I can't recall the last time we sat at the kitchen table and had a meal together. I prefer to eat at around six or seven, and she prefers to eat before she goes to bed. Then she'll take the dog for a walk and a shit on the neighbor's yard.

"You shouldn't be doing that," I say.

"It's dark. No one can see," she replies.

"Yeah, but it still isn't right. One of these days someone's going to catch you."

She shrugs.

My daydream of relocating to Thailand and beginning a new life maintained a powerful hold on me. Whether Chaiya would be there to greet me when I arrived or whether she would remain a part of this rather complicated equation, well — that image began to fade like a photograph let out in the sun. Heartbreaking and disappointing, it was to be expected. Time, distance, the fact that we barely knew each other — better to end it now before I spend any more time and energy on it. And money.

"Babe, I need money to pay my son school. Can?"

"Babe, are you working? I need money to pay my room. Can?"

"Babe. How r u? I need money to buy soap and medicine. Can?"

Whenever she asked, I gave. And gave. And gave.

$3,000 baht.

$7,000 baht.

$5,000 baht.

$15,000 baht.

Most times, I was the one that was acting the fool. I was the one who broached the topic of money. I would ask her if everything was okay, how was she feeling, did she have enough money. How else was she going to respond? Of course she needed money. The answer was always yes, yes, yes. Please send more. Goddamned fool that I was, I had voluntarily become her own personal ATM machine.

The money I was sending her was money I was supposed to be saving to repair the house, pay down my credit card debt and that IRS bill. My overall credit card debt had ballooned to over fifteen grand. What the hell was I doing? I must have lost my brain somewhere over the Andaman Sea. Flushed it down the toilet in one of those hotels on Phuket.

I maintain a spreadsheet of my daily budget projected two years into the future. I've maintained this file since the days when the wife and I really needed to track where every dollar was going. Back then, buying that new video game could mean not being able to afford diapers for Sara that next week. What was it going to be? A carton of Marlboros or a tank of gas? We were operating on very small margins.

Things are better now. I'm sitting in front of my laptop computer with the spreadsheet open, looking over my latest budget projections for 2022 through 2024. Things will soon be looking a lot better. Much more financially stable over the next few months and into the next year.

Then I see an email notification pop up in the corner of my screen. The subject line briefly flashes: "Bangkok Airfare Alert."

Flights from Dallas to Bangkok are just over a thousand dollars. I book another trip for March 2023. Charged it to my American Express card. What the hell. I still have six months to plan, save, and budget.

I dropped a hint to my manager, telling him in an email on another subject that oh, by the way, I'm planning another overseas trip in March 2023. No response.

I tell the wife, and she laughs. "Oh, my god. They're going to fire you."

She still hasn't renewed her passport, and she still isn't interested in visiting Thailand.

I'll be out there for a month. 30 days. I'll need to budget.

Hotel: $60 x 30 = $1,800

Food: $60 x 30 = $1,800

Airfare to Saigon, Hat Yai, Phuket: $150 x 4 (including return flight to Bangkok) = $600

If Chaiya comes with me, that will be another $600.

Total: $4,800. Or call it $5,000, even.

$5,000US will be my target.

Then, another $2,000 for Chaiya and her mother. (Or around $80,000 Thai baht.)

Adjusted target: $7,000 to $8,000US.

I'll need to have that amount saved up by March 2023. I could probably do it for much less, but that target is realistic. I'll aim for that.

I'm assuming that I'll still have a job come March, and that can always change. I've been working as a consultant at Verizon for over five years now, and maybe it's something about hitting that five-year mark — my patience and tolerance for playing well with others takes a steep nosedive, especially when it comes to putting up with nit-picky middle-managers and company yes-men of the brown-nosed variety. I've grown too old to give a shit. The house is paid. The wife is working. The pressure is off. For the first time in thirty years, I can afford to fuck off and not worry so much about mundane things like having a job and paying bills. I can afford not to give a shit anymore.

So yeah — there is a very strong chance that I might decide to quit or — and this is more likely — be fired by then. If any of these occur, I'll extend my stay in Thailand to two to three months. I will likely not have any income coming in, so my budget will need to be as tight as a hamster's ass. I self-published my first book, *Flea Market Weirdos and Other Stories,* in September 2022, but who knows if that's going to bring in any money. I've got at least two more books planned — the one you're holding in your hand, and the other set in an alternate earth history scenario with Lemurians, Atlanteans, cockroach spies, and Inner Earth mythology. None of this will be much help for me if I find myself in Thailand without a job. And that could happen much sooner than expected.

Chaiya is in Malaysia. She texted me and said she's working at one of the nightclubs in Kuala Lumpur. She sends a few photos from inside the club. There's a stage up front where a band is playing live music. There are a hundred girls working in the club.

"Too many girls," she complains.

I ask her if she moved there.

"No. Come back next month. Contact for 24 day."

I later surmise that she meant 24-day CONTRACT. She'll work as a contract "PR girl" (the official job title used to refer to bar girls in the contracts they sign with the club). When her contract is over, she'll return to Hat Yai. Then return to Malaysia to do it all over again.

Things have cooled considerably between us since last December. For me, there is not so much longing now as a feeling of deep regret for a missed opportunity. This was a painful wound, one that will heal eventually. But my compass remains set for Thailand. That is my true north.

How did I allow myself to get so distracted? Nearly an entire year has passed with her constantly on my mind. This sort of obsession is not sustainable. I have been lost in the weeds.

Her birthday is next week, October 5th. I was planning to surprise her by wiring $36,000 baht into her account (a thousand baht for each of her 36 years). Just under $1,000US at the current exchange rate. But she texts me a few days before, complaining that she hasn't made any money at the club these past few nights. I asked her if she wanted her birthday gift a little early.

"Yes, I need now," she replies.

I thought it would make her happy, but she texts me a few days later and says she's moving to a new room.

I text her back, 'Why do you need to move? Did you find a cheaper room?"

Then she asks if I can send her money for airfare so she can move to her new room. Her new room is in Johor Bahru, near the Malaysian border with Singapore.

I'm confused. "You're working at a new club?" I ask.

"Yes," she says. Her friend says the money is better in Johor Bahru.

Something must have been lost in the translation. What she means is that she's going to start working at another club, not a new room. I sometimes forget that she speaks very little English.

But I'm still confused. I had just sent her $36,000 baht two days ago. And she's already run out of money?

"No money for food," she says, "Can?"

I reply simply, "No."

"Okay, I will ask my friend," she says. She doesn't text me the rest of the day or night.

I don't care. Life continues.

Part Three

—

Thailand / Malaysia
March - April 2023

The excitement and anticipation of seeing her again isn't there anymore. I'm already feeling exhausted and anxious. That's all our relationship has become. We were so close to making it work. I thought, anyway.

Caught that flight from Dallas/Fort Worth International to Tokyo-Narita. My original itinerary had me making a connecting flight at Haneda International, which is a two-hour bus ride from Narita. But to my surprise, when I got off the plane at Narita, I saw a Japanese Airlines gate agent holding up a piece of paper with my name printed in large bold letters. Turns out that connecting flight to Bangkok would be flying out of Narita instead of Haneda, and it would be departing within the next two hours instead of the original eight-hour layover. Not only that but the flight to Bangkok was mostly empty, and I had an entire row of seats to myself. The only hassle was getting through the immigration line when I got to Bangkok. Evidently my flight arrived at the same time as a flight from Korea, and I kept getting bumped and jostled by Korean dudes jostling their way to the front of the line.

By 2am, I was downtown on Sukhumvit and had checked into my room at the Red Planet Hotel, right across the street from Terminal 21. Made my way to Soi Cowboy and bar-fined a girl named Kik. We went to eat at a Thai-style shop around the corner. Everything else was getting ready to close down, and I was hungry.
I blew through my entire week's budget within those first few hours, and I'll just leave it at that.

—

I'm trying to stick to a $2,000 baht per day budget. I did a lot better today, my first full day back in Thailand.

Breakfast at the coffee stand in the BTS Asoke station:
Coffee: $35 baht
Chicken, rice, and egg plate: $45 baht
Stuff I purchased throughout the rest of the day:
Bottle of water: $40 baht
2 chicken skewers: $20 baht

Slice of pizza and a Coke at Pala Pizza Romana: $175 baht
Subway ride on the MRT: $40 baht
Baby wipes and large bottle of water: $43 baht
Shampoo, shave, and massage at Hwangjae Massage: $700 baht (plus $200 baht tip)

So far for today: $1,258 baht

―

Don Mueang International, Bangkok
Waiting for my 3pm flight to Kuala Lumpur.
I'll be in Malaysia for seven days. We were planning to meet, but I think she's busy working at the W Club. It doesn't matter if I see her or not. I will make other plans and enjoy my time in that area of the world.
I didn't do as much exploring as I was hoping to during these past few days in Bangkok. Walking around becomes too oppressive beneath the sweltering heat of the mid-day sun. Most of the time I end up retreating to the safety of my air-conditioned room back at the hotel.

―

The juice lady at the front of the alleyway leading to the Red Planet Hotel is a sneaky little scammer. The first night I bought a bottle of freshly-squeezed orange juice from her. She charged me $40 baht. The next night she charged me $60 baht.

Then last night I asked her how much for a bottle of the same stuff.

"$80 baht," she said, smiling.

"$80 baht! Last night it was $60. And before that you charged me $40!"

She laughed. "Okay. $60."

I'd pass her on my way back to my room in the afternoon as she was setting up her little cart. She would still be standing out there past midnight when I was coming home.

"Sawadee!" I'd shout to her.

"Hey!" she would shout back, smiling.

$40 baht, $80 baht. What does it matter? We're only talking a difference of a dollar or two, USD. The old woman is out there twelve hours a day, every day. It was worth the two bucks to see her smiling slyly when I caught her trying to rip me off.

Caught the MRT train to Chinatown yesterday.

I was on my way back to the subway when I passed a shop that had shelves and shelves of little white boxes. It looked like the parts department in a hardware store. I went in and poked around and discovered that each box contained eyeglasses of various prescriptions. I asked a woman stocking shelves if they had my prescription. She stopped what she was doing, seemingly annoyed at my interruption. I showed her a copy of my prescription that I always keep on my phone. Frowning, she nodded and retrieved a pair for me to try on. They were a little too round for my taste — like large John Lennon/Harry Potter spectacles — but they worked just fine. Good enough for reading. And the price was more than reasonable: $200 baht (about $5 USD). I'm wearing them now as I write these words. They don't usually stock a prescription as powerful as the ones I need back in the States (+600/+800). The prescription pair I picked up from Walmart cost me just under $500 USD for the lens and the frame.

I arrived in Kuala Lumpur, Malaysia yesterday evening. It was a leisurely two-hour flight from Bangkok's Suvarnabhumi

Airport on AirAsia. The cab ride from Kuala Lumpur airport to my hotel in the city center felt like it took longer.

On the cab ride over, I texted Chaiya, asking if she wanted to meet me for dinner. No, she replied. She has to work. She'll only have time to meet me for lunch or dinner. Then she has to go to work at the club. She said I could meet her at her work if I wanted to. Some place called the W Club. It was beginning to feel like she was luring me into another bar girl trap. I flew halfway across the planet for this bullshit. I said, thanks but no thanks. There were enough clubs near where I'll be staying, I texted back. I'm thinking this is the end of this particular dead-end road, a so-called relationship that consisted of two or three text messages a day for over a year. What a waste. We had become two complete strangers on opposite ends of that Internet connection.

Oh, well. I blocked her out of my mind. I couldn't quite bring myself to block her number completely from my phone just yet, but I wasn't going to let another failed relationship keep me from having fun while wandering around the world. I wasn't the one who was trapped.

—

I'm staying at the Indie Hotel in the Bukit Bintang district, a busy nightlife area a few blocks away from the downtown shopping district of Kuala Lumpur. It reminds me of North Beach in San Francisco, that being my only point of reference since I have often steered clear of anything resembling "trendy night spots." (Although I've made one notable exception for Thailand.)

There are a bunch of bars and restaurants and a walking street lined with food stalls and outdoor eating areas just down the road from my hotel. The crowd is a mix of high society Asians (a lot of well-dressed older men with much younger women) and dark-skinned Indians, also well-dressed, who look Samoan. They are tall and broad shouldered and flash bright white, toothy smiles, unlike the small, skinny Indians from Mumbai or Bangalore who come to work as software engineers back in the States.

I had a burger and a pint of beer at one of the trendy restaurants, then wandered into another place a few doors down that had live music. There I sat, nursing pints of beer and watching young couples and groups of single women dancing and waving their arms around enjoying themselves. This was no pickup joint or lady-drink bar. Everyone kept to themselves, which was perfectly fine with me. I was drunk by the time I got back to my hotel room. The drunkest I'd been in a while.

—

Mexico has Oxxo stores.
Thailand has 7-Elevens.
Malaysia — or at least in Kuala Lumpur, anyway — has KK.
Oxxo, KK, Circle K all have similar branding with the red (and yellow?) logos. I wonder if they're all owned by the same multinational corporate conglomeration?

—

Walked to Petronas Towers yesterday morning. Got there in a roundabout way. I got turned around in a few spots, distracted as I was wandering through the air-conditioned corridors that run like giant hamster mazes elevated over the city streets. These corridors wind through the city center and connect the highrises like a neverending airport terminal. Now the bankers and businessmen can wear their fancy suits without sweating like pigs and showing up for their sales meetings looking like they just ran a marathon.

Not exactly a "green" solution with all the energy they're burning to keep those walkways nice and cool. But I have to admit, it is nice to get out from under that oppressive Malaysian heat.

Wandering around Kuala Lumpur, as in Bangkok, you get a cardio workout just by walking from one place to another, trudging up and down steep concrete stairways, trying to get to those air-conditioned corridors. And much like Bangkok, there aren't very many places in downtown Kuala Lumpur where it's safe to cross the street with designated pedestrian crosswalks. You're taking your life into your own hands whenever you cross the street at street level.

I didn't mind the workout. If the typical American had to do that every day, they could eat as many McDonald's cheeseburgers as they wanted and wouldn't have to worry so much about diabetes or heart disease.

—

Dripping with sweat from the heat and humidity. Whenever I get back to my hotel room, I immediately strip off all of my clothes and jump into the shower. I've been taking three or four quick showers every day since I arrived in Southeast Asia.

—

I've already blown through a thousand dollars of my travel budget within the first week. I think I'll be okay.
$1,200: Charles Schwab brokerage
$1,300: Cash budget
$800: Capital One
$3,300 to last me through April 15th.
$3,500 counting the $200 I have on my Wise debit card.

—

Went way overboard and spent about $500USD at Chaiya's club. The W Club @ Solaris.

I met her for dinner at this Thai shop next door to the club. I caught the waitress giving Chaiya a sly smile when she spotted her walking in with me. I knew then that she was probably a regular there who regularly ate there with other customers.

I ordered a beer and told the waitress to bring whatever Chaiya wanted, to which she quickly replied, "She always orders the red wine."

Chaiya was on the other side of the room getting napkins and utensils and didn't hear the exchange.

"You eat here a lot?" I asked her when she returned.

"Oh, no," she said. "This place is too expensive."

Later at the club, one of her girlfriends joined us at our table. Next thing you know, I'm buying drinks for two girls. Then Chaiya ordered a tray of tequila shots. $1,300 Malaysian ringgit. Or about $275USD.

But my Wise debit card was declined. Evidently, I had reached the daily maximum limit that I could withdraw. Then it was a mad scramble as one of the club's security guys personally escorted me to the nearest ATM.

Still declined.

So he got one of his other security buddies to drive me twenty minutes back to my hotel, so I could use another credit card. He drove me all the way back, where they promptly presented me with the portable register and charged the new card.

I was afraid to think what those security goons would have done to me if I couldn't pay the bill. Take me out back and beat me to a bloody pulp? Chaiya didn't seem too concerned. She had already downed a handful of shots and was halfway to getting plastered.

—

I'm here until April 2nd.

Chaiya says she'll work until April 7th. Then she'll catch a bus back to Hat Yai.

I have a room booked for April 13th at the Baan Boa Resort Hotel in Patong.

Not sure where to go or what to do between April 2nd and the 13th. I still have a few days to figure it out.

Dinner with Chaiya yesterday evening. $90US for sushi, oysters, and soba noodles at a Japanese restaurant in the Lot10 shopping mall downtown. Then I bought her a pair of $90US New Balance sneakers and $90US worth of makeup at the Lancome and Bobbi Brown stores at the mall across the street. Shopping, eating, and drinking seem to be the only things to do in Kuala Lumpur.

Then she caught a Grab taxi back to her room, but not before dragging me to the grocery store to buy ingredients for making tom yum.

Afterward, I stopped by Rockefellers bar and nursed two pints of Tiger and a plate of french fries for $99 ringgit ($21US).

Another expensive day of going way over budget. Good thing tomorrow is payday. That $3,187.92US paycheck can't come soon enough.

—

Happy birthday to me. My 53rd turn around the sun.

Chaiya made it clear that she wasn't interested in coming with me to Penang on the 2nd. And she doesn't want me to ride the bus with her back to Hat Yai. She basically doesn't want me around except to take her shopping and send her money. I fell for the oldest bar girl trick in the book.

The tarot card readers on Youtube suggest that the situation no longer serves me (or people born under the sign of Aries, in general), and it is time to let it go.

Time to let it go.

This toxic situation has dragged on long enough.

Sever the connection and let it go.

My mind is free once again. Unburdened by heartache and anxiety. I am free once again to explore the beauty of the living world. I've been spending too much time living in my head.

My updated itinerary for the remainder of this trip:

April 2 - April 5: Penang, Malaysia

April 5 - April 13: Kata, Phuket
April 13 - April 18: Patong, Phuket
April 18 - April 21: Bangkok

—

Spent my birthday walking around the Central and Petaling districts in downtown Kuala Lumpur. Another hot and muggy day to go wandering about in that soul-crushing heat. Whenever I return to my room, my clothes are soaked through and dripping with sweat. I usually change out of my day shirt, hang it to dry, and change into my evening shirt later. But it's been too muggy and my clothes are still damp nearly two days later. My hotel room lacks a balcony, so I've been hanging my clothes to dry in the room, which doesn't seem to be as effective as hanging them outside, which is what I normally do when I'm in Thailand or Mexico. Beach bum problems. I'll wait until evening before going out again.

Dinner was a burger and fries with a pint of Tiger beer. I stopped by a few more bars and drank a few more pints before calling it an early evening. I was secretly hoping to hear from Chaiya, and I kept checking my phone for a text message from her. Nothing.

I think it's better this way. I can move on to something (or someone) more positive and productive.

I don't know what changed. Maybe she realized the ultimate futility of a long distance relationship. Maybe she's got a new guy. Maybe it's both. Whatever. It's not worth expending any more time and energy fretting over it. I'm on a month-long vacation in one of the most beautiful regions of the world. I can't allow myself to be distracted with bar girl nonsense.

—

Batu Ferringhi
Penang, Malaysia

I've been staying at the Oceanview Beach Resort Hotel since April 2nd. Tomorrow I fly to Phuket where I booked a room in Kata for the next five days or so.

My Wise debit card was hacked in Kuala Lumpur, and the thieves withdrew $800 ringgit ($170US) before I noticed what was going on and put a freeze on my account.

I've only got $995 worth of credit left to last me until April 15th, next payday. If not, I've got to make that $995 last until the 20th, which is when I'm scheduled to fly home. Fortunately, I paid in advance for all of my airfare and hotel stays, so I don't have to worry about being stranded somewhere without a place to sleep.

Batu Ferringhi is a chill little beach town. The beach is decent and mostly devoid of any beach-goers. The water is brown and murky, but very warm. Both days I went swimming, I was the only one in the water. There are mostly Chinese tourists here, and they only take pictures on the sand. The girls are dressed in fancy lace dresses with wide sun hats, and their boyfriends wear pants with the cuffs rolled up to avoid getting wet. Meanwhile, I'm there in the background splashing around in the brown murkiness, like some chubby Filipino sea monster. Maybe it's because this is a Muslim country that Batu Ferringhi isn't the party beach town that it could be? Just a few doors down from my hotel there's a Hard Rock Cafe - Penang. At some point, someone put in the effort. Maybe Covid is what killed off the party beach vibe. Who knows.

Chaiya wants me to meet her mother in Hat Yai, so I booked a three-day excursion out that way. April 15th to the 17th. I might just fly back to Bangkok from there since I'm scheduled to return on the 18th. I'll need to move some flights around. Not sure how much that's going to cost me.

Penang, Malaysia
Batu Ferringhi
Oceanview Beach Resort, Room 726

I'm really glad I brought along this little folding stainless steel coffee-drip filter. Way better than relying on that instant coffee crap that most hotels provide in their rooms. And I don't have to go prowling the early morning streets in a strange town looking for a place that's open that sells fresh coffee. There's a Starbuck's here, but it's about a fifteen-minute walk up the street.

The Indian guy working in the restaurant across the street calls me over for lunch. He tells me he can serve me beer as long as there aren't too many Malays eating there when I order. I'm lucky since I'm the only one there. I order the lamb masala with rice and chase it down with two cans of Tiger beer.

I'll be living on a backpacker's budget the rest of this trip. Sixteen days on $995. That works out to about $62US per day. Or $2,100 Thai baht per day.

But Chaiya wants me to take her mom and family out to dinner. And then she wants to buy her and her mom dresses for the Eid celebration. $10,000 Thai baht a piece.

Honey Resort, Room 101
Kata, Phuket
Thailand

Been here since the 5th. Checking out on the 10th and heading up the road to Patong.

95% of the tourists here are Russian. If it weren't for the hired help working the bars, restaurants, and trinket shops, you wouldn't even know you were in Thailand.

I spend the mornings on Karon Beach. Hide out in my hotel room most of the day until early evening when I head out to the night market. From there, I head to the walking street of pop-up bars a few blocks over.

Went way over budget (again) these past few nights, buying drinks for bar girls and playing board games. Tonight I will just eat dinner, then go back to my room. I hope.

Ventured down another street of bars — or "walking streets" as they're called. Stumbled upon one that looked more like a pool hall — it had more pool tables (about eight of them) than the little round drink tables. I played a few games with a little old lady who ran the table on me. She laughed and yelled out every time she made a shot, which was most of the time. A smiling bar girl hovered nearby, sitting at a nearby table and cheered her on. They were the only two women working in the place. I bought each of them a drink and told the old lady I would return tomorrow for a rematch. I was back at my hotel room and falling asleep by 9pm.

—

I've been averaging around $1,000 Thai baht per day for breakfast, lunch, and dinner. If I go out drinking, add another $1,000 baht on top of that. If the bar girls get a hold of me, add another $2,000 baht on top of that.

Went for a short swim this morning. Sunburn settling in on my back and shoulders. Crispy, crackly feeling. Like a barbecue potato chip.

Breakfast at Kata Villa. $140 baht for:
- Two eggs
- Two strips of bacon
- Two slices of toast
- Two slices of cheese
- Two slices of ham
- Two cups of orange juice
- One cup of coffee

I retreat to my air-conditioned room and wait out the heat of the day, watching tarot card readings on Youtube, most advising me to "walk away from this connection."

Yes.

Heartbreaking and unfortunate, but it must be done. (How in the hell did I go tumbling down this rabbit-hole of New Age bullshit? As Edgar Cayce always said: MIND IS CREATOR!)

Late lunch at the Thai place across the street:
- Red curry chicken with rice
- Fried squid
- Big bottle of Singha
- Total: $470 baht

Heading out to the bars later tonight.

Played another few rounds of pool with that little old lady. I learned her name is Da. The lone bar girl, who looks more Vietnamese than Thai and is always smiling wide with her braces, goes by Patsy.

Da ran the table on me again, taking me three games to two. Then the dreadlocked guy sitting at the bar, looking wild and disheveled, took me up on a game. (The previous night, I thought he was a crazed homeless guy making trouble with the bartender.)

If I won, he would buy a round of drinks for everyone in the bar. If he won, I would only have to buy him a drink.

He played one-handed, setting up for each of his shots by balancing the cue on the edge of the table or just holding it one-handed in the air. He still beat me, but instead of just buying him a drink, I went ahead and bought everyone a round — him, Da, and Patsy.

His name is Bob, and I learned that he's the owner of the bar.

I said to Bob: "Man, you're really good with those one-handed shots."

He pointed to a trophy up on the mantle behind the bar. He'd won tournaments playing one-handed.

—

Patong Beach, Phuket

I checked out the night market on the other side of Bangla Road, across the street from Bangla Boxing Stadium. I wanted to watch Muay Thai boxing last night, but the flyer that I got from one of the touts was for another location up in the hills, Patong Stadium, which according to the guy standing out front was a 15-minute tuk-tuk ride away.

Dinner earlier was a small rack of ribs at the night market near my hotel. More bone than meat. $450 baht with a large bottle of Singha. Afterward, I wandered through Bangla Road and stopped for a few drinks at the Red Hot bar. Stopped in at Suzie Wong's. Place was crowded as usual. Standing room only. Mostly guys and a few white couples. When I was there a year earlier, I sat between two bikini-clad young women — one a Thai/Chinese and the other a Filipina. They let me finger their pussies and play with their tits while we relaxed with a few rounds of drinks that I'd bought them. I left each of them a $1,000 baht note before heading out into the night.

Nothing new or particularly exciting this time around. I made the long, sweaty walk down the beach and was back in my room by 10pm. As always, I slept alone.

Baan Boa Resort, Room 313
Patong Beach, Phuket

Another $3,000 baht day yesterday. One thousand went to a decent after-lunch massage with an attempted "happy ending." Unfortunately, the two beers I had at lunch made it impossible for me to finish. I noticed the poor woman becoming exhausted as she kept switching from hand to hand. She had broken into a sweat and looked as if she was struggling to strangle an eel. After a while, I put my hand on hers and said, "It's okay. Never mind." She smiled gratefully and got up off of me.

But her massage was top notch, exactly how I like it — slow, very slow, and firm.

Some place near the entrance to the OTOP marketplace and bar complex, dinner was a sad excuse for an overpriced pizza. It was just cheese and salami draped over what looked and tasted like a large cracker drowning in tomato paste. I spent the evening and rest of my $2,000 baht playing games and buying drinks for a girl I met at Crystal Bar. I was back at my room by 11pm with $70 baht left in my pocket.

My final week in Thailand went by in a flash. I was too exhausted in the mornings to write coherently about any of it.

My disappointment over Chaiya — well, heartbreak — let's just call it what it is — all those shitty feelings and rollercoaster emotions slowly faded to the background as I made new acquaintances and sought new experiences here in the Land of Smiles. She continued to text me each morning and at night, asking me what I was doing, how I was feeling. She thought I was still planning to meet up with her in Hat Yai, but I told her that I was flying back to Bangkok straight from Patong instead. I had booked and paid for a flight plus a two-night stay in Hat Yai, but I wrote that off as a loss (a few hundred dollars, at least) and wasn't going to bother her about it until she asked. I told her I was tired of catching planes and waiting around in airport terminals. I was running out of time, and I just wanted to chill and enjoy my remaining time. She texted back with a crying emoji.

"It's okay," I texted her. "Bad timing ya. Maybe next time."

She responded with more crying emojis and apologized. She was sorry she couldn't spend time with me, but she had to work. She had no choice. She was the only one supporting her mom and her boy.

I don't think I was ever angry with her, or spiteful. It's like I said — just bad timing. I just felt numb after a while. Disillusioned.

I spent my remaining evenings in Patong at Crystal Bar in the OTOP bar complex. This is where I met Ice.

I was looking for a place to shoot pool that first night. Just some place to chill out and play a few games, like I did when I was in Kata. Something low-key. No hard sell or come-ons from the girls. I wasn't looking to meet any girls.

In the distance, toward the back of the complex, I spotted a lone pool table and a girl sitting alone on a barstool next to it. I walked up and asked her if she wanted to play a game. She gave me a confused look at first, and one of the other girls shouted something in Thai to her. Then she understood that I wanted to play a game of pool with her. She got up and racked the balls on the table. We played a few games until a group of tourists complained to the katoi mamasan that we were hogging the table. They looked like any other group of tourists in this part of Thailand — obese, sunburned, wearing tanktop t-shirts, arms and ankles riddled with tattoos. White. Farang men.

Some with their equally obese wives or heavily tattooed Thai girlfriends.

The katoi mamasan, a heavy-set woman, came to our table and informed us very sternly that we need to give other customers a chance to play.

I shrugged. Okay, whatever.

We finished our game and took a seat at a nearby table. I ordered another drink for me and one for my new friend, who took a seat next to me with a Connect 4 board game and cups of dice in her arms.

And so it began innocently enough.

I returned every night for the remainder of my stay in Patong for an evening of Connect 4 and dice games with her. She didn't dress like a typical bar girl — heavy makeup, barely clothed with ass and tits hanging out all over the place, every inch of her back or thighs covered with dragon tattoos or whatever. She was dressed conservatively and looked more like the college-aged Thai girls you see at shopping malls in Bangkok. She often wore a beige jumper with suspenders and a t-shirt underneath. She wore very little makeup but didn't need to — she was young and beautiful. She had an alluring innocence about her, which I'm sure other customers picked up on as well.

I noticed she had a few regulars and would-be suitors. Some of these guys would come in and sit very close to where we were sitting. They would sit facing her, looking at her expectantly. Almost needy. As if I was about to walk off with something that belonged to them. Then she would lean into me and whisper very quickly into my ear, "I'll be right back. I have a customer."

She'd sit with the guy for a few minutes. Let him buy her a drink. Maybe let him cop a feel. Grope her a little. Then she'd come back next to me and resume whatever game we were playing.

She remained at my side most evenings I was there. I was content to just play boardgames with her and buy her drinks. At the end of each night I would return to my hotel room alone with a nice cool buzz.

My last day in Patong I took her to lunch at the Thai restaurant where Chaiya used to take me, a place called Sam Chor Restaurant on Sainamyen Road, just down the street from the hospital. I told Areeya about it (or Ice, as she prefers to be called) a few nights before.

Last night she asked me almost accusingly why I didn't call her for lunch as I had promised. I said I was waiting for her to text me.

The next day she texted me as soon as she awoke. It was a little past 1:30pm.

I had just returned from the beach and had eaten a rather large late breakfast at the Coffee Club.

She asked if I still wanted to meet at that Thai restaurant. I said sure, thinking she wanted to meet for dinner later that evening, so I laid down and took a nap.

She texted me a few minutes later: "I have arrived."

"You're at the restaurant now?"

"Yes."

It was barely 3pm, and I was still groggy from sleep. I rushed and put on my clothes and caught a tuk-tuk to the restaurant. It was just down the street and around the corner from my hotel, but in that Thai heat it would have been a very sweaty fifteen-minute walk.

Ice was waiting out front when I got there. She was wearing her usual beige jumper and white tennis shoes, looking every bit the innocent Asian schoolgirl.

We took a seat at a table near the wall. Our waitress, smiling knowingly, handed us a set of torn and ratty laminated menus. She probably didn't remember me, but I recognized her from the previous year when I last ate there with Chaiya.

In the evening and on into the wee hours of the early morning, this place is crowded with farang tourists and their bar girl dinner companions. The waitress will only speak with the bar girl when taking the orders, but when it comes time to settle the bill, she'll hand the check to the farang, whom she assumes will be the one paying. As if we are all harmless, retarded man-babies with uncontrollable sexual urges and wads of cash. We are merely tolerated while being catered to, like giant lumpy maggots that return a decent money to time investment. How can we expect to communicate coherently in a foreign language? We are too stupid and fat.

I don't recall the specific dishes that Ice ordered, but it seemed like she ordered everything on the menu that contained shrimp. (Thai girls always order enough food to feed three or four people, family style — even if there's just two people sitting at the table.)

I was still full from that huge early afternoon breakfast I had before going to the beach earlier. In fact, I felt bloated from the sausage, eggs, toast, and beans, but I went ahead and ordered the fried lobster, secretly hoping I wouldn't vomit all over the place.

The bill was $2,500 baht, and I left a $500 baht tip. Our waitress grew visibly excited when she saw it. Or maybe she was excited about something else, but she was giggling hysterically as she brought the check back to the register and showed the other girls. When we left, she gave us an enthusiastic wave. She might very well have been laughing about something else, but I like to think that small gesture made her day.

On top of lunch, I had also promised Ice that I would take her shopping. I asked her if she wanted to catch a taxi to Central World in Old Town Phuket, but she said she was okay with just going to Robinson's.

She was talking about the Jungceylon Shopping Center just down the street from my room at the Best Western. The place had recently reopened, like everything else in the country and around the world, since the height of the covid pandemic. When I was there in November 2021, Big C was the only store in the complex that remained open. The rest of the place was a ghost town, shuttered and left in the dark. Yellow caution tape was stretched out across various areas, blocking off the closed sections. I had no point of reference in those days since it was my first time there, but Patong itself had been reduced to a ghost town. Many shops and restaurants were forced to shut down. Bars had to close by 11pm.

For a first-timer like me, the Covid situation was a blessing in disguise, although I didn't realize it at the time. It seemed as if I had the entire island and all of its pristine beaches to myself. Plenty of available seating in every restaurant. Heavily-discounted rates on all the hotel rooms. In the bars along Bangla Road, ten girls for every farang.

Being my first time there, I thought it would be like this all the time. Barely two years ago. How things have changed. Now the beaches were packed solid with tourists, Russian being the main language I heard spoken throughout Kata and along Karon Beach. I'd never seen so many Russians gathered in a single place. To be honest, a fair number of them could very have also been from Ukraine. I couldn't tell the difference.

It was a strange dichotomy to see so many unfriendly, unsmiling faces in a country known as the Land of Smiles. The Russian invasion of Kata was so complete, I could barely walk down its narrow sidewalks without bumping into one of them. Often I would just step off the uneven curb into the street, narrowly avoiding being hit by a speeding motor scooter or tuk-tuk.

But no one hassled me, and I was left alone for the most part. I watched from a distance as they enjoyed themselves — mothers doting on their kids in restaurants, fathers splashing around in the water with their kids at the beach.

Having lunch at the Thai restaurant across the street from my room at the Honey Resort Inn, I watched a father struggling with his young son. He was trying to get him to eat a bowl of soup. The father was leaning over him, trying to spoon-feed the boy, but the boy was having none of it. It was clear he wanted no part of that soup. The father was growing visibly frustrated as he patiently held spoonful after spoonful of soup in front of the boy's face. The father's voice was stern and sounding increasingly threatening as he addressed the boy in their native tongue. The boy whined softly. He buried his face in his hands. He didn't want to eat that weird foreign stuff his father was trying to feed him. The boy turned his face away from his father and laid his head on the table.

I watched the drama unfold while working on my "American breakfast" — two slices of toast, a slice of ham, two strips of bacon, and a tiny thimbleful of pork 'n beans. With coffee and orange juice.

April is the warmest time of the year in Thailand, and today was no exception. Even while seated in the shade beneath the covered outdoor dining area and directly in front of one of the large floor fans, which forced me to anchor my napkins to the table with my plate, I sweltered in the heat, beads of sweat dripping from my forehead and onto the tabletop. How long would it take me to acclimatize to this environment? Probably never. Even back home in the States when the temperature gets just a little warm, I tend to sweat a lot. Maybe it's my high blood pressure? Overactive sweat glands? Who knows. I always carry a handkerchief with me to wipe my face, and I often wear a hat, not only to block the sun, but also to soak up the sweat from my head.

I could see that the boy's father was also feeling the heat from that midday sun. He was a tall, thin man with dark, close-cropped hair and a trimmed beard. His face was flushed red. From anger, frustration, or the heat. Perhaps all three. He finally gave up on trying to get his son to eat his soup and focused on his own meal. The boy's mother returned shortly. She'd been across the street exchanging money. When the boy saw her, he lifted his head from the table and resumed his whining. She grabbed him and held him close to her bosom, as if she hadn't seen him in years, stroking his hair consolingly. Then she lifted the spoon from the bowl of soup and held it enticingly in front of his face. Like a baby bird, the boy tilted his head and allowed his mother to feed him the rest of the soup. The father watched in disbelief. He threw his arms in the air, shaking his head and smiling.

At last — a smile, a laugh, crying, movement in the soul. Up until that moment, I was starting to think all Russians were stone-faced, unemotional and unfriendly robots, trained from birth to be killers or cogs in the machine. The ones I'd seen on the beach or walking along the narrow sidewalks or perusing the food stalls — they were as gray ghosts wandering silently through private purgatories. They were like people waiting to die, resolved to that inevitability.

Sweating, I paid my bill and retreated to my air-conditioned room, waiting for night to come.

—

At first, Ice was quiet and subdued as she walked alongside me. We perused the shops at Jungceylon mall. She looked at shoes, t-shirts, dresses, hats — not trying anything on. She'd just pick it up, glance at it briefly from different angles, then set it back down.

I asked her if she saw anything she liked. She shrugged and shook her head, no. She was timid, perhaps unsure of how she was supposed to behave in this situation. Maybe this was the first time a customer from the bar had taken her out for a shopping spree. Although I suspected this wasn't the case — she wore a relatively expensive Apple smart watch on her wrist to go along with her iPhone, items a college-aged Thai person couldn't possibly afford on a bar girl's salary. But that didn't bother me. I just wanted to do something nice for her before I returned to Bangkok. I had enjoyed her company these past few nights at Crystal Bar, playing Connect 4, shooting a few games of pool, or playing dice games. It was all innocent, which was a welcome change from the mind games and drama I experienced with Chaiya down in Kuala Lumpur.

In sharp contrast to Ice, Chaiya was like a seasoned professional, as skilled as a pickpocket in quickly working over a guy in the club to get what she wanted, whether it was money, drinks, or both. At least with me, anyway. She played me like a goddamned fool. When we went out to eat, Chaiya always made a point to order the most expensive item on the menu. When I took her shopping, it was like a shark feeding frenzy. And I was the unsuspecting live bait. Chaiya did not hesitate. She knew exactly what she wanted. She knew the brand names of the most expensive makeup and perfumes and would interrogate the girl working behind the cosmetics counter on the relative merits of this particular shade or scent of one particular brand versus another. Then she would wave me over to see what I thought, knowing full well that I was absolutely clueless in anything related to women's fashion or style. I think she did this just as a prelude to getting me ready to pay.

Then Chaiya would instruct the clerk to ring it all up, at which point, as if on cue, the clerk automatically turned to me and asked for my credit card. (Is it only in Asian countries where retail workers assume that it is the man who will be paying?) Like a fool, I would hand over my card not realizing until I signed the receipt that I had just charged over a hundred dollars U.S. to my credit card. Chaiya was like a lioness, working with a surgeon's precision to get at the choicest organs of her prey. She didn't waste her time with Dollar Store discount crap.

Ice, on the other hand, was not as polished, her skills not as honed. In Robinson's, she spent a few minutes asking the old woman who worked in the pharmacy questions about Maybelline or L'Oreal makeup in the cosmetics aisle. She showed me the price of each item she wanted to buy — cotton balls, toothpaste, cleaning solution for her contacts, a packet of rouge, and eyeliner.

I said, "Sure. Get whatever you want." There couldn't have been anything in the pile that was worth more than a few bucks.

Where she seemed uncomfortable with a near-stranger buying her things a moment ago, now she warmed to the idea. Smiling wide, she grabbed my hand and led me back to a shop where she'd been eyeing a purse. I grew hesitant. The last few times I took Chaiya shopping — at Central World in Phuket Town, at the local mall in Hat Yai, and at Terminal 21 in Bangkok — she had a knack for choosing handbags with price tags well over the $200USD mark. And here I was once again, in another mall with another girl, and still a damned fool.

But Ice, I could tell, was still a little timid and shy. She hadn't been working the bar scene as long as Chaiya and hadn't yet acquired that same degree of sophistication and ruthlessness. Ice was only 25, while Chaiya was pushing 36. Even at 25, Ice seemed much younger.

She found the handbag she'd spotted earlier and held the price tag up for me to see.

"Is this okay?" she asked.

The price of the bag was $1,200 Thai baht. Or about $36US.

"Sure," I said, quietly relieved.

She held up an identical bag, but in a different color. "Which one you like?"

She held the lime-green bag in one hand and was holding up a pink one.

I pointed at the green one.

"But pink is my favorite color," she said, shooting me a look as if that were something I should have known. So I bought her the pink one.

We strolled around the mall for a little while longer. She took my hand in hers as we walked. When we rode the escalator, she snuggled her face into my arm. Were we a couple now? It felt good to have an attractive young woman snuggling up to me like that. No wonder so many old men came over here to retire. The poor saps were wasting away from neglect and loneliness in their home countries.

"Sugar daddy," she giggled.

"What?"

"You my sugar daddy," she repeated and squeezed my arm.

"No, no, no," I protested. "I'm not anyone's sugar daddy."

Was that what I had become? Or worse — was I behaving like a simp? Just some lonely old dude on his third trip to Thailand in two years, creeping on women young enough to be his daughter?

I was becoming increasingly annoyed at taxi drivers, hotel clerks, and restaurant staff continually asking, "You come here alone?"

What they really meant to ask: Was I another weirdo sex tourist visiting Thailand to have sex with their women? Was I one of the thousands of wrinkled, gray perverts coming in on overseas flights, perspiring with anticipation and beady-eyed eagerness? Barely able to control their erections and ready to ejaculate all over the first unsuspecting bar girl who asks for a drink?

Mongoloid animals! Borderline rapists and pederasts!

Indian men wander down one of the many Walking Streets in packs of no less than four or five abreast, like little brown goblins, wide-eyed and ogling the girls perched on bar stools at the front of every club. They want boom-boom and will not spend more than $500 Thai baht. The girls wave them off with mild annoyance.

At another bar, a drunk Aussie or two sit in the shadows. Sunburned and morbidly obese, like beached elephant seals. Tattoos on arms and calves like scrawlings on a roasted pig, bloated and pink. Bloated, pink flesh stretched tight and ready to burst. It's 11 o'clock in the morning.

In the touristy areas, you will often see bar girls hanging on the arms of farang men. The girls cling tightly to these walking ATM machines. Some of these guys are actually good-looking, to be honest. Young and fit. There might actually be some genuine boyfriend-girlfriend chemistry going on. Mutual attraction. Mutual lust. Not all of these guys are obese schleps or 70-year-old retirees. Geriatric perverts looking for a nurse-maid and end-of-life happy endings.

What did that make me? Where did I stand within this spectrum? Here I was, nearing the end of a third month-long trip to

Thailand in two years. Was it really because I needed to see Chaiya again? Or was there some deeper urge? Sex tourism was certainly a part of it. That couldn't be denied. But then there was everything else — the beaches, the food, the VIBE. The fact that everything was so cheap and affordable compared to the cost of living back in the shitty, third world United States. Life was easy in Thailand, but it was easy because I brought a large stack of U.S. dollars with me. I was just another "two-week millionaire."

But now my money was running out. I wasn't in dire straits or as desperate as I was on my previous visit back in April 2022, when I lost both of my ATM debit cards and barely had a hundred dollars in cash to my name, but I also couldn't be spending thousands of Thai baht on some bar girl's shopping spree.

It was my last day in Phuket, and I would be flying back to Bangkok the next morning. I tried explaining this to Ice, who spoke very little English, using various combinations of hand gestures and the Google Translate app.

"Tomorrow, I go," I said, speaking like Kimosabe in a 1950's western.

Ice just looked up at me, smiling innocently. I don't think she understood a word I said.

"I have to go to work," she said.

"Right now?" I said.

"Yes."

The sun was still high up in the sky. It was barely four o'clock in the afternoon.

"Why do you have to work so early?" I asked.

"It's my job," she replied.

Outside I flagged down a tuk-tuk for her and she looked surprised when I didn't get in with her.

"You not come bar with me?"

I smiled. "It's too early. I rest in my room little bit. I come later."

She nodded and left with a pile of shopping bags in her lap and in the seat next to her.

Chaiya texted me while I was walking back to my room. "What RU doing?"

I responded with a video showing a view of the sidewalk I was walking down. "On the way back from the beach," I said. "Last day in Patong."

Later that evening I returned to Crystal Bar to see Ice. I spotted her from a ways off. She was perched on a bar stool in her usual spot near the front of the place. When she saw me, she ran up and gave me a big hug. She brought out the Connect 4 and cups of dice. We played for a few hours, drinking and enjoying our time.

I wished I had met her sooner. I could have taken her on day trips around the island. We could have had dinner in Kata or Rawai. But it was too late. There was no more time. I was flying back to Bangkok in the morning.

And she was still so young. Only twenty-five. I had too many years on her. I tried to imagine where she would be in another five, ten years. How her looks would change. How her personality would change. This town would corrupt her soon enough, and there were too many old farang eager to be a part of that process. Wrinkled white devils.

For now, she was still soft and innocent looking, despite the fact I later learned that she had an 8-year-old son. You could still see the baby fat around her face. When she walked across the bar, it seemed as if she did so with some trepidation, as if she were unsure of her footing or herself, like a child that enters a room full of adults.

I watched her now as she walked back to the bar to fetch me another drink. I was getting better at Connect 4 and had won two out of the last five games. Two free drinks for me.

I was drinking rum and Coke tonight and was starting to feel more than a little buzzed. My month-long vacation was finally starting to feel — not so lonely. Maybe I should stay in Patong for a few more days? Spend more time with Ice. Bangkok could wait. There was nothing for me there but a plane ride back to the States. But I was running low on cash. Changing my hotel and flight reservations would likely add another few hundred dollars to my teetering credit card debt. This will be it until next time. If there is a next time. No sense trying to make something into more than what it is. Just let it go and move on.

Then Chaiya texts me again and asks what I'm doing. When I was in Kata last week, she had asked if I was still planning to see her in Hat Yai. I had already booked a flight and paid for a hotel room. But I told her no, time was running short and I just wanted to relax and spend the remaining days near the beach in Patong. That plane ticket and hotel reservation would go wasted. Another three hundred bucks down the drain. I didn't care. I had grown weary of waiting around in airports and checking into strange hotel rooms. Patong felt like home, and I was content being lazy on the beach.

Was I getting burned out from traveling already? It had only been three weeks.

No, it couldn't have been that.

I was burned out from Chaiya and our nonexistent relationship. When I went to see her in Kuala Lumpur, I got the feeling that she didn't want me around. My last memory of her was looking over my shoulder waving good-bye at her in the W Club as I was being escorted out of the VIP lounge area. No hug, no long good-bye. She remained a ways behind me up the stairs and simply held up a hand — "Bye." — like I was just another customer that she was finally glad to be rid of.

I couldn't figure it out. Why did she remain so cold and distant and yet continue to text me every day about nothing in particular? I was tired and heartbroken.

I made a new friend. (In fact, I had made a few.) But Ice was just a bar friend. We hadn't yet gone for a little "boom-boom in the room," and we probably wouldn't. At least not during this trip. She was fun, competitive, and playful. She wasn't moody and irritable, like Chaiya. Perhaps a bit too young for me, but therein lay part of the allure.

I texted Chaiya a quick video shot of my view sitting at the table crowded with drinks. Then I glanced up to see where Ice was with my drink and saw that an older white guy had intercepted her near the bar. I spotted them just as he was reaching his arms around her to give her ass a few tight squeezes. He buried his face against her neck, kissing her. The lech was latched onto her, slowly kneading her ass with both hands. Then Ice spun around quickly, looking in my direction — I think she was checking to see if I saw them. I turned my head, pretending to be looking in the other direction. I continued watching them from the corner of my eye as she took him by the hand and led him to a seat at the opposite end of the bar. She stood nestled between his knees while he continued to kiss and grope her. The bartenders (one of whom was her brother) and other bar girls kept looking in my direction, probably wondering how I would react. I waited a few minutes, but when I saw her pull up a bar stool next to him, I got up and left. No sense hanging around. I was just another customer.

Oh, well. It was my last night in Patong, and I would probably never see her again. I took the long walk back to my hotel, ruminating once again on heartbreak and disappointment.

Walking down those narrow, uneven sidewalks, I grew annoyed at being jostled and forced into the street to avoid the crowds of Indians and other tourists. I felt driven to violence, like I might punch one of them or throw one into the street and into the path of speeding tuk-tuks. Was it the alcohol? Was it heartbreak? I held myself in check and retreated to my room. Anger management in the Land of Smiles.

Ice texted me a few minutes later. Where had I gone? She thought I had stepped away to the restroom and was waiting for me at our table. I responded that I had an early flight tomorrow. (My flight back to Bangkok wasn't leaving until 3pm).

I miss you.

Miss you, too.

Kisses, hearts, and hugs emojis.

Blah blah blah. Nothing but bullshit and lies.

Traveling between northern and southern Thailand is as simple as catching a one- or two-hour flight on Thai Airways if you've got the hundred bucks or so to spare. The planes are clean and modern, and there's enough leg room on the seats to feel like you're not having to contort yourself into a tiny wooden box. The flight attendants, tall and leggy, are like car show models catwalking up and down the aisle offering tea, Chinese biscuits, or heated moist towelettes. My experience was consistent, whether I was traveling from Bangkok to Hat Yai or Phuket, or flying into Thailand from

Malaysia or Japan. I imagine it must be a similar experience traveling throughout Southeast Asia, a harkening back to the golden age of airline travel, when flying on a jet plane was a privilege enjoyed solely by the wealthy and elite.

This is in stark contrast to air travel in the United States of Ass-Monkery, where the experience nowadays is akin to riding on a school bus for juvenile delinquents with behavioral problems, where the flight attendants are more like vengeful school marms running over toes and ramming elbows with their large metal food carts filled with little plastic containers of ultra-processed horse shit and miniscule cans of lukewarm Coca-Cola. $7 bucks a pop. Cash only.

Imagine being stuck in a large metallic tube going five hundred miles an hour, forty-thousand feet in the air with a bunch of obese mental retards who can't stop blathering or complaining about the stupidest shit, fighting over overhead bins, arguing over armrests, some of them drunk off their asses, many of them over-medicated. Imagine riding on a Greyhound Bus with wings, and you'll get the picture.

The flight attendants are haggard-looking and overworked. Many appear to be a decade or two past their prime, old ladies and the occasional homosexual (no longer so carefree and flamboyant six hours into a fifteen-hour overseas flight) pushing heavy food carts down narrow aisles. They are weary of having to say the same things over and over again to moronic and oblivious passengers. They are weary of having to remind passengers to fasten their seatbelts and to not congregate near the restroom areas (this is how terrorists formulate their most devious plans). They are weary of asking the same fucking question: "Coffee or tea? Chicken or the goddamned beef stroganoff?"

I don't know how long it takes — years, maybe a few weeks — but after a while, having one shitty day after another will seep into your personality and turn you into a shitty, miserable person. Years spent breathing in stale recycled air that smells like it was vented straight out of a gas station bathroom. Who knows what havoc this wreaks on a person's mind over the course of years and decades? All while being forced to wear polyester pantsuits and a fake smile? The only other job in America remotely similar is working the graveyard shift at a Waffle House in the Deep South.

Riding on a Third World chicken bus can hardly be as hazardous or violent as air travel in the U.S., where one must constantly be on guard against being attacked or confronted. (Americans love to confrontation, liberals and conservatives alike, if only to voice their often misinformed opinions to one another.)

When in doubt, take the aisle seat. You'll have a better chance of escaping the lunacy that has become life in the United States.

This country is slowly becoming one giant police state housing the criminally insane. Too many people have been shoved through the public education system, graduating with a high school diploma and still barely able to read or write at a fifth grade level. They will remain trapped in generational poverty and indentured servitude for the majority of their prime adult years, working part-time jobs at fast food restaurants. Allowed to exist, allowed to earn poverty wages, allowed to live in hovels at the whim of their masters — the bankers, the politicians, and billionaire CEOs. This isn't democracy — it's a fucking pyramid scheme.

—

Back in Bangkok.

It took me a little over an hour to get through immigration at the airport. The place was crowded with dour-faced Russians, bug-eyed Indians, and six-foot-tall Asian women in leather mini-skirts and knee-high boots. Difficult to know for sure if they were going straight to work in Nana Plaza or if they were on their way to an S&M party hosted by some wealthy Japanese businessman.

Three days left on this month-long trip. Just another two-week millionaire on vacation. Short timer, none the wiser.

This was my third trip here in two years. It still isn't enough. I must return as soon as possible. One month isn't enough. I need to stay longer. There is too much to see, too much to do. It is an entirely new world that beckons to be explored. I might as well be on another planet because that's what it feels like. And it isn't just Thailand. It's the entire region of Southeast Asia. I've been bitten by the bug. I've got yellow fever.

The food. The women. The cheap cost of living. The beaches. By comparison, every other beach vacation I'd taken — from Maui to Playa Del Carmen to Costa Rica — all of those places faded into the dim, distant background. 2nd place runner-ups. Also rans. Nothing could possibly compare to what I discovered, and what millions of other travelers are discovering, in Southeast Asia.

If there is any truth to the old adage that in your old age you will regret all the things you wanted to do but didn't, when it comes to my experiences in Thailand, I regret nothing. I take it all in with one deep inhalation. It all rushes in like a tsunami, like an entire universe. And in one vast exhalation, I give birth to an entire universe of flashing neon diamonds and exploding stars. I see a new reality opening up before me, the thin film of my old life peeling away from my eyes like yellowed wallpaper, worn with age and neglect. I have entered a parallel universe, one that was only a fifteen-hour plane ride away.

—

I spent the last few days hanging around Sukhumvit — along the touristy expat area bounded by Soi Cowboy, Terminal 21, and Nana Plaza. I was doing okay money-wise. I had a swanky room at the Hotel Clover with a 7-Eleven right next door. I probably could have spent another five weeks there if I'd wanted, but — who was I fooling? The money would run out sooner rather than later.

A sad reality slowly dawned on me during this trip, and it was awakening to the fact that there was no practical way for me to survive in Thailand unless I kept my job back in the States. I had allowed the place to lull me into a sweet hallucinatory dream those first few visits, but now I was a bit more resistant to her charms. And a lot more jaded. I was feeling....grouchy.

It would have been easier to blame the hordes of Indian tourists, some of whom I couldn't help noticing were rude and boorish and often treated their native hosts like shit. Or the unsmiling Russians with their cold aloofness and how they crowded the beaches like herds of pale, white sea cows. But really, what I was pissed off most about, what really soured my mood, was the way Chaiya treated me when I went to see her in Kuala Lumpur. It felt like I had become a stranger to her, one that she firmly kept at arm's length. She had become distant and cold. Why was I wasting my time, energy, and MONEY on her? There were a million other women in Thailand ready to take her place. She was easily replaceable.

—

Three more days in Bangkok. I needed three more months. Three more years. I needed more time in this brand-new reality, this parallel universe that I had just recently discovered.

When you find the reality within the dream, hang on to it tight and don't let go.

My life back in the States felt like a previous existence, a past life, a discarded corn husk. I still missed my wife, as strange and paradoxical as that seemed. I missed my granddaughter and our dog, Bootsie, who was getting up in age, ten years old now and developing cataracts in one of his eyes. (He would develop a cough over the summer, which would grow progressively worse. He passed away shortly before Thanksgiving later that year.)

I would miss Texas, too. Driving around Garland and old northeast Dallas. Rummaging through thrift shops and Mexican flea markets. Taking lonesome road trips down to Galveston and Corpus Christi. Driving out to Hunt County and points eastward, looking for vacant land and mobile homes on acreage.

It seems like cardboard cutouts to me now. Flimsy inanimate memories like flimsy inanimate objects blown over by this brand-new reality I had just discovered. Was it all just a bunch of non-interactive stage props this entire time? Illusions in the matrix waiting for me to see through it? See beyond it?

I couldn't make the move just yet. I still needed to make money. If and until I could make the break, I would remain chained to that cardboard existence.

I have begged and pleaded with the wife to renew her passport. She refuses to travel anywhere without our granddaughter.

And nowhere longer than a two or three-hour plane ride away. I'm afraid I must leave them behind when the time comes.

The weather in Bangkok is normally hot and humid. In April, the middle of the hot season, it's ten times worse. I'd been in Thailand for nearly a month and still hadn't acclimated. If I went out for any length of time — across and over Sukhumvit to Terminal 21, or down the block to the nearest Starbucks — I would be drenched in sweat by the time I got back to my hotel room. I was taking three or four showers a day. Not long hot showers, but quick cold-water rinses to wash the sticky mugginess off of me.

Bored of looking at tourists along Sukhumvit, I decided to catch the MRT subway past Chinatown and pay a visit to Wat Arun, another Buddhist temple. Might as well do some touristy things while I had a few more days. I didn't want to waste all of that time creeping around Soi Cowboy and Nana Plaza. Might be a good idea to copy the locals and "make merit" after weeks of hedonism and being a lazy beach bum.

Making merit is the Thai practice of leaving donations or money and saying a few prayers at a Buddhist temple with the hope of improving one's karma. Basically paying for one's sins, but I wasn't interested in buying my way into Heaven or Nirvana. The ties that bind are often the ones we tied ourselves. Anyway, money was tight, so I took a day trip out to Wat Arun, hoping to record some content for my Youtube channel.

I made my way down to the MRT station near Sukhumvit and Asoke, one of the main transfer points between the MRT and the BTS subway systems. Extremely busy, extremely crowded place. People everywhere, coming from all directions, rushing to and fro. Meanwhile in various spots along the elevated walkways and concrete stairwells, you will see some of the saddest, most pitiful looking beggars you'll likely see anywhere in the world.

An infant cradled in the arms of an old woman. They are covered in dust and grime and sit amongst a pile of filthy blankets. Passers-by toss a few coins into a tin-pan tray. It's crowded here. Lots of foot traffic. I worry that someone might trip over the pair. It's only ten in the morning, and I know this woman will still be here with her child until around midnight, when I stumble past her on my way back from Soi Cowboy.

Along the elevated walkway crossing over Sukhumvit, a man and his wife pause while he fishes a $20 baht bill out of his wallet. He turns back and hands the bill to a young woman sitting on the ground. Her eyes are squeezed shut, and her front teeth are jutting out of her mouth in strange angles. Then you notice her arms and legs, which are under-developed and horribly misshapen. She is like a nightmarish ginger root, stubs of bony flesh where her arms and legs should be with fleshy nodules growing out of them. I caught sight of her as I passed by and as the man was leaving the $20 baht bill in her tray. I was jolted with an initial disgust followed by delayed feelings of pity and sympathy, feelings which require some level of relational understanding, of which I found little. I could not even pretend to comprehend the suffering and struggle this poor young woman must endure just to survive. (Was she even aware of her suffering?) I might as well have been gazing upon an alien lifeform. She appeared to be blind and deaf as well — she was completely unaware of her immediate surroundings and was oblivious to the people leaving money in her tray. And then I thought, how did she get there? I couldn't see how she could have gotten to that spot on the elevated walkway unless someone carried her and left her there. I learned later that many of the beggars you see on the streets of Bangkok are recruited by a sophisticated network of organized gangs that assist in placing them at targeted spots throughout the city to ensure the highest amount of profits. Of course, the beggars are still beggars at the end of the day, but someone must be making enough money to warrant such an effort.

—

I worked my way through streams of people fast-walking out of the MRT subway making their way over to the BTS skytrain on a seeming collision course with people moving in the opposite direction. People rushed up the steep concrete stairs from the street or rode the escalators packed in tight, one after another, an endless conveyor belt of office employees and shop workers, restaurant help and hotel staff.

Having just strolled from my hotel around the corner, I was already breaking into a sweat, and yet here I saw women in sweaters and young men in suits and dress shoes. I would have collapsed from heat exhaustion if I had to wear such clothes in hot, humid weather like this. Where's the nearest beach? Which subway takes me to the nearest beach? I knew better than to wear anything other than my usual outfit — swimming trunks, Teva sandals, synthetic t-shirt, and my army surplus boonie hat. My testicles felt as if they were about to overheat at the mere sight of people walking around in blue jeans or skinny jeans. How could anyone do that to their genitalia? Let them breathe!

I also always double-check that I have a bandana in my pocket and a small hand towel in my backpack. The hand towel is for wiping the sweat dripping from my face and neck whenever I'm walking around anywhere outdoors for longer than a few minutes. I might look all hot and sweaty, like I just came off a five-mile run, but no, just walking from the hotel to the train station.

The bandana is for wiping my hands and mouth if I'm out eating somewhere. Napkins are few or nonexistent at many restaurants and food stalls. A few places offer rolls of toilet paper, which may seem clever at first, but are actually worse than useless. Instead of fingers covered in grease and hot sauce. Now you've got fingers covered in grease, hot sauce, and soggy bits of disintegrating toilet paper.

I caught the train heading south. Or was it west? On Google Maps, I could see that I needed to head downward and to the left to get to the station nearest to Wat Arun. So….southwesterly, I guessed.

The train was jam packed. Standing room only. Most people were still wearing their Covid surgical masks, so I donned mine, not wanting to look like an inconsiderate jerk, like people of a particular political persuasion from the States asserting some self-proclaimed God-given right to this or that constitutional amendment. Spewing anger and hatred, like a watery shit-stain trailing across a Walmart parking lot. Diarrhea of the mind.

I grabbed hold of one of the wrist straps hanging down from a pole extending along the ceiling of the car and enjoyed the ice-cold air-conditioned air blowing down my short sleeve t-shirt and chilling the sweat on my armpits. A welcome respite from the street-level heat and mugginess.

I noticed most of the passengers were women — anime schoolgirl types, scowling fashionistas, grandmothers, housewives, and working mothers. It seemed I was the only tourist headed in this direction. Bar girls and their customers were still asleep.

The train slowly emptied itself of passengers the farther away we got from Sukhumvit, and by the time we got to my stop at Itsaraphap station, there were just two other old ladies and myself on the train. I rode two sets of escalators up to street level and was blasted with a wall of heat. That fifteen-minute walk to Wat Arun would be a sweaty one. Already toweling off the sweat dripping from my face and neck, I stopped by 7-Eleven and picked up a two-liter bottle of water to prepare for the coming ordeal.

If you've seen one temple (or wat) in Thailand, you've seen them all, but I had nothing better to do these last few days, so I figured I might as well spend some time walking around in this outdoor steambath and get some exercise. But man, that sun was shining bright and hot in that clear blue, noonday sky. What little shade my army surplus boonie hat provided was of little use — soon I would be wringing the sweat out of it like a wet dishrag. I should have brought an umbrella to block the sun's rays.

Just outside the temple complex at Wat Arun was a row of gift shops selling rice paper and bamboo umbrellas and women's traditional Thai gowns. The shops lined a maze of narrow roads and alleyways, and I had to pay mind not to get my toes crushed by cars inching by the crowds of people making their way to the temple.

I noticed a few women dressed in traditional Thai gowns. I assumed they were a part of some ceremony taking place on temple grounds, but I soon realized that most of them were just day-tripping tourists, dressed up to take Instagram photos amongst the colorfully tiled spires of Wat Arun — husbands and boyfriends in tow, obediently following them around, snapping pics with high-end cameras from every angle.

But like I said, if you've seen one wat, you've seen them all. It probably wasn't the most opportune time to be taking photos. The midday sun beat down on the place with a merciless vengeance, washing everything out with blistering heat and blinding sunlight. I was drenched in sweat from climbing around the steep, narrow steps of the spires. I must have made it into the background of a few of those tourists' shots that day. I'm the sweat-soaked slob hunched over and panting from near heat exhaustion, squinty-eyed and looking for a spot of shade to hide in.

I did manage to snap a few shots and record a few video clips for my Youtube channel. An intelligent, culturally sensitive traveler would have done some research on the place. Maybe provide some thoughtful commentary on the temple's historical significance. I am not that sort of traveler. I've never had much interest in Googling for important dates and bits of trivia about a place. Unless you've got a specific itch to satisfy, some interest or curiosity, the history of a place will only feel as relevant to you as your own relative distance to it in time and space. (Beyond a handful of rednecks and American history buffs, does anyone still give a shit about Civil War battleground sites?)

When I visit a city for the first time — or for the hundredth time — I like to see what it's like right then and now: Today. What food is there to eat? Where are the cool, unknown spots that no one knows about yet? Unknown alleyways and side streets that have yet to be explored? Where are the crowds, the people? Where is the nightlife? Where is the life? What is the energy of the place? Where are the interesting sights and scenes? Of what use is it to know that a thousand years ago, this might have been the center of a great basket weaving civilization when all there is now is row upon row of market stalls selling the same generic over-priced tourist trinkets, bearing the same ubiquitous "Made in China" stamp?

So go enjoy those market stalls. Buy a few trinkets for the nieces and grandkids back home. Enjoy yourself! And if those places turn out to be overrated, overpriced shit holes — leave. Go somewhere else and be grateful that you have the ability to travel halfway around the world for weeks or months at a time while the vast majority of Americans slave away at low-wage jobs with no healthcare and no vacation time.

Wat Arun, like most temples in Thailand, is not entirely stuck in the past. These are not merely vacant buildings harboring some abandoned philosophy or former way of life in the form of old plaques and forgettable memorabilia, with attached gift shop milking tourist dollars trying to escape the muggy heat. Wat Arun remains an active, functioning temple replete with Buddhist monks in orange robes drifting in to pay homage and say their daily prayers. The general public are also welcome to come and pray and give merit. The cynic in me sees it as a money-grab, perhaps not as greedy or hypocritical as Christian mega-churches back in the States. Organized religion is all about control and power. Except with Buddhism, I think, there's a lot more wiggle room.

Sabai sabai.

―

I wanted to see Som before I left. I met her a few weeks earlier at one of the go-go clubs in Nana Plaza where she worked as a dancer. We didn't do anything naughty. Yet. But she was fun to joke around and drink with. Wiry and energetic, she wore her hair cut in a short bob and had a large dragon tattoo, covering the entire length of her back. Classic Bangkok bar girl. She was completely at ease walking around the club in platform heels and wearing little more than a string bikini.

She worked at the Whiskey A Go-Go, one of the less busy clubs tucked away in a corner behind the stairway landing between the first and second levels of Nana Plaza. Whenever I stopped by, it was usually just me and one or two other guys in the place. The girls would be lined up on the narrow walkway stage. Standing around, looking bored. Hardly dancing and mostly just gazing at themselves in the mirrors that ran the length of walls on either side of the stage.

Bar girls who are also Bangkok natives carry a certain pride about them. They have that take it or leave it, no strings attached, big city attitude. Ask them where they're from, if they are from Isan, and they will likely respond with a mild annoyance that no, they are not some country bumpkin that just stepped out of a rice paddy from some far-flung province. They don't need foreign men. They only want their money. Bangkok girls are not desperate beggars, like the bar girls in Patong or Pattaya, who swarm lone white men like flies to shit.

This was how Chompooch explained it, leaning into me half naked and yelling into my ear over the blaring house music. She was one of the other girls working at the Whiskey A Go-Go and was easily the most attractive woman in the place. She could pass for a car show model. And maybe she was — maybe go-go dancing was just a side hustle. You definitely would not mistake her for some farm girl who just got off the bus from Isan.

I noticed her the previous night while I was sitting with Som. Chompoon was up on the stage in front of us, slowly gyrating her hips and watching herself in the mirror while I watched her from the booth, admiring her China doll face and porcelain skin. Som's hand was on my crotch, slowly massaging my cock over my shorts.

Som and Chompooch were polar opposites. Som was dark-skinned, short-haired, and had a feral look in her eyes. Chompooch was more reserved and on the classier side of the bar girl spectrum — strip club environment notwithstanding. She carried herself with a kind of grace. Whereas Som was like a wild animal — energetic and aggressive. The sort of girl who was unafraid to take matters into her own hands, so to speak, as I felt her hand roaming over my crotch area.

I got to the club relatively early, as I usually do — around 9 o'clock. The place was empty except for a handful of girls. And I noticed — Chompooch. The girls began chattering amongst themselves when they saw me walk in. I took a seat on the wooden bench against the wall where I usually sat with Som.

The mamasan came over to me, waving. "Som no here," she said.

"Oh, okay," I said. "Where she go?"

"She left thirty minutes ago. Maybe she come back later."

"She go with customer?"

"I don't know. You want drink?"

I ordered a rum and Coke with ice. When mamasan returned, she asked if I wanted one of the other girls to come sit with me.

I pointed to Chompooch.

"That girl there," I said. "The one with the nice ass."

The mamasan got Chompooch's attention and waved her over.

Chompooch held her hands together and slightly bowed her head (the traditional Thai greeting known as a "wai") before sliding in next to me on the wooden bench. We clinked glasses when they brought over her drink. She was respectful and reserved for someone wearing a string bikini and stiletto heels. I resisted the urge to ask her what a girl like her was doing in a place like this.

I felt suddenly shy in her presence. This was a woman whose beauty and grace commanded respect, regardless of how skimpily she was dressed or how just a few minutes before, she was slowly gyrating her ass onstage. She possessed an aura of royalty. I couldn't help thinking about all the men, the farang men, the stinking white devils, who had pawed and groped this statuesque beauty, and the others who'd had their way with her in filthy short-time rooms with semen-stained sheets and mildewed carpets. She didn't seem the type, but who was I fooling?

We sat awkwardly next to each other for a few minutes with a small space between us. Then we started making small talk, yelling into each other's ears over the loud music. Where was I from, how long was I staying, blah, blah, blah.

She was born and raised in Bangkok, she said, but I kind of already figured that out.

I told her that I'd been in Phuket for the past few weeks and asked if she'd ever been there.

She shook her head, no.

"Too many Indians on Bangla Road," I said, leaning into her so I could yell in her ear. She smelled good and not in a cheap perfume kind of way. Her mere presence was at once calming and alluring. There was a delicate feminine energy about her, and I felt myself slowly being drawn into her, entranced.

"You don't like Indians?" she asked.

"Too many Indian men," I said. "They like to travel in packs. All together in groups of four or five. They very rude to the girls."

I was thinking now of a group of Indian men sitting at a row of tables in the dining area at the Best Western in Patong. It was late in the morning, and I had just arrived in a taxi from over the hill in Kata and was waiting for my room to be ready. One of the men yelled for their waitress to come over to their table, as if he were calling to a dog. He flicked his hand over the mess of food and plates and spilled ashtrays on their table, indicating to her that he wanted it all cleaned up. These were six grown men, but their table looked like toddlers had been eating there. With another wave of his hand, he dismissed her, as if he were shooing away a fly. She spun around and headed back to the kitchen, and I could see a look of disgust and annoyance on her face. Clearly, she was upset.

Meanwhile, the men were standing around and pacing around their table, treating the place like their own private club. To be fair, it was early and the dining area was empty except for me and them. I wondered if they would have behaved differently had the place been crowded with other guests, farang customers who could not be so easily bullied like the kitchen staff?

On too many other occasions, whenever I witnessed tourists haranguing hotel or restaurant staff, those tourists were often of Indian descent. It almost seems like these Indian tourists pick up on the fact that Thai people tend to be more passive, non-confrontational and overly polite, and these boorish Indians take advantage of it.

I asked Chompooch what she thought about Indian customers.

Her response was a diplomatic one. "There are good and bad ones," she explained. "Just like everyone else." In fact, she added, she counted many Indian and Arab men as her friends.

I asked her if she'd ever been to Pattaya.

She wrinkled her nose, no.

If you mentioned Pattaya to anyone even remotely familiar with Thailand and its infamous nightlife, you might get the same reaction. Pattaya is known as a sex tourism hotspot, especially for older white men in their sixties and seventies. Liver-spotted, pale, wrinkled, and hunched over. Suffering bad knees, aching backs. But still — looking to get their freak on for one final hurrah before they keel over from Viagra-induced heart attacks. The bar girls might as well be nursemaids. Have them trained in CPR and diaper changing.

Chompooch made clawing and grabbing motions in the air. "Everybody like that," she said.

"The men?"

"No, the girls! They grab the men and drag them into the bar."

She laughed.

I laughed, too, nodding my head. I understood what she meant. Bangkok girls, like Chompooch, seemed more cosmopolitan and possessed a certain kind of class. They're not as desperate or needy as those farm girls from the countryside.

Chompooch was warming up to me. She gently rested her hand on my knee while we talked and let her fingers gently brush against my inner thigh. Then I knew that she knew exactly what she was doing. She sidled in a little closer to me. Nice and cozy. Man, she smelled good, and her bare skin against my leg felt soft and smooth. My Spidey senses were tingling.

She told me about an after-hours club she likes to visit when her shift is over.

"Aren't you tired?" I asked.

She giggled, "No."

"What time do you go home?"

"Four. Sometimes six."

"In the morning?" I knew that's what she meant, but still — I was incredulous.

She giggled again.

These girls were like vampires. I couldn't wrap my mind around it. Maybe I was too old. But even then, when I was in my twenties and getting hammered in Tenderloin bars in San Francisco, I rarely stayed out past midnight. I was usually roaming around by myself in those days, and maybe that was part of the reason. No one ever invited me to any of the cool after-parties. I was never invited to any parties, period.

Chompooch took out her phone and showed me a few photos of her at the club. Some place called The Mixx.

"Do you work there?" I asked.

"No, I just go for fun."

But I could see from the photos that she was clearly wearing some sort of matching outfit with the other girls. Here she was in bunny ears and white lingerie. Here was another of her in a string bikini. In many of the shots, she was standing between guys who appeared to be of Arab or Indian descent, smiling in silk black shirts and holding their drinks up to the camera. I could almost smell the Axe Body Spray and pungent cologne through her phone.

"You should go," she said.

"Okay," I said, although it looked like the kind of place you would only visit if you were with a group of hyper-macho alpha males, judging by the photos of those dudes on her phone. Bunch of tech bros and crypto weirdo types. Not the kind of place for a 53-year-old loner like me, whose fashion style could only be described as "homeless beach bum camping in a Walmart parking lot."

I asked her if she wanted another drink. She nodded demurely. I motioned to mamasan to bring us another round when I spotted Som standing in the doorway. She was dressed plainly in a gray sweatshirt and skinny jeans.

She spotted me sitting with Chompooch and came straight for us. She remained standing in front of our wooden bench, glaring at me.

"I told you I work early tonight," said Som. She continued glaring at me and didn't even bother acknowledging Chompooch sitting at my side.

We had been texting back and forth earlier that day. The night before, we talked about meeting for lunch, so I texted her in the afternoon to see if she still wanted to meet. She didn't respond until around five o'clock saying that she was working.

That's the thing about these vampire bar girls — I'll never understand what is "early" or "late" to them. They keep unpredictable hours that are nearly impossible to sync up with. They are like cats simultaneously existing in multiple dimensions, completely unmindful of the fact that foreigners like myself are limited to a linear space/time reality here in the third dimension.

Also, I think I may have violated some kind of bar girl etiquette by sitting with Chompooch when I had been sitting with Som the previous few nights.

"Mamasan said you not here," I explained weakly.

"I no work tonight," said Som. "I helping at new club upstairs."

Maybe it was true, maybe it wasn't. Maybe she had disappeared for a short-time rendezvous with a customer and was just now returning. She could have said she'd been kidnapped by aliens. It wouldn't have mattered. None of it was relevant to the transactional nature of our relationship, which had been simmering from the previous when we were busy massaging each other's genitalia.

I texted her when I arrived at the club, but she didn't respond. Surely, mamasan would have mentioned if Som was doing something innocent, like helping out upstairs at the new bar? Who knows? It didn't matter. In the bar girl space/time continuum, everything was a continuously shifting whirl of miscommunications and half-truths. Chaotic, frenetic, and unpredictable.

Som's glare softened when I offered to buy her a drink.

"Okay," she said, squeezing past Chompooch, her butt in her face, and sidling up next to me. "I have to go back upstairs. Birthday party for one of the girls."

She still hadn't greeted Chompooch or acknowledged that she was even sitting there. Is this how bar girls assert their dominance?

Chompooch quietly and without protest slid over to make room for Som, who had wrapped her arm around mine and was looking up at me with big, vengeful eyes. She had successfully reclaimed her property.

Here, sitting beside me, were two diametrically opposed types of bar girls. Chompooch was fair-skinned and demure. She looked and carried herself as if she didn't belong anywhere near Nana Plaza. You could tell she was a short-timer, only here to make some extra cash on the side, while she lined up bigger and better things completely unrelated to sitting in bars and getting drunk with strange men night after night.

Som, on the other hand, was in her natural habitat. Dark-skinned and heavily tattooed. Feral. She, too, took pride in being a Bangkok native. When I asked her if she'd ever been to Pattaya or Phuket, she gave me a sideways look, like I was crazy.

"No," she said. "All my friends here. Everything here."

Bangkok was the center of their universe. Those other tourist hotspots might as well have been distant planets at the far end of the solar system.

There could be worse places to call home.

Thoughts of my flight back to the States hit me with a pang of anxiety as I realized my month-long vacation was drawing to a close. Another dream slowly fading away.

Som and I got to laughing and joking around with each other, like we'd been doing the previous two nights. She was like a frisky, wild animal. I tried to include Chompooch in the playful banter, but with Som sitting between us, it was like oil and water. Their styles were too different — Chompooch sat with her legs crossed, her hands resting on one knee, delicate and demure, staring off into the distance.

Meanwhile, Som was busy pawing at me and making exaggerated love-making noises. "Uhh! Uhh!!"

We'd both break out in laughter. We were laughing so much, my sides were hurting.

Chompooch smiled politely.

I bought them another round of drinks, after which Chompooch quietly excused herself. I slipped her a thousand-baht note as a tip, and she gave me a respectful wai before slipping off to sit with the other girls, who were waiting for customers.

Som still had yet to acknowledge her. She hadn't even bothered looking in her direction the entire time Chompooch was sitting with us. There was definitely something going on there, but it was my last night in Bangkok and I didn't concern myself too much with it. Shortly after, we caught a tuk-tuk back to my hotel, but I was too drunk and couldn't perform, so we sat in bed watching TV for a little while before I released her back into the night, like the feral creature she was.

Another Thai daydream was drawing to a close. This was my third trip to Thailand in two years. At some point during this trip, the spell wore off. I saw things now with a discerning eye. My cynical self came through and pulled me back to reality. It wasn't all just one long sleep-walk along exotic beaches and burying myself face-deep in Thai pussy, though this could be the entirety of your experience if you chose to have it that way.

I had been entertaining fantasies of traveling to Bangkok and other far-off distant places for a few decades now, at least since my twenties when I started reading about backpackers traveling the world on the cheap — buying "round the world" tickets, sleeping in hostels, catching midnight bus rides with other backpacking vagrants, and partying it up with the natives.

My old drinking buddy, Eric, who I used to drink and shoot pool with at a bar called The Outsider, told me about his plan to retire in Thailand. This was back in the 1990s, and we were in the heart of the Tenderloin district in downtown San Francisco, before the City became overridden with tech bros, fentanyls junkies, and sidewalk shitters. What little awareness I had of Thailand at the time was limited to a few massage parlors in the neighborhood that were staffed with Thai women.

Eric would go on and on about Thailand in between games of pool and chain-smoking Marlboros. I'd humor him, nodding occasionally. I was obsessed more with Korean girls at the time. In fact, many of the bars along Geary Street in those days were owned and operated by Korean women who were themselves former bar girls or sex-workers in those same massage parlors. (I don't know if this is still true today.)

Jinny, a Korean woman in her forties who owned The Outsider bar on the corner of Geary and Larkin when I was drinking there every night, once explained that these women bar owners had formed something akin to an investment club. They would pool their money together and allow members to take out loans for repairs to their respective places or loan out as a down payment to women looking to open their first bar. At the time, the average startup cost to open a bar in that area was about a hundred grand, she explained.

I had no idea these women were playing around with such large amounts of cash. Here I was, some 27-year-old punk in a black leather jacket and Skinny Puppy baseball cap, working his first tech consulting gig making $35 bucks an hour, and living paycheck to paycheck. I thought I was rich, drinking every night and eating $5 hamburger sandwiches at Little Henry's across the street.

I knew Jinny had money. Her boyfriend, a Korean guy ten years her junior, would drop her off in front of the bar each night, driving her Mercedes-Benz SUV. And she owned a Victorian flat in Lower Haight. She was doing pretty good.

Some nights, she would get a little too drunk and come around from behind the bar, sliding up on the barstool next to me. On one such night, she asked if I'd be interested in renting out one of the rooms in her house. She would charge me a discounted rate: $300 a month.

I told her it sounded interesting, but I liked the studio I had on the corner of Post and Jones. (Even though I was paying $710 a month for the place.)

Then she leaned in and whispered into my ear that she wanted to take me back to her house and fuck my brains out.

"What about your boyfriend?" I asked.

She waved it off. He won't know, she said dismissively. Grinning, she pulled down the front of her blouse and flashed her tits.

The next night I told Eric what had happened with Jinny, and he became visibly annoyed. I told the story jokingly, but he wasn't laughing. In fact, he looked angered. He cut our usual pool playing early that night and went home. I realized then that he probably had a crush on her.

He and I were always talking about calling it quits in San Francisco and getting the hell out of the Tenderloin. I talked a big game about giving up all of my belongings and getting rid of my apartment. I'd just stuff what I could into a backpack and go traveling around the world. Nothing holding me back. Nothing holding me down. No attachments, no problem! I was a free man!

Instead, I got married, had a kid, moved to Texas, and bought a house. To sum up the past 25 or so years.

Whatever happened to Eric and his dream to retire in Thailand, which had now become a dream of my own?

He was from somewhere out in the Midwest. Wisconsin, if I remember. Not sure how he ended up in San Francisco. He worked as a clerk in some office downtown. Administrative office worker. The sort of work I was doing before I moved into tech. Overnight, I went from making $17 an hour to $35. I was living like a king. No more eating frozen burritos from the corner liquor store for dinner. Those days were gone.

But I get the feeling Eric wasn't making a lot of money. He was older than me by ten or fifteen years and walked with a slight limp. His wrist hung a little limply. Not because he was homosexual, I don't think, but more so from childhood polio or something. What the hell did I know? I'd never met him anywhere outside of that bar in the two or three years we spent drinking and shooting pool on a near nightly basis.

He lived in a studio apartment right across the street from The Outsider bar. His rent was probably similar to what I was paying for my place — $500 to $700 a month. He'd never been married. No kids. Just another lonely clerical worker in downtown San Francisco. There were thousands of people just like him. Just like me. Where did they all go?

For every lawyer or investment banker, there must have been at least ten people on the administrative side to support them — file clerks, secretaries, data entry clerks, word processors (the people, not the software application), paralegals, mailroom clerks, copy machine operators. There was a time when you didn't need a college education, and you didn't need to be making a six-figure salary to live like a normal human being in San Francisco. Or anywhere else in the country, for that matter.

Living in the United States has become an increasingly shitty proposition. The anger and stupidity on full display now on a daily basis. The morbid obesity and drug addiction, crime and homelessness.

It might be possible to overlook all of it — just keep walking and pretend everything is fine, everything is peachy-keen, even when you're sidestepping human feces on the sidewalks, avoiding eye contact with drug-addled panhandlers, looking past tent cities along the freeways and cardboard shelters in abandoned doorways. You would likely forgive all of it if only you could find an affordable one-bedroom apartment that wasn't infested with cockroaches or crackhead squatters. Even this is slowly becoming a diminishing possibility. Bankers, lobbyists, and politicians have ripped the entrails from the still-quivering corpse that is the American middle-class.

My drinking buddy, Eric, foresaw his own obsolescence nearly thirty years ago. Hence, his plan to escape overseas to Thailand. It seemed like a far-fetched and hackneyed plan to me at the time. As far as I could tell, he'd never been outside of San Francisco or his Midwest hometown. A kind of postcard daydreaming that people engage in when they have nothing else to hope for and not much of anything else going on in their lives, except boredom and monotony. So they stare at that postcard and try to imagine the life they could have had. This was Eric. Tall and lanky, shaded prescription glasses — he was like a depressed Eric Clapton.

I wonder where he is now? I never got his last name, so wouldn't be able to look him up on social media.

What would I say to him? Hey, man! Remember me? That skinny Filipino kid you used to drink and shoot pool with every night at The Outsider? Did you ever make it out to Thailand? I've been there a bunch of times. Planning to retire there, too. Whereabouts are you staying? I'll look you up when I'm there next. What's it like living out there as an expat? Is it all that you had imagined?

Was Thailand all that I had imagined? It was at once beyond anything I could have dreamed of, and yet it was as if I had willed the place into existence. Every bar and back alley I wandered through. Every beach I went swimming at, whose sand I sunk my toes into. Every bar girl I chatted with. Every tuk-tuk driver who took my $400 baht to take me to the other side of town. The night markets. The food stalls. Every hotel room I awoke in each morning and feeling that brief moment of bewilderment until I remembered where I was.

It all felt like something I was simply reliving. I have been here before. I felt comfortable and at ease. I knew this place. It felt like home.

Feeling burned out and tired, I needed to go home and get back to work. Rather than spending money, I needed to get back to making it. This sad realization hits me whenever I'm coming up to the end of another month-long visit. Five grand poorer, heartbroken, and beat down.

I'm at Suvarnabhumi Airport now. The other travelers look sinister and unfriendly. They, too, must be heading back to the United States or some European country. Grouchy white people. Grouchy farang. A collective cloud of gloom hangs over us all.

I spend twenty minutes standing in the wrong line, waiting to check my North Face duffel bag. I had asked one of the ticketing agents at a nearby counter if the long line of people queuing up was for Japan Airlines.

"Yes," she replied, visibly irritated. "It is Japan airline."

I slunk back and waited in line only to discover when I got to the counter that this was the line for a Japan airline alright — Nippon Air. Japan Airlines was directly behind and on the other side. No wonder I couldn't find the damn counter, even though a few people had pointed me in this general direction.

So I went and stood in that line for another half-hour. By now, it was getting close to the official check-in time. More and more people were queuing up.

When it was my turn to check in, the ticketing agent seemed to be taking longer than usual to check me in. He stared at my ticket, then stared at his computer screen, then he looked back at my ticket. Then he stepped away to speak with one of the other agents. They came back and now both of them were staring at the computer screen.

After a while, the agent looked at me and said, "Sir, it looks like your ticket was canceled."

What?

No, seriously — "What?"

"Did you miss your flight when you were coming from Japan?"

"No," I replied. "I've been in Thailand for the past month. How else would I have gotten here if I had missed my connecting flight in Japan?"

Now I was as confused as they were. I didn't understand.

The woman, who was a team lead or manager or something, asked me to take a seat off to the side while they checked in the remaining passengers and tried to figure out what the hell happened with my reservation.

Here's what happened:

My original itinerary had me flying into Japan and landing at Narita International. From there I had a connecting flight out of Haneda International, which was a two-hour train ride from Narita. I only had a six-hour layover and would have to navigate Tokyo's subway system. This was the trickiest part of my itinerary, something I would rather have not had to deal with so early in the trip.

So I was pleasantly surprised when I was coming off the jetway in Narita and spotted a Japan Airlines agent holding up a small placard with my name printed in large, bold letters: ABELAYE.

The agent politely informed me that my flight had been changed and that I would be flying out of Narita instead of having to travel to Haneda. The flight would be leaving in two hours.

Such luck! Things were finally going my way. Those Youtube tarot card readers were right — the universe was finally opening up to me. Beck's "Loser" echoed through my mind: "Things are gonna change / I can feel it."

My stroke of good fortune continued when I boarded that flight to Bangkok and discovered that I had an entire row of seats to myself.

That "stroke of good luck" was precisely why I found myself sitting at the Japan Airlines ticket counter one month later, wondering why my flight got canceled. Evidently, when they rebooked my connecting flight from Haneda to Narita — they neglected to remove my name from the passenger list on that Haneda flight and marked my ticket as a no-show.

And here is when I learned a very important lesson about airline travel policy:

If you happen to miss a single connecting flight on a multi-leg itinerary, the airline will cancel that entire itinerary. All future flights. All return flights. Everything.

So basically, my return flight home was canceled a month earlier when I got on that updated flight from Narita to Bangkok. I was wondering why I couldn't complete the 24-hour check-in on their website the day before. I kept seeing a message on-screen: "Please contact the airline."

The ticketing agent finally figured out what was going on and explained all of this to me after an hour of waiting around and watching the long line of passengers get checked in ahead of me. They tried to fly me on stand-by, but the flight was packed and my seat had already been sold. The seat that I had already paid for.

In a way, I almost didn't mind. Maybe this was the Universe's way of telling me that I needed to catch a taxi back to Bangkok and spend the rest of my life in Thailand. I kept asking the ticketing agent if I should come back some other day. I had my American Express card and enough cash to spend a few more days in Bangkok. I wouldn't mind spending another evening with Som. Or Chompooch.

"No. No need for that," the agent replied. His fingers were flying across his keyboard, typing furiously as he searched for flights. "We'll get you on a flight tonight."

That wasn't the answer I was hoping to hear. I wanted him to say, "Oh, there won't be any seats available on any flights for at least another week or so. Go back to Bangkok, and we'll contact you if something opens up."

I could live like a king along Sukhumvit and Asoke, eating street food and spending my days riding the BTS and MRT to distant points on the map, finding new side streets and back alleys to explore. Nevermind a week or a month. I needed another five to ten years to explore this town, not to mention the rest of the country and all the countries neighboring it — Laos, Cambodia, Vietnam.

My fantasizing was interrupted by the agent waving a handful of boarding passes at me. He found a flight routing me through New York. Instead of a day's worth of traveling from Bangkok to Narita to Dallas, I would now be spending the next two days flying from Bangkok to Narita to JFK to Dallas. I was not looking forward to this, but at this point I'd been waiting near the ticketing counter for over two hours, and my brain was fried. I already felt like I needed to take a shower and a nap.

Leaving Thailand is always a heartbreaking pain in the ass. What is it about these tropical beach vacations that makes us feel like we're leaving home? I'm sure there's some overly intellectual, rational explanation for it, a scientific term that some graduate student in academia came up with in order to put a name to it.

What are its causes? An obvious one would be the suspension of day to day responsibilities and obligations. Or ridding oneself of the mindless tedium of daily chores and errands to run and replacing it with a leisurely stroll along the beach after an early morning swim in the ocean.

Or perhaps that emotional feeling of "leaving home" has at its root a metaphysical or spiritual origin, some psychic connection we make to a memory of a time when life on this planet did not revolve solely around making money. When life was about simply existing and experiencing the beauty that Mother Nature (Gaia) had to offer. A time in human civilization when FEAR had not yet entered the collective consciousness.

It is Fear that rules the land now. Our minds have become infested with it. It controls us, like an insidious bacterial infection. Those in power, especially here in the United States, use fear to control us, to keep us in check. We, the collective consciousness. We are of little use to our corporate overlords if we are not in a state of constantly producing. Constantly working to satisfy their goals, not ours. They are paying us to do a job, after all. They didn't hire us to take beach vacations.

The Fear creeps in and whispers into our ears: Do not allow yourselves to be distracted by the tropical paradise and the easy living. Beware the spectre of homelessness and starvation hovering over you like a black cloud. How can you stand to look yourself in the mirror if you do not put in an honest day's labor? The good Lord rewards hard labor. Let us pray.

Let us pray for the men and women who died for your freedom, fighting for the rights of banks and corporations to utterly crush those Third World mongoloids who refuse to give us their land and precious resources or to go into debt in the name of the mighty U.S. dollar. Amen.

Let us pray for Jesus Christ, who died for your sins and was nailed to a cross and on the third day emerged from that cave proclaiming himself to be the Easter Bunny and, hiding in bushes, shat golden eggs for all to find and thus be saved from eternal damnation. Amen.

God be with you. And also with you. And also with the pastor who likes to slip his finger up the buttholes of choir boys and sniff their testicles. So pink and so soft. So fresh and tender. Amen. Oh dear God, amen!

—

The more you travel, the more you learn to appreciate the freedom you possess and the spiritual connection you have to the world around you. And the more you begin to realize that religion is a giant cartload of antiquated horseshit and that spending the most productive years of your life slaving away for some soulless corporation is the most counter-productive thing you could possibly do with the limited time you have on this planet.

Nobody died for your freedom. Nobody died for your sins. Nobody died that didn't have it coming to them — to paraphrase Al Pacino's Tony Montana character in "Scarface." Guilt and shame are useless feelings, forced upon us by those who wish to control us and keep us in our place. Don't let the assholes of the world ruin the things that bring you happiness and joy. Don't allow anyone to interfere with the things that bring you peace in this fucked up world.

Keep it light. Keep it simple. Nobody gets hurt.

Unfortunately, too many of us fail to realize this until it's too late. We spend decades looking forward to "retirement" — telling ourselves (fooling ourselves, really) that we'll finally get to do all the things we've been wanting to do for so many years. And when retirement finally arrives, we discover that our bones have become too brittle. Our knees ache. We've got arthritis in our fingers, blood in our stool. We fill our time filling prescriptions to treat that case of gout in our ankles or goiter in our necks. We can't let ourselves stray too far from the nearest pharmacy. Got those prescriptions to fill. Got to find some way to treat the pain, address those ailments. How are you going to manage a 15-hour overseas flight, stuck in that tiny cramped airline seat, bent like a pretzel? Never mind surviving a trek up Kilimanjaro.

And so we spend what little time remains of our precious lives living as shut-ins in our homes (for those fortunate enough to have a home). Waiting for that next doctor's appointment. Waiting to die.

There is, however, a segment of the geriatric population that refuses to lay down and die. Mostly male. Mostly white. Mostly over the age of sixty-five. You'll find them in places like Pattaya or Patong, creeping around girlie bars along Bangla Road or in Nana Plaza, sitting on bar stools overlooking the street, nursing their beers.

They will very likely have in their possession a handful of magical blue boner pills in one pocket and packets of condoms in the other. The scent of Thai pussy rouses them from death-like stupors. Gets the blood flowing through graying skin. These old perverts want to go out with a bang — banging freelancing streetwalkers, drunken bar girls, pancake-tittied massage parlor hags. There'll be no sitting around waiting to die in retirement homes for these dudes, unless those retirement homes are staffed with dark-skinned, raven-haired girls in string bikinis, sporting dragon tattoos on their backs and walking around in stiletto heels handing out painkillers.

If it were not for Thailand the Land of Smiles, these old pervs might otherwise be eking out the rest of their lonely days sitting around drafty and crusty old houses back in England or Germany — cold, gray, and conservative. Day in, day out. Looking at the same old cold, gray neighbors. Eating the same old cold, gray food. Death couldn't come soon enough to take them away from their cold, gray worlds.

One night, back in Patong, I was eating a pizza in a little restaurant/bar near the OTOP market. It was weirdly situated with a large sliding glass door for an entrance with a steep asphalt ramp leading up to it. It looked like it might have been steps at one time, but someone decided to pave it over with asphalt, and now it had the appearance of a very large, very steep speed bump. Your typical Thai storefront, basically — watch out for uneven steps, broken or cracked sidewalks, or any other number of random, unexpected walking hazards.

I look up from yet another disappointing plate of pepperoni pizza and spot a scrawny old man, hunched over and leaning on a cane, struggling to get through the sliding door entrance. A waitress comes over and helps him through the door, then ushers him to a seat at a table directly in front of mine. We are the only two customers in the place.

The man is German, judging by his heavy accent, and speaks to the waitress in a low, coarse tone. He has a question about something on the menu, but the waitress doesn't understand what he's asking — she doesn't speak German. He is hunched over the table, his face leaning over the menu while he runs a gnarled finger over each menu selection. He continues peppering her with questions and pointing at something on the menu. The waitress keeps shaking her head — she doesn't understand. Finally, through hand gestures and broken English, the waitress takes his order.

She returns a few minutes later with the old man's order — a pizza and salad. He digs in with his fork and butter knife. Or tries to. His hands are trembling, and he can't get a good grip on the utensils. He has grown too old and feeble. The waitress sees him struggling and goes over to cut his pizza into tiny, bite-sized chunks. His face hovers low over his plate while he tries to guide that first piece of food into his mouth with a trembling hand and fork.

Here is a guy who can barely walk and appears incapable of feeding himself. He must be in his late eighties or early nineties. What is he doing out here by himself? Did he travel all this way from his homeland in this condition? Can he manage a walk along Patong Beach without falling over?

Perhaps the more likely scenario is that he's living in Patong full-time, an expat retiree eking out the rest of his days in a rented room in a residential motel somewhere on the cheaper side of town. Maybe the old pervert is still looking to get his kicks on Bangla Road, coming out on a Friday night and reminiscing about the things he used to do with those bar girls that he can only now watch ruefully from a distance with watery gray eyes.

Or maybe he's a retired schoolteacher looking to spend his final days in warmer climes. It's got nothing to do with sexual perversion or getting hammered in bars.

Yeah, maybe.

Life is better here in the new world. You don't need to be a geriatric sex fiend to appreciate that. Why waste away in the motherland, where cold gray days are especially harsh on brittle bones and creaky, arthritic joints? Better to risk falling down in the Land of Smiles, where any number of nice young women will eagerly help you to your feet. No, they don't need your money — but their scooter needs repairs; they have to pay for their kid's school; their electric bill is due. "Any amount helps, ya? If can give little bit? Kahp khun kahp, tirak."

The smile and scent of a Thai woman sitting alone in a bar loosens up that farang wallet and adds years to a waning life. Sends the blood rushing through calloused veins, Brings new life to old dead skin. Hordes of old men in their sixties and seventies roaming around Patong, rejuvenated. Buttoned-down shirts flagrantly unbuttoned. White-haired and bare-chested along the Andaman Sea. Bleached-white dentures and sunburned skin beneath an Andaman sun.

New life in the new world! Women, beer, weather, and cheap food. What more could you ask for?

Confidence! Vitality! An old man feels thirty years younger. Hell, maybe he'll get a tattoo. Something sentimental. Maybe the name of his granddaughter. Or the name of that Thai bar girl, who later became his wife, who let him take her up the ass. Maybe he'll take this new girl out to one of the islands for a few days. They always love that.

Enjoy it while you can, old man. You've got maybe a good five to ten years left (fifteen, if you're lucky) before Death comes to strip away your senses and whatever remains of your physical abilities. Bar girls don't make good nursemaids. Changing adult diapers and giving sponge-baths isn't what they signed up for when they went to work at the Lusty Lady or the Sweet Cherry nightclub. Doesn't matter how many extra Thai baht you're willing to tip them, these girls lack the interest or training. They have their own children and extended families to care for.

And so you end up alone in a pizza joint on a Friday evening, struggling to cut through a slice of pepperoni pizza as if it were a piece of shoe-leather steak. Your waitress patiently assists you, like the Angel of Death biding her time.

I had another long layover in Tokyo's Narita airport before that flight to New York. It was too early in the morning, and none of the shops were open for business yet. I wandered around the vacant terminal like a zombie in the morning light glaring through the large airport windows.

Nothing says you are in Japan more than stepping into one of their public restrooms. Each stall is a completely enclosed space through which you enter via a sliding door, like walking into a Japanese restaurant. Like your own private little sushi bar, except you're there to conduct business at the other end of the digestive process.

The toilets are an over-engineered marvel of dubious technology left over from the 80's or 90's. The toilet that I used at Narita was so old, the white plastic sections had faded into discolored shades of beige, like old desktop computers or dot matrix printers from thirty years ago. I was perplexed by the three layers of seats on the one toilet and the large plastic push buttons along the edge of the bowl, each one labeled with a graphical depiction of what it supposedly did. I wasn't in the mood to experiment and figure it out. I did my business and avoided pressing any buttons. Too much shit just to take a shit.

I am twelve hours and one flight into my three-flight, two-day journey home. Feeling grumpy, numb, and irritable. My skin feels oily and clammy. The best I can do is wash my face. My balls will have to wait another day.

I realize that part of my discomfort and unease stems from the fact that I am wearing pants again. For the past month, I'd been walking around in little more than swimming trunks and flip-flops. Returning to the world of shoes, pants, and socks has me feeling burdened and constricted. I can feel my pants rubbing against my legs. My overheating feet are suffocating in the shoes and socks. I glance around at other people in the terminal. Everyone seems just fine wearing similar clothing. I, on the other hand, feel as if I'm being subjected to a passive form of torture. The feel of these clothes against my skin is slowly driving me insane. I suffer my madness quietly in that airport terminal as the morning wears on and the place begins to fill with other travelers.

I try to distract myself with people-watching, always a good way to pass the time in airports. I'm fascinated by the variations of people's choice of luggage and packing styles.

There are few distinct types:

The unapologetic over-packer: These people will pack two large suitcases, a rolling carry-on, and a backpack for a week-long trip to Cancun. Fashionista types fall into this category and most women who aren't butch dykes or tent-dwelling vegans.

The guilty over-packer: These people are too attached to their belongings and feel a deep sense of shame about it. They are unable to let go of childhood toys or old girlfriends. They have the strongest potential to appear on episodes of "Hoarders" in later years. When they arrive at their vacation destination, they spend their time worrying about their jobs and the work awaiting them upon their return. They long ago forgot how to have fun and spend large portions of their vacation suffering from depression and mild anxiety.

The fugitive/deportee: This person is traveling with only the clothes on his back. He may or may not be handcuffed and traveling in-custody with an armed escort. He very likely is not traveling for leisure. Like the Mexican and Guatemalan restaurant workers I used to drink with in Tenderloin bars thirty years ago, who had grown accustomed to being deported back to their respective home countries and would make plans to return to San Francisco "very soon." For them, airline travel was an absolute luxury. But traveling with luggage was not even a consideration when planning a week-long hike across the desert and trying to sneak back across the border. Carrying too much baggage could prove to be a death sentence in this scenario.

The "one-bag" traveler: This person aspires to the fugitive mode of travel (above) and is completely enamored with the idea of traveling light and using only one bag to travel indefinitely around the world. However delusional this may be, they watch every Youtube video: what to pack, how to pack it, what to pack it in. They are familiar with all the brand names and only buy gear that has the best online reviews. Before even stepping foot outside their front door, they will plunk down $300 for a backpack that fits within the maximum carry-on size limits, according to the only specifications, which they will have obsessively and thoroughly researched beforehand.

Our itinerant one-bagger arrives at the airport with what looks like a small house on his back. His pack is loaded down with a hundred pounds of gear he'll never use. Like a soldier being deployed to the front lines in Iraq, except this guy's self-deploying to Khao San Road in Bangkok.

One-bag travelers fool themselves into believing they're traveling carefree and light. Secretly, they are hurting. Their shoulders are raw and sore. Their backs are in pain from carrying unnecessarily heavy loads that they are not in any kind of shape to be carrying. They dread having to walk from one end of the terminal to another. Or having to stand in line for more than half an hour at a time. Or having to walk from the bus station to their hotel and then having to lug their "one bag" up three flights of stairs to their room, where they collapse from exhaustion.

And for those who are not as disciplined, who are relatively new to the minimalist mindset, one-bag travel is not as efficient or practical as it might first seem. You have to think strategically when loading your pack, not only from a weight perspective, but also from an ease-of-use point of view. That pack with the built-in laptop sleeve might seem like a cool idea until it's time to get through the TSA checkpoint. Then you find yourself scrambling to undo the straps and zippers on your backpack and having to unpack your packing cubes and compression sacks so you can get your laptop out so it can be X-rayed in its own little gray tub. Likewise, if you're at a bus station and want to change into a pair of sweatpants and shoes for the ride, you'll have to unpack all your shit there on the bus station floor to get to what you need. Such seemingly simple tasks are much easier to accomplish when you have a rolling suitcase or large duffel bag instead of an unwieldy and overpacked 40- or 50-liter backpack.

And when you arrive at your destination and get situated in your hotel room, what are you planning to carry your stuff in on your excursions around town? If you're planning to use that one bag, you'll need to unpack all your shit and stash it somewhere in your room. For me, personally, I try not to keep any of my belongings in any hotel dressers or closet spaces. Maybe I'll hang a shirt or two in the closet, but that's it. I prefer to leave everything packed in my duffel or pack.

The one-bag traveler ultimately realized three things:
1. They're still packing too much crap and trying to cram two bag's worth of shit into one. This defeats the purpose of one-bag travel.
2. It's actually more practical to bring along more than "one bag." Maybe a small satchel or packable daypack for those beach days or wanderings about town.
3. They are not fit enough to carry their one bag for long distances. Sore knees, aching shoulders, back spasms. All of these are signs that you've packed too

much stuff and/or you lack the physical stamina to carry it around.

Out of the various types of travelers mentioned here, one-bag travelers are probably the most delusional of the bunch. In their minds, they are minimalist jet-setters flying from one end of the planet to the other with little more than a credit card and a change of underwear. In reality they are hoarders, secret midnight snackers, pound cake gobblers trying to stuff fifty pounds of gear into a 20-liter sack.

I've been riffing on these one-bag folks because I, too, am a one-bag wannabe. I obsess over backpacks and duffle bags, soft-side briefcases and leather satchels. I have entertained countless daydreams of traveling light and carefree through Southeast Asian jungles, Chinese train stations, Greyhound bus depots, or traversing old world Europe's inimical cobblestone streets that so many budget travelers use as a rationale for carrying a backpack versus a rolling suitcase.

"How well does it handle cobblestone streets?"

"Can it survive Europe's cobblestone streets?"

"The cheap-looking wheels on that rollaway suitcase won't last long on Europe's cobblestone streets!"

In my own travels, I've had to contend more with broken, uneven sidewalks in Cancun and Bangkok, speeding motor scooters and sidewalk restaurants with little plastic tables in Vietnam, dogshit in Playa del Carmen, homeless people and drug addicts sprawled across the sidewalks in San Francisco. Cobblestone streets have never factored into any of my travel considerations. A rolling suitcase, I realized much later, works just fine for about 90% of the kind of traveling I do.

The root of my obsession goes back decades, when I was in my twenties, and is likely the result of having lived a number of years in a tiny ten-by-twelve foot "efficiency" studio apartment in San Francisco's Tenderloin district. Living in such a cramped space forced me to live a minimalist lifestyle, not by choice but out of practical necessity. And that wasn't the only limitation. I was forced to live a barebones lifestyle because of my barebones salary (squeaking by on $8.50 an hour in those early days).

"I can't afford it, and even if I could, there's no room for it," was the constant refrain I often found myself mumbling whenever I came across a nice, solid-looking wooden writing desk, or a nice, tall bookshelf for all the books I hoped to buy, or a comfy looking queen-sized bed I hoped to sleep in that didn't have a soiled, warped mattress.

It became my mantra: I can't afford it. There's no room for it. I don't need it.

This is what would-be one-bag travelers ultimately come to realize. It's not the bag or its carrying capacity or the base weight of your gear or the brand names of each item in your pack. One bag travel is all about the mindset. Focus on the traveling, not the stuff.

You really do not need all the shit you think you do. Take that 50-liter backpack jam packed with seven pairs of jeans and ten pairs of socks and underwear and replace it with a 25-liter pack with one pair of jeans and three pairs of socks and underwear.

Instead of a shitty two-week vacation to Florida. Save up enough cash to fly to the other side of the world for a month. Tell your manager and your coworkers to fuck off. You'll see them when you get back.

Do these things and you will begin to understand the spirit of one-bag travel.

This being my third month-long trip to Thailand in two years, I've got my packing list dialed in, and I've figured out what works for me. Here is the bare minimum list of things I pack for a month-long trip to Thailand while staying in hotels and swimming at the beach nearly every day and going out bar-hopping each night. I've packed and repacked this stuff so many times, I can recite it from memory:

Clothing:
- 1 pair of Columbia traveler's pants
- 2 pairs of swimming trunks (with the sewn-in mesh underwear)

- 1 pair of basketball shorts (for laying around the hotel)
- 1 cotton t-shirt (for laying around the hotel)
- 3 short-sleeve, button-down shirts. (I prefer synthetic rayon material because it's extremely light-weight, stays cooler, and dries faster.)
- 3 synthetic t-shirts
- 3 pairs of underwear
- 3 pairs of socks
- 1 pair of light-weight running shoes
- 1 pair of flip-flops
- 1 pair of Teva sandals
- 1 boonie hat
- 6 bandanas
- 1 baseball cap
- (I don't usually pack a jacket, but I'll sometimes pack a hoodie if I know I'll be traveling to cooler climes or riding on a bus that blasts super-cold A/C.)

First Aid kit:
- Small selection of bandages
- Small strip of gauze
- Packet of alcohol wipes
- Aspirin
- Allergy medicine
- Small tub of Vaseline
- Small bottle of hand lotion
- Lip balm
- Packet of baby wipes
- Immodium

Toiletries:
- Small toothbrush
- Small tube of toothpaste
- Dental floss
- Backup pair of glasses

- Small nail clipper
- Reading glasses
- Prescription medication

Gear:
- Pacsafe TravelSafe (3 liter model)
- Paracord (25 feet)
- Mini-flashlight (USB-C rechargeable)
- 4 compression straps
- 3 Sea to Summit stuff sacks
- 1 sleeping bag liner
- 1 Borah bivy sack
- Pens, pencils, notepad

Tech:
- Primary cell phone (Samsung Galaxy series)
- Backup/secondary cell phone (for use with my Thai SIM card and using the Grab app, which requires a local Thai phone number)
- Bluetooth keyboard
- Bluetooth mouse
- Powerbank
- Bluetooth earbuds
- Charging cables
- Portable coffee filter

Documentation:
- Backup copies of my passport, driver's license, and vaccinations records. (I keep three copies — one in my luggage, one in my day pack, one in my Pacsafe TravelSafe.)
- Printouts of my travel itinerary.
- Digitized copies of my passport, driver's license, and vaccination records stored on Google Drive and on my cell phone.

- Digitized copies of my travel itinerary stored on Google Drive and on my cell phone.

Clothes are the heaviest items on the list and take up the most space. I aspire to be like the hardcore maniacs who can get by with just a single change of clothes crammed into a 20-liter backpack. I'm not quite there yet, and I'm not sure I ever will be.

On my first two trips, I'd brought along my Samsung Galaxy tablet, but I realized on this trip that I can get by just fine with just the two cell phones. I was able to check email, watch Youtube, and use Google Sheets to work on my budget. That's about 90% of what I use my laptop for when I'm back at home.

The portable coffee filter was a new thing I tried on this trip. It came in handy when I was in Kuala Lumpur and Penang and didn't feel like foraging for that first cup of coffee every morning.

Despite my "one bag" packing list, I've never really been a fan of that budget backpacker look or pack mule aesthetic. Unless you're planning a trek through the Himalayas or are about to spend the next six months working as a merchant marine on a freightliner, your pack rarely ever needs to be greater than a 30 or 35 liter capacity. Anything more, and you might as well use a rolling suitcase or split your stuff into two bags. Of course, this all depends on where you're headed and for how long. The packing list for a month-long trip to Alaska in the winter will look a whole lot different than the packing list for a week-long beach vacation in Cancun. This much should be obvious. The trick is to figure out what you can pack that works in both scenarios and use that as your baseline. Buy whatever else you might need as you go along. No need to cram in the entire contents of your house. Everything is temporary. Short-lived. Use it while you can. Give it away when you no longer need it. Your baubles and jewels and all the rest of your belongings are the chains that weigh you down. Move fast, move light.

Start with the most important things and work your way from there:

- Plane ticket
- Passport
- Credit cards
- Vaccination records

That's it. That's all you really need to literally, physically move from one place on the globe to another. You can pretty much buy everything else when you get to where you're going. And if you can't, well — you probably didn't need it, anyway.

For this trip, I used my small North Face Base Camp Duffel, which is actually quite large at about 50 liters. I also brought along a small, 20-liter Mountainsmith day pack and a Pacsafe fanny pack that I wore like a cross-body sling.

I'm constantly trying out new bags and backpacks in different configurations for traveling, but time and again, I find myself going back to the Base Camp Duffel — mainly for its comfort, durability, and practicality for traveling. It's simple, with one big zippered opening, and the compression and backpack straps aren't overly complicated. You don't have to fuss around with unbuckling straps and getting all tangled in the process just to get to your stuff. You do need to push the backpack shoulder straps out of the way to fully unzip the bag, but access is still relatively quick and easy, and that's a small trade-off for the ability to carry it comfortably like a traditional backpack.

When I'm in the hotel room, I never completely unpack my stuff. I'll hang a few shirts in the closet and maybe stash my toiletry kit in the bathroom if there's enough counter space near the sink. I'll leave everything else in the bag, which reduces the chance of losing or leaving something behind. The North Face duffel is perfectly suited for this use. I use it like a catch-all trunk when I'm in the room.

The only wonky thing about this configuration of traveling with basically two backpacks (a clear violation of the one-bag travel rule!) came into play whenever I was in transit. Obviously, I could only wear one pack on my back, so that meant I had to lug around the other backpack in my hand or wear it around front like a kangaroo pouch. Doable but goofy looking, which I didn't mind. The deal-breaker for carrying bags in this fashion is realized when you're trying to take a piss at a urinal in the airport restroom. Unless you want the pack you're wearing on the front to stick out into the urinal and get wet, you'll have to set it down on the floor, where it will still get wet.

This was an unexpected requirement I didn't realize I needed. I would add it to my list of other requirements when considering what kind of luggage to use: the ability to urinate in a public urinal without having to set my bag down in a puddle of piss.

And how will I feel lugging my luggage or backpack down crowded city streets? In the past, I would visualize in my mind the kinds of scenarios I might encounter while traveling with my gear. Nowadays, these considerations are based more on my own personal experience:

- Lost in Mexico City and trying to find a hotel I'd reserved in the Zona Rosa district, I was literally going in circles, having gotten turned around more than a few times on the various roundabouts, while lugging a rolling suitcase and my 35-liter Maxpedition Vulture II tactical backpack. I wasn't exactly traveling light on that trip. Having booked a spur-of-the-moment ten-day vacation through Mexico and Costa Rica, I didn't have time to carefully plan what I would bring along. I just stuffed everything into my pack; what didn't fit went into my suitcase — desert tan combat boots, a five-pound laptop, a jungle sleeping bag, and a few paperback books. The suitcase alone weighed just over ten pounds. I spent nearly two hours wandering around those circular streets, trying to find that hole-in-the-wall boutique hotel. Feeling thankful I'd brought that rolling suitcase and equally relieved I wasn't lugging all of that weight on my back, it provided a place to sit and rest when I needed to catch my breath.
- Once, in Playa del Carmen, I made the mistake of booking a morning flight back to the States, which meant I had to catch a bus to the airport at six in the morning if I hoped to make the flight on time. It was

a fifteen-minute walk from my hotel to the ADO bus station through darkened city streets. In some places, I had to use my mini-flashlight to traverse the uneven sidewalks, which were riddled with ankle-breaking potholes, random metal pipes jutting out of walls, or an occasional sharp concrete slab sticking out of the ground. More importantly, I was able to side-step all the dogshit littering the sidewalks, which seems to be a real problem in Playa. I was traveling light on this trip — only carrying a North Face backpack and my Tumi satchel. I would have been struggling if I'd brought a rolling suitcase and the racket it would have made rolling down those quiet, early morning streets — Clack-CLACK! Clack-CLACK! Clack-CLACK!

- I can get away with using a rolling suitcase when I travel to Thailand, especially going to Bangkok or Phuket. In the three roundtrip flights I'd flown from Texas and the numerous flights I'd taken within the region, I've rarely had to lug my gear farther than the nearest taxi or tuk-tuk waiting to take me from Point A to Point B. To and from the airport or to and from the hotel.

There is one scenario that's always playing out in the back of my mind: What if I have to walk five miles loaded down with all of my gear? Do I possess the physical stamina to do it? Is my gear configured in a way that would allow me to walk such distances comfortably and efficiently?

I put this to the test once over a decade ago, back in 2010. I loaded up my old North Face backpack that had been sitting in my closet and simply walked out the front door of my house. For this trip, I vowed not to drive a car or take any taxis — I would only walk or use whatever public transportation was available. I had nothing else to do. It was the time of year, right after Christmas and a week before the New Year, when everything is in limbo, schedules and projects go into a suspended state of animation, and I'd been itching to do some solo road-tripping. I'd taken the family on a few beach vacations early in the year, but I wanted to do something a little grittier and more adventurous. So I decided to catch a Greyhound bus somewhere. Wasn't sure where at first. I'd decide on a destination when it came time to buy the ticket. This was going to be my "hobo road trip."

I left the house and headed for the commuter rail station about three miles down the road and over the freeway. From there, I caught a train to downtown Dallas and walked the few short blocks to the Greyhound bus station. The place was packed with weary-looking holiday travelers, a random assortment of homeless people, and guys who looked like they just got out of prison.

Initially, I thought I'd head to New Orleans or El Paso. Somewhere where I could do a quick trip up and back in three or four days' time. I stood in line to buy a ticket, still trying to decide where I wanted to go.

When I got to the counter, I asked the agent when the next bus was leaving.

"11:30 to Laredo," she said.

So I bought a roundtrip ticket to Laredo for $70 bucks. Returning on the 31st, New Year's Eve.

That previous summer, we'd spent three weeks in a condo resort in Lahaina on Maui. Total cost for the three of us for that trip was a little over $7,000. The budget for my hobo road trip was $300. This would be an adventure, I told myself, not a vacation.

I found myself seated next to an old guy who was grumpy and irritable the entire ride down. Every time he adjusted himself in his seat, the smell of shit wafted across my face. I didn't realize until later that he was probably using a colostomy bag.

(In 2014, my father discovered he had stage four colon cancer and had part of his lower intestine removed. For the last year of his life, he had to use a colostomy bag, and there was always the faint smell of feces around him. Then I recalled that guy I sat next to on the Greyhound bus four years earlier and understood the reason for his discomfort and foul mood.)

It was a nine-hour bus ride with stops along the way in Waco, Austin, San Antonio. By the time we reached the bus station in

Laredo, it was late in the evening. I stumbled off the bus, my legs cramped and sore. In fact, my entire body was cramped and sore from sitting upright with knees bent for hours and hours. It felt like I'd endured a form of mild torture. I slipped on my backpack and limped out of the bus station and into the night.

I was using a Blackberry cell phone back then. Internet access was slow and impractical on that tiny screen, but I managed to book a room at a Motel 8 about three miles away and an hour-long walk along a main road that ran parallel to Interstate 35. The streets were dark, and the sidewalks were uneven and cracked, giving way to bare dirt and thick patches of overgrown weeds in places. There were a few houses scattered along the way, older homes surrounded by chain-link fences and metal bars on the windows. I reached the hotel around midnight and checked in.

I spent the next two days wandering around on foot. No taxis, no buses. Just walking around aimlessly, like a bum with nothing better to do.

Laredo seemed like a sleepy, podunk town. Mostly hispanic. Mostly poor. At least around the downtown area where I was situated. Not a whole lot going on.

Curious about the Mexican side, I walked over the International Bridge into Nuevo Laredo. On the other end of the bridge, a lone Mexican border patrol agent stood next to a small folding table. He asked for my passport and motioned for me to dump the contents of my backpack into a plastic bin resting on the table. Stifling a yawn, he gave each a cursory glance and waved me through. He seemed bored and disinterested. He couldn't have been older than 20 or 25.

If I ever needed to leave the United States undetected, this is the route I would take. I would pay cash for everything and avoid using ATM machines or credit/debit cards. Leave the cell phone at home, buried in a sock drawer or something. Better yet, send it somewhere headed in the opposite direction — like Portland, Maine or Portland, Oregon. The first thing government spooks will do is subpoena your cell phone records and trace your phone's beaconing signal off of every cell tower all the way down to the border. Why make it any easier for them? Pay cash for everything. Avoid airports and computerized checkpoints at the border. Use burner phones and throwaway Internet accounts.

Once you make it to Mexico, it should be easy enough to move undetected to points further south via local buses, taxis, and ferry crossings — Guatemala, Costa Rica, and on down into South America — Colombia, Venezuela. The trick, I think, is crossing the ocean if you want to go explore, say, Cambodia or Morocco.

This train of thought was taking me down a road that was less about hobo travel and more about how to travel like a fugitive. My urge to ESCAPE and GET AWAY hadn't yet reached that level of toxicity. Or desperation. I was okay with just pretending and fantasizing for now.

Crossing from Laredo into Nuevo Laredo was like that Wizard of Oz transition from black-and-white into technicolor. Where downtown Laredo was mostly empty and bereft of life, with many storefronts displaying "For Lease" or "Going Out of Business" signs in their front windows — Nuevo Laredo, by contrast, felt like a Cinco de Mayo celebration. There were crowds of people shopping and lounging around in the central plaza area with their families. Many shops had loudspeakers setup out front, blasting Tejano music. A few, I noticed, were walk-in dental clinics with dental chairs setup like chairs in a barbershop for all to see.

It was late morning, and a late-December chill lingered in the air. I stopped in at a busy-looking diner along the edge of the main plaza and ordered a bowl of menudo.

Halfway through that bowl of soup, my stomach started gurgling again. The night before I put a little too much of that extra spicy green salsa on a plate of tacos I was eating at some hole-in-the-wall place near the hotel. I was on the toilet most of the following morning. I thought it was done doing its thing to my insides. Evidently not. My sphincter puckered up tight, struggling to hold back the unholiest of drips.

The thing I noticed about Mexican restaurants is that when they leave the check on the table, they don't come to pick it up right away, even if you've clearly set your cash sitting on top of the bill near the edge of the table. They'll politely ignore you and your payment for a while. Maybe they want to avoid making it seem like they're pressuring you to leave. Maybe they want to give you time to digest your food or pick your teeth with a toothpick.

I couldn't afford to wait. There was a biohazard emergency slowly working its way through my lower intestine. I stood and asked the waitress, "Los banos?"

She pointed to a door near the cash register and just behind a table where a small family was seated. The door swung inward, giving a clear view of what lay inside — a single toilet, peeling wallpaper, and a half-roll of toilet paper. The room was about the size of a small closet. Fearful and reluctant, with family members watching, I went in. Dear Lord, have mercy upon me.

I undid my pants and sat down to do my thing and nearly immediately slipped off the toilet. The toilet seat wasn't attached to the toilet.

I could hear the family on the other side of that thin, hollow door, speaking Spanish to each other in low, hushed tones. There was no TV or music in the dining room. Inside the toilet closet, there was no fan to mask the sounds. It was as if I were seated at the table with them, punctuating the conversation with diarrhea squirts and slow, gurgling farts.

I probably wasn't in there for more than ten or fifteen minutes, but it felt like an hour of squirting and shitting, my stomach knotting and contorting. The smell was horrendous, and I was preparing to apologize to the family just outside the door for their meal I was about to ruin when I swung the door open wide and let out that foul stench.

When I finished, I did my best to clean up with that half-roll of single-ply toilet paper and gingerly pulled my pants up. I needed another shower, and I needed to throw my underwear away.

The family on the other side of the door was talking and laughing, unaware of the disaster that was about to take place mere feet from where they were enjoying their meal.

I reached back to flush the toilet. Nothing happened. A single bubble floated to the surface through the murky brown and black water in the bowl. The water kept rising. I watched in horror as the stuff slowly rose to the lip of the bowl.

Holy fucking shit. What the hell was I supposed to do?

Just behind the toilet tank was a tiny plunger. I gently lowered it into the brown and black mess until I felt it hit the bottom of the tank, just over the hole. Then I gave it a firm shove, but the fucking thing was one of those Made in China Dollar Store plungers, and the hard rubber cup just flipped itself inside-out and created a ripple of waves splashing back and forth. I set it back in its plastic holder behind the tank and got the hell out of there.

My waitress was at the cash register ringing up another customer. She smiled at me, "Gracias!"

I smiled weakly and left.

That was in 2010. I haven't been back to Nuevo Laredo since.

—

Maybe it's something in the air. Or something in the water. Or maybe it's all the ultra-processed, artificial ingredients they're dumping into fast-food cheeseburgers and french fries. Or maybe it's the high fructose corn syrup in the soft drinks. Add to that mix cable news ("news") stations bombarding viewers around the clock with horseshit and biased opinions wholly endorsed and paid for by banks, corporations, and insurance lobbyists.

It could be any number of reasons, but it will be clear you've landed on U.S. soil. People are more agitated, more easily annoyed. The griping and the whining intensify. There are more frowns than smiles. People are more red-faced than suntanned.

Nowhere is this more evident than when you've landed in a U.S. airport after spending the past month overseas in Southeast Asia. The contrast couldn't be more stark after you've spent the past month lounging on a beach, where everything is "sabai sabai" and where you've been wearing little more than a flimsy pair of flip-flops and tattered swimming trunks the entire time.

I awaken from my Thai daydream and find myself in the dull gray purgatory of the immigration checkpoint at JFK International. An immigration officer is shouting instructions at us like we're prisoners being transported to another prison. Indeed, we shuffle slowly through the line as if we're shackled at the ankles.

Welcome back to the United States! Incarceration nation! Confederacy of Dunces! You don't know freedom until you've gone FULL RETARD! Yee-haw!

No one is happy to be here. I take my place in the long line of people queuing up. There must be a hundred people in front of me. My connecting flight to Dallas leaves in less than three hours. It will take me nearly two hours to work my way to the front of the line and one of only two immigration counters that are currently staffed by agents and processing travelers. I glance at my phone and see that it's just past noon. The other agents must be on their lunch break.

In other countries in other airports I've traveled through, if there were a number of international flights arriving at the same time — Mexico City, Cancun, Bangkok, Tokyo, Kuala Lumpur — it would be all hands on deck. Airports would beef up the staffing at those busiest times. Not so at JFK. At least not on the day that I was there.

"Time for my legally mandated lunch break. Have fun, losers!"

"I'm sorry. This counter is closed. You'll have to fuck off and wait for the next one to open up. Someone will be right with you."

"That particular task is above my pay grade. You'll need to find someone else to help you. Sorry."

"GET IN LINE! GET YOUR PASSPORTS AND BOARDING PASSES OUT! NEXT! I SAID, NEXT!"

America might be owned by billionaires, but it is run by low-wage bureaucrats, bitter office clerks, and bottom-of-the-rung petty tyrants, each with their own little plastic name tag attached to their shirt pockets. Their souls have been ground to a pulp. What little joy they find is derived from the suffering they inflict upon small animals and members of the unsuspecting public who are completely at their mercy. One spiteful customer service rep can ruin the day for hundreds of people just as easily as a terrorist flying a plane into a New York City highrise.

"Fuck you. They don't pay me enough to give a shit."

Such is the state of customer service in America. Home of the free, land of the brave. Yee-haw.

The customer is always right, and you — you poor under-paid, uneducated, pimply-faced, fast food-eating piece of shit. You, who never knew a mother's love, whose very mother treated you with scorn and disdain. You, who barely graduated high school and can barely read or write at a fifth grade level. You better learn some interpersonal skills. We're not paying you nine dollars an hour to stand around with your finger up your ass. Clock in and get to work!

This agitated, low-key aggressive attitude is contagious. I feel as if I'm beginning to lose my mind as well. Or maybe it's because I've been traveling for two days and haven't slept in a bed or showered.

I barked at a Russian couple who were commenting on an old Chinese woman literally dragging a huge hiking backpack behind her as she snaked her way through the line. There were a number of columns that the line of people zig-zagged around, and the old woman would set her pack down against the column, then snake her way along the line until she came back around. Then she'd take the backpack and slide it over to the next column in front of her.

The Russian couple notices her doing this at some point and exchanges glances with each other. The man looks at the bag, then looks at the old woman who is shuffling away, then looks at the bag again.

"Should we be concerned?" he says to his wife, jokingly.

"Maybe we should call TSA," the wife replies.

They both speak with thick Russian accents. Any normal person, who had showered and was well-rested, might have found their remarks to be boorish and a little insensitive, but nothing more than that. It was obvious the couple were just joking around. But in my fogged, sleep-deprived brain, I began thinking to myself as I worked my way through the line just behind the old Chinese woman:

We ought to be more concerned about Russian spies that have infiltrated the highest levels of the U.S. government! And the Russian oligarchs who come to the U.S. and throw their money around, looking down their noses at other immigrants that come here to find better lives for themselves and their families! Foreign billionaires are the reason working class families in the U.S. can no longer afford to buy a home! Foreign corporations are buying up all the available inventory causing home prices to skyrocket!

Middle-class Americans have been further degraded and downgraded into two lower sub-classes: renters and van-dwellers. Below that, you have the sidewalk-shitters, the mentally ill, and the drug addicts, most of whom spend their lives bouncing between homelessness and incarceration. In another generation or two, these will make up the majority of American society. Nation of beggars. Begging for time off from shit jobs. Begging for a little more time to come up with the rent. Begging insurance companies to help cover the cost of ass cancer treatment and diabetes medication.

And here is this young Russian couple, looking smug and confident. With their child in tow. A ten-year-old boy. Oblivious like the spoiled offspring of the wealthy upper-class. It's not his fault. I'm sure his parents love him dearly, they who look down their noses at the old Chinese woman struggling with her humongous expedition-sized backpack.

I read the look on their faces. "We are not like those kinds of immigrants. We are white and educated and have high-paying jobs. You can let us into your country. We will assimilate quite nicely. We will host cozy dinner parties with our closest friends and colleagues, all of whom are also white, educated, and well-paid. Go ahead, look them up on LinkedIn. We might even incorporate an Indian or two or a Black person into our circle of friends, as a token of our diversity. But heaven forbid if any of those monkeys try to sleep with our women. Scandalous! Absolutely scandalous!

The Russian woman is going on and on about contacting security about the giant backpack sitting there on the floor.

"Relax!" I scowl at her. "She's coming back to get it." (Meaning the old Chinese woman.)

I've had enough of these smug Euro-elitists and their stinking white privilege. I'm exhausted. My skin is clammy, and I haven't brushed my teeth in two days. I'm running low on cash, and I need to get back to work, so I can be yelled at by Indian bosses. No longer am I daydreaming about Thailand. I'm thinking now about war and bloodshed.

The Russian woman is taken aback. She glances at her husband who glances back at her. They remain silent for a moment. Then she continues, pretending like she didn't hear me, as if to signal that she is not accustomed to being so rudely addressed by Third World mongoloids. No acknowledgment necessary.

We continue snaking our way through the line. Every time we pass each other, the Russian couple glance at each other and share a smirk. I'm sure they were fine, normal people. I was the one suffering from sudden onset mental illness.

Meanwhile, a tiny gray-haired woman, hunched over and dragging a rolling suitcase behind her is slowly cutting through the line. She, evidently, doesn't feel like zig-zagging with the rest of us. She's ducking under the cordoned ropes and gently pushing people aside.

"Excuse me," she says, "I have a flight to catch. Excuse me, please."

"You're not the only one, lady!" I yell.

People are giving her the angriest, dirtiest looks. But they let her pass. Probably because of her age and her hunched back. She looked like an old, decrepit question mark cutting in front of everyone.

It will be another hour before I get to the immigration counter. What does it take so fucking long for American citizens to re-enter their own country? And why do they treat us like animals? The billionaires are holding us down. The ghetto rats are dragging us down. American society has become a diaspora of mental illness and drug-addled derangement.

I'm tired. I need a shower. I need to brush my teeth.

I retrieve my duffel bag from baggage claim and rush to catch a shuttle train to another terminal on the other side of the airport, where domestic flights are departing. Wait in line at the ticket counter, and then another long wait to get through TSA security. I glance back to see how many people are waiting behind me and spot the little old hunchbacked woman with her rolling suitcase. I arrived at my gate with fifteen minutes to spare.

As we're boarding the plane, one of the other passengers complains that they forced him to check his duffel bag, which was about five feet long and three feet wide.

"I probably coulda fit it under the seat in front of me," he says to another gentleman who isn't carrying any luggage. He's just wearing a sportcoat and smiling with his hands in his pockets. I noticed him in the terminal earlier. Smiling, he bowed and waved me to go ahead of him as the gate agent called out our seating numbers.

He's still smiling as he says to the duffel bag guy, "It doesn't matter. This airport is garbage. I'm never flying through JFK again."

—

Part Four

**Thailand / Vietnam
March - April 2024**

Itinerary (in order of cities visited):

- Thailand:
  - Bangkok
- Vietnam:
  - Danang
  - Bana Hills
  - Hoi An
  - Hanoi
- Thailand:
  - Hat Yai
  - Patong, Phuket
  - Bangkok

March 21, 2024
Hotel Clover Asoke, Room 906

My flight landed at Suvarnabhumi Airport yesterday morning at 10am. By 1pm, I was checked into my room at the Hotel Clover Asoke and had roamed down to Sukhumvit for a slice of pizza at Pala Pizza Romana & Bistro near Terminal 21, near the BTS and MRT interchange.

Dinner was a plate of fish 'n chips at Fitzgerald's, down the street from Nana Plaza. Finished the evening at Penny Black, one of two bars on Soi Cowboy that has a live band playing every night.

All in all, I spent about $200USD my first night back.

Chaiya will be flying in from Hat Yai later this afternoon. I bought her that bottle of perfume she'd been asking for. Some fancy Tom Ford bullshit that cost $300USD at the Ulta store in Allen, Texas. (Which caused me to bring a checked bag because I didn't feel like answering questions trying to take it through the TSA line at the airport.)

I also ordered a bouquet of roses to be delivered to the room before she arrives. Should be here within the hour.

The goal for today is to see what kind of camera gear I can find at Central World. I brought along my Nikon Z30 for this trip. First time traveling with a "real" digital camera.

—

April 2024

I did not write a single line in this notebook other than that short entry on my first day in Bangkok. I was too tired, too drunk, too burned out.

I'd spent those first few weeks with Chaiya, who accompanied me to Vietnam. That was a bad decision. Her behavior became increasingly cold and distant until things came to a head in Hat Yai. More on that later.

My itinerary went something like this:
- March 18 - 24: Bangkok, Thailand
- March 24 - 27: Danang, Vietnam
- March 27 - 28: Bana Hills, Vietnam
- March 28 - 30: Hoi An, Vietnam
- March 30 - April 2: Hanoi, Vietnam
- April 2 - April 3: Bangkok, Thailand
- April 3 - April 5: Hat Yai, Thailand
- April 5 - April 15: Patong, Phuket
- April 15 - April 17: Bangkok, Thailand

I like to use Bangkok as a kind of base camp and launching point for heading out to other cities in the region. Bangkok has the infrastructure and the modern conveniences one would expect to find in a world class city — electronics and tech, restaurants and bars and street food, efficient transportation, 7-Elevens and shopping malls. And it's usually cheaper to fly into Bangkok than it is to fly into Phuket, usually by about a thousand dollars. The Russians have flooded Phuket since their leader decided to start a war with Ukraine, and the cost of airfare and hotel rooms have skyrocketed.

—

Some quick notes on a few of the cities we visited:

Bangkok:

- Terminal 21/BTS Asoke station: This is the center of the city. Restaurants, hotels, bars and nightclubs all converge within this four- or five-block area. A little too touristy for some travelers' tastes, but it's where I prefer to stay whenever I'm in town.
- A BTS day pass costs $150 Thai baht as of April 2024 (or about $4USD). Good until midnight. You won't have to think twice about venturing up and down the Sukhumvit line —

Nana Plaza, MBK and Siam shopping malls, the Ekamai district, Emsphere, etc. Just scan the card and go. It's so much easier than having to fish around in your pockets for loose coins to pay the 40- or 60-baht fare.
- The Penny Black bar located on the northern end of Soi Cowboy is my go-to spot for a quick drink to begin or end my evenings. There's almost always a live band playing, and you don't have to worry about bar girls hassling you for drinks.
- I stayed at the Hotel Clover Asoke for the days I was in Bangkok. Next door is a 7-Eleven. Down the block is a Foodland. Access to the BTS Asoke station via the elevated walkway is just an easy stroll up the escalators in the Exchange Tower building just around the corner. No need to go trudging up those steep concrete stairs at the street level and trying not to succumb to the heat and humidity.
- Pro tip for making life easier for getting around Thailand, Malaysia, or Vietnam:
  - Bring along an unlocked cell phone (or pick one up at Big C).
  - Get a Thai SIM card. I've been using AIS for the past few years without any complaints. Their service has been reliable. Coverage is decent, and the price is very affordable.
  - Install the Grab app and link it to a credit card. You'll need a local number to do this. Hence, the need for a Thai SIM card.
  - Now, whenever you need to go somewhere, like with Uber or any other ride-sharing app, just select a pickup point, destination, and let Grab do the rest. The cost of the trip will be calculated automatically. No need to haggle over prices, currency conversions, or worry about getting short-changed. As long as you've got your credit card linked to the app, there's no need to deal with cash at all. The Grab app handles the entire transaction.
- MBK Center in Siam Square is the place to go for all things electronics or photography related. They also sell some really good knock-off clothes and luggage on the top floor.

Danang, Vietnam:

- The Mandila Beach Hotel, as the name suggests, is right across the street from Khe Beach. Our room was up on the tenth floor, and I was awoken each morning by Vietnamese music being blasted from boomboxes and exercise instructors shouting instructions over loudspeakers. It's barely six in the morning, and the beach is already crowded with Vietnamese locals and Chinese tourists doing their morning exercises or going for early morning swims.
- ATMs were hard to find in this city. The few that I did manage to locate were either out of service or appeared to be running outdated equipment from a few decades ago. I could hear the machine making strange clicking and whirring noises as it responded to my request. Then it would make a slow grinding noise as the little door opened and reluctantly dispensed my cash.
- My Wise debit card didn't work anywhere all throughout Vietnam. I contacted Wise support, who explained that the reason is because Vietnam has their own unique and antiquated way of processing transactions that is incompatible with the way the rest of the world processes transactions. So I was stuck running up the debt on my Capital One credit cards since they also didn't accept American Express in every other place except the hotels.
- Danang was the first city we visited in Vietnam. In fact, it was my first time seeing Vietnam, period. The sheer amount of traffic and noise pollution took some getting used to. It made Bangkok traffic look calm and peaceful by comparison.
- Many of the Vietnamese I met seemed a little guarded at first, but once that initial hesitancy wore off, they were as warm and welcoming as the Thais. I wondered if this guarded behavior might have its historical or cultural roots in the fact that Vietnam has been occupied at various times by the Spanish and the French, and more recently by that period they

commonly refer to as the American War. (What us Yankees call the Vietnam War.) But I'm no historian, so what the hell do I know?

Danang didn't quite live up to the hype that I'd read about online. The food was just okay. The customer service skills of restaurant staff and store clerks could only be described as unenthusiastic at best. The overall attitude seemed to one of bored disinterest, at times bordering on outright disdain. It was as if they were unaccustomed to dealing with foreigners, much less tourists in a touristy part of town, which seemed to contradict the popular notion that Danang is a favorite destination for digital nomads. But again, maybe this attitude of mistrust is rooted in the lingering feelings leftover from the American War.

To be fair, we were only in Danang for a few short days, and I didn't get the chance to explore as much of the city as I'd wanted, seeing that I was with Chaiya, who was content with venturing no further than the hotel's breakfast buffet each morning before retreating back to the room.

The initial impulse when visiting a place for the first time is to compare it to all the other places you've visited. Maybe this is due to some natural urge to find some familiarity within the unknown or alien. Or to keep your brain from exploding from sensory overload.

"Oh, this beach is like the one in Playa del Carmen."

"The road to Patong reminds me of the highway leading through the mountains to Jaco."

"The pad thai in that shophouse along Nanai Road is a lot spicier than the way they make it back in Dallas."

But at some point, you come upon the realization that every country, every city has its own unique personality and possesses its own unique vibe, and such comparisons are ultimately pointless. The sooner you're able to relate to a place on its own terms, the sooner you'll come to appreciate it for what it is. Some places — I found Danang to be one of them — are not so easily forthcoming, not so easy to figure out. They're a bit more subtle, and finding that vibe might take a little more time. I resisted the urge to make sweeping generalizations based on a handful of bad first impressions. Danang is a city that definitely warrants a second visit.

    This is one of the reasons that I prefer to travel solo. When I'm alone, I'm able to get a better feel for a place without my impressions and experience being tainted by the opinions and biases of whomever I happen to be traveling with. When you travel with family and friends, you're basically traveling in an insulated bubble. It won't be as easy to absorb the sights and sounds of any new environment. Maybe they don't feel like eating at the same restaurant. Maybe they want to go shopping instead of the beach. Maybe you'd rather go drinking when they want to go on a dinner cruise. And if your situation is anything like the vast majority of Americans working shit jobs for shit pay, who are extremely fortunate to get a two-week vacation (laughable by most other nation's standards), any deviation from the plan, any argument over where to eat or what to see, wastes precious little vacation time. Make use of that time. Be greedy with it. Be selfish. It's your time after all. Use it wisely.

    Chaiya and I had our first tiff in Danang. She had hired a driver who would be taking us around on a number of planned activities over the course of the next few days. Initially, I thought we had only hired him to drive us from the airport to our hotel. I became annoyed when Chaiya said that he would be picking us up at the hotel to take us to dinner after just dropping us off a few minutes earlier. I told her that I would rather just walk around the area around the hotel by myself and find a place to eat. She, in turn, grew angry and said that she had spent a lot of time planning our itinerary for this trip. I told her to go by herself if she wanted. I wasn't stopping her. She ended up staying alone in the hotel room while I went out and got something to eat at one of the beach-side restaurants across the street.

    What I was really angered about was that I happened to look over her shoulder while we were waiting to get through the immigration line at the airport, and I saw her texting some guy on her phone. I could see the last few messages from him were crying or laughing emojis (I was too far away to see it clearly), and she had responded in Thai. She quickly glanced over her shoulder to see if I was looking, but I turned away and pretended not to notice. I didn't mean to spy on her like that, and I never did mention it to her, but that put up a big red flag for me for the rest of the trip and was the reason I didn't want to be anywhere near her that first night.

Bana Hills / The Hand of God:

The only interesting thing about Bana Hills was the thirty-minute cable car ride up the side of the mountain. We were treated to spectacular views of the rain forest below as we glided silently overhead. Everything else about the place was fake as shit and hopelessly contrived, like wearing Mickey Mouse ears on a Disneyland kiddie ride.

Judging by the architecture of the buildings and the pseudo-classical music quietly playing from speakers hidden all over the place, I figured the place is meant to be a replica of a town in the Swiss Alps. There's even a fake cathedral where I presume people can come to pray before a make-believe god or maybe even get married. Very strange to encounter something like this in the middle of Vietnam. I don't know the story behind the place or why the Vietnamese decided to build it. I was too lazy to Google it; it wasn't worth the energy. Best to just experience it for what it is and let it pass like a cloud of mist. Chaiya suffered from diarrhea the entire time, so her experience was a little more uncomfortable than mine.

The next day we awoke early and caught a second set of cable cars to see the main attraction — the Hand of God. You've likely seen photos of it on the Internet. A set of giant concrete hands that appear to be holding up a concrete walkway jutting out from the mountainside. There are probably a million photos of the place on Instagram, and I added another handful of my own.

Go ahead, take the shot. Why not? How do you choose to experience the world? Through your own eyes?

The Hand of God, like most everything else in Bana Hills, is man-made. Mildly interesting, but not worth the price of the ticket or fighting the hordes of tourists, in my opinion. We would have been better off staying in Danang for a few more days, or even Hoi An where we would be traveling to the next day.

Chaiya's stomach was still turning when it was time to ride the cable car back down the mountain. Twenty minutes of watching her writhe and squirm. She literally ran to the nearest toilet when we finally reached the base of the mountain.

Hoi An:

Hoi An was my favorite place of all the cities we visited in Vietnam.

We stayed at the Wyndham Garden, right across the street from the beach, where the sand was clean and the water was nice and calm, if a bit chilly. I only went swimming on one of the three days we were there. As in Danang, Chaiya refused to visit the beach at all and instead chose to remain in the hotel room for most of our stay.

By now, Chaiya had grown completely cold and distant and had retreated to sleeping on the far side of the bed. She rarely left the hotel room except to take advantage of the breakfast buffet each morning or to join me for dinner later in the evening. She had absolutely no interest in walking around the town and seeing the sights.

I asked her time and again if something was the matter, if anything was wrong. She would only smile slyly and mumble a quick "No."

But something had to be the matter. Something was wrong. Something must have changed. Was it something I said or did? We were getting along just fine those first few days in Bangkok, but now it felt like she was pushing me away, keeping me at arm's length. Did she leave a husband or boyfriend back in Malaysia that I didn't know about? Was she secretly a lesbian and only coming along with me for the money and distraction? A temporary break from getting drunk every night in those Kuala Lumpur nightclubs?

"It seems like you're not having any fun," I said. "Do you want to go back to Hat Yai or KL?"

Every time I asked her this, her response was a simple head shake, "No" — and then she would go back to staring at her phone. After a while, I stopped asking her if she wanted to join me on my wanderings around town and began venturing out on my own. I knew the answer would be a quiet head shake, "No."

The sex was few and far between. She wasn't as into it as those first nights in Bangkok, when she would grind her hips into my face, quietly moaning and gripping the side of my head with both hands as I went down on her. After showering, she would slip into bed wearing nothing under her bathrobe, and I knew she was ready.

By the time we got to Hoi An, she had taken to sleeping in her street clothes. If I attempted to snuggle next to her in bed, she'd get up to go sit in a chair. And still, I kept asking her, "If you don't want to stay with me, I can buy you a plane ticket back home."

And again the quiet head shake, "No." Then back to staring at her phone.

I was baffled and disheartened. How did I end up with this mental case? Sitting with her at a restaurant, or in our hotel room, or riding in the back of a taxi — I felt like I was by myself, completely alone, like there was no one else sitting there next to me. I became filled with feelings of isolation and loneliness. It was like she was projecting this laser-focused beam of emotional energy, something that she seemed able to wield alternatively like a weapon or defensively.

In previous conversations, on the rare occasions when she felt comfortable enough to open up to me, she had made vague comments about being left alone on a daily basis when she was a young child. Her mother had to work, she explained, and would lock her in the house, leaving her completely alone until her mother returned later that evening. She was around four or five years old at the time, she explained. She added that she had spent most of her life alone and was always by herself.

Goddamn. And I thought I was a loner.

I could never ask her more about it. She would quickly change the subject or signal that she was done talking about it by getting up and busying herself with something else. During our time in Vietnam, I don't think we had a single meaningful conversation the entire time we were together. It was as if I'd been vacationing with a complete stranger.

I waited until sundown before venturing into Hoi An's Old Quarter by myself. I took my time wandering through the side streets and back alleys and took tons of photos, having brought along a new toy for this trip, a Nikon Z30 mirrorless digital camera, which ironically, was Chaiya's idea. We had planned to do a number of "photo shoots" during our trip. She wanted to go shopping for a traditional Vietnamese dress, she said, and take a bunch of photos — on the Dragon Bridge in Danang, along the Hand of God in Baha Hills, basically all the touristy Instagram spots. We were making all sorts of plans via text message before our trip, while I was still in Texas and she was still working the nightclubs in Kuala Lumpur.

So much for that idea. I was reluctant to mention the subject seeing how icy our relationship had become, but feeling a little sporty one day, I asked her anyway. Her response was as expected — a frigid, "No."

She had been lugging around a huge, shiny yellow, hard-sided rolling suitcase. I wondered what she could have possibly been carrying around in that thing because I'd only seen her wearing two outfits the entire time we were together — a pair of jean shorts and a t-shirt or a plain-looking beige polyester business suit. She didn't dress up at all during our trip. She appeared to have lost all interest in going anywhere or doing anything. I couldn't figure it out. It was driving me mad.

Surprisingly, she decided to come out with me the following evening. I thought she'd be interested in having dinner and then going for a ride along the lake in one of the lantern boats, but she retreated to our hotel room before the night even got started. It was too hot, she said, and she was annoyed with the crowds of people. She looked bored and kept her distance from me, often sitting off by herself. I gave her some money for the cab ride back to the hotel. I stayed back to go wandering by myself with the excuse that I had to find an ATM and get more cash. We left each other in the middle of the street without a kiss or goodbye. We both just turned around and headed in opposite directions. There in the crowded Old Quarter, crammed with tourists and street vendors rubbing shoulder to shoulder, enjoying the sights and sounds, relaxing outside in front of the restaurants and bars — I never felt so alone. It would have been better if I had come to Vietnam by myself.

Despite the fact that I suspected her of harboring some muted hostility toward me, she insisted on accompanying me to Hanoi. At this point, I just saw her as another piece of luggage that I had to lug around. I kept my distance from her at the airport and wandered around the terminal while she waited at the gate, staring at her phone.

―

It seems the people of Danang haven't yet grown accustomed to being a popular tourist destination. From the rickety old ATM machines to the awkward way hotel and restaurant staff interact with English-speaking guests, to the peculiar choice of products they decide to sell in airport convenience shops.

One such shop in Danang airport looked more like a Chinese medicinal/toy store — packaged boxes of roots and herbs and various flavors of tea. On the back row, toy soldiers arranged randomly on the shelf alongside miniature airplanes and little dolls. I could find nothing that a traveler might actually need prior to boarding his flight — aspirin, baby wipes, tooth paste, chewing gum, deodorant. It was more just a random hodge-podge assortment of things you might need if you were a Vietnamese grandmother on her way to visit her grandchildren in the countryside. None of it made any sense to the mind of a Western traveler.

―

In Hanoi, we were unprepared for the crowds of people and insane traffic. The sheer intensity of noise and constant beeping of horns, which seemed to increase ten-fold compared to the noise level in Danang or Hoi An. Motor scooters zipped by our taxi like a million buzzing insects.

I had a room reserved at the Hanoi Pearl in the heart of the Old Quarter. Streets in the area are closed to motor traffic on weekends, and only pedestrians are allowed. Our taxi driver stopped in the middle of the street a few blocks from our hotel and motioned for us to get out. At first, I thought he had just grown tired of sitting in traffic and didn't feel like taking us all the way. He pointed down a closed-off street and made sweeping motions with his hand to go down and make a left.

Chaiya was her usual distant and moody self. Again, she would just sit in the hotel room, content with just staring at her phone all day and night.

"What's the point of traveling if you don't want to go out and see anything?" I said to her.

She merely shot me a blank look and went back to staring at her phone. So I left her alone in the room, and again, I found myself racking my brain and trying to think if it was something I'd said or did. She gave no hints or explanations.

—

On weekends, the Old Quarter is jam-packed with people. Many of the sidewalks are blocked off for people dining on little plastic tables and chairs, and the crowds overflow into the street. People have to squeeze by, rubbing shoulder to shoulder and twisting sideways this way and that. Within minutes of leaving the hotel, I found myself in the middle of such a crowd, trying to avoid getting my toes run over by motor scooters revving their engines through the same mad pile. I was suddenly reminded of wading through the mosh pit at an Iron Maiden concert in 1987. The experience was essentially the same.

I found (and fought) my way out to some side streets and back alleys soon enough. Breathing room at last. I slowed down and wandered a bit, snapping photos of the silhouettes in doorways and old women squatting low over the street as they scrubbed pots and pans. Children rode bicycles, steering around the pot-holed asphalt. Some kicked a ball around. Pot-bellied men in undershirts sat sprawled out on tiny plastic chairs — some napping, others staring blankly into the distance. Above the street, the backlit glow of a curtained window here or there. The front entrances to shop houses left wide open with a clear view into the living quarters and private lives of its inhabitants — sitting on sofas watching TV, children playing with toys on tiled floors, a housewife preparing a meal. And in the distance, the constant and incessant beeping traffic and honking horns, like an unseen swarm, now muted and seemingly worlds away.

Without Google Maps and my cell phone, I could have been lost out there for days and would never have found my way back to the hotel. I suspect this is one of the biggest reasons global travel has exploded in recent years. Everyone and their fucking grandmothers are creating Youtube channels or trying to be Instagram influencers, recording everything they do from all over the planet. Google Maps and Google Translate have literally changed the way we interact with the world. Barely a decade ago, I wandered for hours lost in the circular streets of Mexico City and a week later in San Jose, Costa Rica, my teenage cab driver who picked me up from the airport could not find my hotel and had to stop and ask for directions.

How things have changed. Now Google Maps is able to provide me with real-time updates on my precise physical location to within a few meters as I wander the back alleys of Hanoi, Vietnam. Sure, this newfangled technology might take away some of the adventure and sense of discovery in travel, but it also reduces the amount of panic and anxiety. Not all who wander are lost. Some have purchased the global roaming package on their overseas cellular data plan.

—

We stayed only a few nights in Hanoi. As I was basically alone most of the time, I ended my evenings with a drink at the bar across the street. The place was done up in the style of 1920's Prohibition-era Chicago. Stylized art deco and scant mood lighting that didn't actually provide any illumination — I could barely see my own hand much less count out the money to pay the bill. I realized it was one of those hipster places where the twenty-something bartenders and waitstaff were too cool to smile or make eye contact. Which was fine with me. I didn't feel like making any friends. What I liked about the place was that it wasn't crowded and the air-conditioning blew nice and cold. It felt good to cool down before heading up to the room.

I really needed that hit of rum and Coke before heading back. The situation had degraded to the point where Chaiya and I were barely speaking to each other. As I stepped out for my nightly jaunts around town, I'd simply say over my shoulder, "Be back later." In turn, her responses were reduced to single words: "Yes." "No." "Later." (This last one often came when I attempted to snuggle next to her in bed for a little romance.)

When I got back to the room, she'd be on her side of the bed, staring at her phone or pretending to be asleep. I would take a quick shower to wash away the sweat and stickiness of the humid Vietnamese night, slip into my side of the bed, and fall asleep with that soothing rum and Coke buzz in my head. Not a word said to one another. No "good night." No good night kiss. It was like we'd been married for twenty years and had fallen out of love. I'd been down this road before. I knew the feeling. It is strange, discombobulating. It is a constricting feeling in your solar plexus telling you that something is out of whack. There is a great imbalance of energies present. It is that disturbing feeling you get when you thought you knew a person, and then you realize — no, you didn't really know this person at all. You have been traveling with a ghost, a reflection of something that doesn't really exist.

I had four nights reserved at the Hanoi Pearl. I'd booked it months earlier when I was planning our trip. I wasn't scheduled to fly back to Bangkok until April 2nd, but Chaiya had to be back in Hat Yai by the 1st. Weeks earlier when she was getting ready to meet me in Bangkok, she discovered that thieves had stolen the water meter from her house. While we were in Vietnam, she had a repair guy out there installing a new unit and securing it with a lockable steel cage. The work was complete, and she had to return to pay him and confirm that everything was in good working order prior to her mother and son arriving later in the week. It was the end of Ramadan, and her family was preparing to celebrate Eid al-Fitr.

A look of surprise flashed across her face when I informed her that I wouldn't be flying back with her on the 1st and would instead be catching a flight out the next day.

"Did you still want to see my mom?" she asked.

"Yes, of course," I said.

She was watching me very closely. We had been planning to meet up with her mom in Hat Yai. Chaiya had been repeatedly asking me if I wanted to meet her mom. I'd met her mother and son a few years before, so it wasn't like I'd be meeting them for the first time.

I reassured her over and over again. "Yes, I want to see your mom. I promised her last time that I would see her again. Let's make plans to meet up."

I didn't understand why she was doubting me or why it seemed like such a big deal to meet her mother.

Early that next morning, I awoke with her to see her off. No good-bye kiss. No hug.

Instead, she said, "I need money to pay my house."

"How much was it again?" I asked, still groggy and sipping my hotel instant coffee.

"Thirty-five thousand baht," she said. "As you know, I haven't been working, and I don't have any money."

Her demeanor, usually so stoic and unemotional, I noticed now was slowly peeling away around the edges. Her lips quivered, and her face suddenly had a sunken look to it. I could see the desperation and anxiety in her eyes. I could hear it in her voice.

"I can't give you anything right now," I told her. "I have to move some money around my accounts, and that will take a few days."

I promised her early on, when we were still planning our trip, that I would cover her financially for the time she was traveling with me and not working. I had no intentions of backing down on the deal. In fact, I had set aside about two-thousand dollars to give her and her mom.

But I suspect she had been burned too many times in the past, and she didn't believe me. Her face hardened again, and she turned around and left without saying a word, dragging her huge yellow suitcase behind her. I accompanied her down to the lobby, where we found the bellhop and front desk clerk sprawled out on the couch fast asleep. They leapt to attention when they heard us coming out of the elevator. It was barely five o'clock in the morning, and Chaiya's taxi was already out front, waiting to take her to the airport. She left without saying a word or even looking back in my general direction. I returned to the room and went back to sleep.

—

Wanting to get some practice in with my street photography, I went for a stroll around the neighborhood later in the morning. Even in the daytime, I still found it a challenge trying to maneuver through the crowded, narrow streets and uneven sidewalks, often taken up by shop owners displaying their wares and street food vendors with their food carts and ad-hoc dining areas on the sidewalk crammed with little plastic tables and chairs. Often, I found myself walking in the street and trying not to get run over by motor scooters zipping by.

The morning sun coming through a veiled mist (likely early morning air pollution) made for some interesting play between the diffused light and gray shadows. I took a bunch of photos hoping to capture the beauty that I was seeing. Strange how that works, how everything seems more beautiful and inspiring when you see it for the first time. I felt the same dumbstruck awe when I first laid eyes on Chaiya nearly three years ago. She appeared to me as in a dream, floating right before my eyes, and everything else in my immediate environment — Phuket, Patong, the beach, my travel plans, the life I'd left behind in Texas — faded into the background.

—

My short visit to Vietnam was coming to an end. I'd only caught a tiny glimpse of the place, a brief view into a universe contained within a grain of sand. It was everything all mixed together, like a big bowl of pho — beautiful, crowded, alluring, noisy, mythical, inspiring, frustrating, antiquated, and yes, mysterious. It is painfully cliche to say that I'd be leaving with mixed emotions, but that's the only way I could describe it. There were times during this trip that I felt painfully alone. It was as if Chaiya wasn't even there. I might as well have been traveling by myself. I made a mental note to return, but next time alone. Solo travel is the best way to travel.

The next day, I flew back to Bangkok and stayed for a night before flying out to Hat Yai to meet up with Chaiya. I thought she would have gone back to her own place since the repairman had installed a new water meter to replace the one that had been stolen a few weeks before, but was surprised to find her waiting for me at the hotel. Her big yellow suitcase sat looming in the corner, and her toiletries and makeup were sprawled across the dresser.

I was excited to be in Hat Yai again. It had been two years since I was last there. I asked Chaiya if she wanted to go anywhere, but she declined. She was about to have her period and was feeling a little pain. She retreated to her side of the bed and went back to staring at her phone. Our relationship picked up where it left off in Hanoi — cold and distant.

Later that evening we had dinner at a Mediterranean restaurant around the corner from our hotel. The place had just opened and she'd been meaning to take me there, she explained.

She seemed a bit hesitant when the waiter brought out a serving of hummus and tabouli.

"Ah, I love this stuff," I said, swiping a portion straight off the plate with a piece of naan.

"I never ate this before," said Chaiya, smiling shyly. "This is the first time."

"Just take the bread," I said, tearing off another piece of naan, "and dip it like this."

Here was another gap in her life experience. A minor thing that would have passed unnoticed — a bar girl who had spent most of her life living in southern Thailand could not be expected to be familiar with Mediterranean cuisine. But she had also spent a number of years working in nightclubs in Kuala Lumpur, where she likely learned to carry herself with that air of worldly sophistication and aloofness. Her fashion sense was immaculate, very much similar to the typical gaggles of high society Asian women of wealth and privilege, whom you'll often find strolling through Bangkok shopping malls with armloads of shopping bags from designer shops.

I will admit, before she started following me on Instagram, I was already low-key stalking her account, where I discovered numerous photos of her dining in fancy restaurants and staying in fancy hotels. I know her bar girl salary didn't pay enough to afford those kinds of places, and it was unlikely she'd be visiting such places by herself, anyway. Someone else must have been footing the bill. Maybe the guy behind the camera snapping all those photos. Simps and schleps like me who took her on vacations to Bangkok or Hanoi.

But I knew that she kept her fancy clothes in that beat up yellow suitcase with the broken latch. And I know her elderly mother had to awake at four o'clock every morning to go work in the rubber tree plantation. And I know she suffered from menstrual cramps so painful, she would literally fall to the floor writhing in pain. And I know that she had horrible bouts of diarrhea while I laid on the bed on the other side of that bathroom door in tiny hotel rooms trying to ignore the terrible sound of prolonged squirts and farts, the sounds magnified and echoing off the tiles and fixtures. She likely suffered from some combination of irritable bowel syndrome and too many years spent drinking vodka shots in Malaysian night clubs, where competition amongst the girls is cutthroat.

Chaiya has to compete for customers each night with girls that are only getting younger and prettier, while she slowly grows older and less able to handle all that alcohol. She's nearing forty now, approaching the end of the road. She's finding it increasingly difficult to meet her nightly target, which is set by the club and measured in the number of drinks sold. If a girl goes too many nights in a row without meeting her target, the club lets her go.

She allowed me to see the ugly, vulnerable side of her life, and I suppose that counted for something, seeing how she was normally so guarded and secretive.

In many ways, she was still the poor country girl who grew up in a village in southern Thailand, along the edge of a jungle, in a house with no air-conditioning, surrounded by mud and dirt and chickens, insects, and wild vegetation.

Once, I obtusely asked why she couldn't just find a better job. Work in an office or try to get in at one of the airlines as a flight attendant or ticketing agent.

Not possible, she said. She didn't possess a degree.

I later realized that by "degree," she didn't mean a college education. She never completed primary school, but she seemed more sophisticated and intelligent than other girls I'd met in those clubs. Her demeanor was more demure than her Thai counterparts. In fact, she seemed more Japanese or Korean. Thai bar girls tended to be louder and more rambunctious, at ease around Western men, whereas Chaiya was more soft-spoken and reserved. There was an introverted shyness about her, a quality that I found so appealing. It was this quality that kept her so frustratingly distant.

Despite this appearance of sophistication, this faux worldliness, sometimes the Thai country girl in her came through. One such instance occurred while we were in Hanoi. We were returning to our hotel one evening after dinner and a brief walk around the Old Quarter. Nearing our hotel, I noticed a pile of dog shit on the sidewalk and quickly sidestepped it. I turned to warn Chaiya who was a few steps behind me, but she was distracted looking into storefront windows and planted a foot right into the stuff. She stopped, turned her foot up to look at it, then proceeded as if nothing happened. A few moments later, I had to stop her from entering the hotel lobby. She was about to walk right in. The doorman was holding the large glass door open for us, smiling expectantly.

"Wait," I said, "We need to clean your shoe."

"It's okay," she said, "I'll clean it in the room."

"But you're going to track dog shit all over the place."

Annoyed that I should be so concerned over such a thing, she came and sat next to me on a stone bench off to the side, while I worked to clean as much of the stuff off her shoe using a packet of baby wipes that I kept in my fanny pack for such emergencies. Chaiya watched quietly, expressionless and emotionless as usual.

—

I returned to Hat Yai was to see Chaiya's mother again. I'd promised her two years ago that I would come back to see her. Chaiya would periodically ask me throughout our trip if I still wanted to see her mom.

"Yes, of course," was always my reply.

On our last day together in Hanoi, we visited Aldo, a name-brand handbag shop in the Old Quarter. Chaiya wanted to pick up a gift for her mom. She got her on a video call and was holding up purses for her to inspect. (The wonders of modern technology.) I grabbed a few handbags and began posing like a model. Chaiya turned her phone toward me and giggled uncontrollably. It was the first time I'd seen anything resembling laughter or joy come out of her this entire trip.

It came down to two bags that Chaiya couldn't decide on.

"Which one should I get?" she asked.

"Get both."

"Okay!"

The bags were only about thirty bucks a piece. Not as high-end as we first thought. They might have been counterfeit.

—

Now back in Hat Yai, Chaiya says she needs to pay the cleaners she hired to clean her house. Because she's hardly ever there, mice had infested the place. The entire place was covered in mouse droppings and reeked of urine. The cleaning people did a good job of cleaning the place up, she said. Now it was time to pay them, meaning it was time for me to pay them. The bill came to $8,000 baht.

House cleaned. Water meter installed. Her house was ready for mom and son to come visit. I had offered to put them up in a hotel, but her mom doesn't like to stay in hotels.

I asked when her mom was coming. I had timed my visit to Hat Yai specifically so we could all meet up and have dinner together, which is what Chaiya had been bugging me about this entire trip. But now, she seemed suddenly evasive.

"I don't know," she said. "Maybe tomorrow."

"I'm only here for two more days," I reminded her, "then I've got a flight to catch to Phuket."

"I know," she said and went back to staring at her phone.

—

Later that night we met her friend, Natti, for drinks.

We'd met up with her weeks earlier when we were in Bangkok. Alluring and statuesque, she could pass for a car show model or a life-size version of a Thai Barbie doll. Like many Thais, she was down to earth and friendly, in a goofy sort of way — an endearing airhead.

While we were in Bangkok, she flew in for the weekend from Hat Yai with her Australian boyfriend. But he wouldn't be joining us, Chaiya had explained, because he and Natti had been arguing, so Natti left him alone back at the hotel while she joined us for dinner and drinks. He was an "older" guy, she added. I took that to mean he was in his fifties or sixties.

Throughout the evening, he kept calling and texting Natti to see where she was and what she was doing. Whenever her phone chirped with yet another text message, an annoyed look flashed across her face. Then she'd check the message and immediately show it to Chaiya, Natti all the while complaining in rapid-fire Thai and Chaiya nodding sympathetically.

We were having a dinner of tom yum, papaya salad, and chicken and pork skewers at a local Thai shop in Bangkok's Huai Khwang district, around the corner from a Buddhist temple that Chaiya wanted to visit and give merit. What I gathered from the bits and pieces I'd overheard, and from Natti explaining some of it to me in broken English, was that her Australian boyfriend had flown her out to Bangkok for a romantic weekend and was miffed that she wanted to spend time hanging out with me and Chaiya instead. He was sitting alone in his hotel room, sulking.

"You know what he always say to me?" Natti said to me. "He say, you need me to give you a good life. He say only him can give me good life."

"You don't need anyone," I said.

As attractive as Natti was, I doubted she would be alone for very long. Farang men in Thailand were constantly sniffing around for new....opportunities. They would not miss taking a shot with her.

I was very mindful of my words, knowing that Chaiya was sitting right there next to her. "I think you would do just fine by yourself. It sounds like he's just trying to control you."

"Yes! He very controlling!"

"Don't let anyone control you. Do whatever you want. You are a free person."

"Yes!"

"He sounds a little insecure," I added. I didn't know Natti before tonight, and I literally would not have been able to tell her boyfriend from a hole in the wall. What the hell did I know?

"Yes, he is!" she said.

Then her phone rang again.

"Hi!" she said, waving excitedly. It was a video call.

I could hear a man's voice on the other end. "How are ya, love?" he said, with a thick Aussie accent.

"I'm good!" said Natti. "I'm just having dinner with my friend. You remember Chaiya, right?"

Natti pointed the phone at Chaiya, who shot me a quick glance.

"Hello," said the man's voice, politely.

Chaiya waved and smiled wanly.

Natti turned the phone back to herself and continued her conversation with the man on the other end, who was evidently not the same guy that was waiting for her back at the hotel room. Natti was flirtatious and coy, flipping her hair and tilting her head. She asked her friend if he'd been with any other women lately.

"Only you, darling," came the reply.

Natti giggled and asked how the weather was where he was at.

We finished our meal and went out into the street to catch a Grab ride to the Bangkok Marriott, where we were planning to have a few drinks up on the rooftop bar.

Natti's phone rang, and another annoyed look flashed across her face when she saw who was calling.

"Hi, baby," she said, blowing a kiss at her phone. She had quickly stepped into a dress shop and was pretending to browse through the racks of clothes.

"I just finished dinner with Chaiya," she said. "Now we shopping."

"Your friend, Natti, talks to a lot of guys, yeah?" I commented to Chaiya.

"Just friends," she replied, coolly. "She cannot have guy friends?"

I laughed. "Some old dude isn't calling her all the way from Australia just to be friends."

—

In Hat Yai, we again met up with Natti for drinks and appetizers at an outdoor restaurant crowded with locals. It was mostly a younger, hip crowd from what I could tell. As always, I was the odd man out, quietly eating and drinking, keeping to myself while Chaiya and Natti chatted amongst themselves. I was only invited along to pay the bill.

Natti was gracious and occasionally looped me into the conversation, speaking in English to let me know what they were laughing about. If she saw that I needed another drink, she signaled our waiter to bring me another.

Chaiya behaved as if I wasn't even there. I could have sworn it was a conscious effort on her part, like she wanted me to know she was treating me this way. I could almost feel a tangible resentment emanating from her, directed at me like a focused beam of negative energy. I felt a hollow emptiness in my solar plexus. I was being torn wide open without her needing to utter a single word.

If I said anything or made any sort of comment, she would shoot me a look filled with contempt and disdain and return her attention to Natti, pointedly ignoring me.

Is this how my life would be if I came to live in Thailand? Is this how life would be with Chaiya? Ignored, isolated, and treated like shit?

You might be wondering why I allowed myself to be treated this way. Where's my self-respect? Where's my backbone? Short answer is: I was in solo travel mode. There wasn't time for fussing or brooding. I had flight itineraries to track and hotel reservations to confirm. Despite the hurt feelings and petty slights, I had to keep going. There were still too many things to see and do. And anyway, I was in Thailand, where making new friends is almost guaranteed and broken hearts are easily mended. I wasn't too concerned.

We finished up at the restaurant and caught a Grab ride to the bar around the corner from our hotel. Chaiya and I had stopped into that same place the previous night for a quick drink after dinner at the Mediterranean restaurant. I wanted to stay longer and have a few more drinks, but Chaiya as usual was bored and disinterested.

The Grab driver dropped us off right in front of the bar.

Stepping out of the car, Natti commented, "Oooh, Chaiya. You know every time we come here, things get a little bit crazy!"

"We were here last night," I said to Chaiya. "You didn't mention you'd been here before."

Chaiya either didn't hear or pretended not to and followed Natti into the bar. I trailed after them.

Inside, the place was busier than the night before. All the booths were occupied, so we sat at the bar and ordered drinks.

Then we ordered another round.

And another round.

I was chasing down Bacardi and Cokes with bottles of Singha, while Chaiya and Natti were hammering shots one after another.

A band was up on the stage belting out classic Thai songs with everyone except me singing along. Chaiya and Natti were swaying back and forth in their bar stools and clapping their hands to the rhythm of the music. Natti was singing her heart out. I urged her to go up to the front of the stage and dance along with the other folks that were up there shaking their thing to the groove. She shook her head, laughing. No, she was too shy.

Chaiya was wasted. When the music stopped, she sat slouched over her drink like the town drunk. She was still swaying, but more so from her own drunkenness.

The entire time we were in Vietnam, she showed no interest whatsoever in coming out with me for a drink, but as soon as she met up with Natti, it was like a button had been switched to the "ON" position, launching her into full-scale bar girl party mode — laughing, drinking, enjoying herself, while I watched quietly, ruefully from a distance.

It didn't feel like we were a couple. I felt needy and pathetic. I'd become a "simp." A "white knight." I was the cliched two-week millionaire looking for the bar girl with a heart of gold. I hated the feeling.

Since when did I feel the need to be part of anything, much less part of a couple? For decades I'd prided myself on being a loner. A Bukowski drunkard. A William Burroughs weirdo. A Jean Genet outcast. I was no Melnibonean "Weird of the White Wolf" — I was just weird. Awkward, out of place, isolated, and alone. I was a fifty-four-year-old teenager experiencing the angst of junior high school all over again.

It was just past midnight, and we'd been drinking since eight o'clock. Chaiya and Natti showed no sign of slowing down. Like true Thais, these girls could party. Chaiya was slamming shot after shot. Natti, by comparison, was a little more moderate. She had slowed a little and was taking her time sipping from her girlie drink. That wasn't fast enough for Chaiya. She took one of the shots lined up in front of her and dumped it into Natti's glass.

"Ahh!" Natti laughed. "What you doing?"

Chaiya grinned drunkenly and downed another shot.

"Ooohh....," I said, "you shouldn't mix drinks like that."

Natti nodded, wrinkling her nose, and slowly pushed the glass away from her. Chaiya snatched it up and downed it herself.

Natti and I exchanged glances. I shook my head.

"Slow down, Chaiya," I said, gently.

The band finished their set to scattered applause around the room. Except for Chaiya, who was clapping her hands and cheering wildly. The lead singer, a handsome and rugged looking Thai local, acknowledged her with a smile and a nod of his head. Chaiya smiled back, making kissy faces at him.

Earlier that evening, we stopped by an ATM, so I could get some cash. I gave some to Chaiya so she could pay for her own drinks and not have to bother me all the time. There was a small stack of these bills in front of her on the bar. She peeled one off the top, ran around the bar to the front of the stage, and like a school girl shyly presenting a flower, held it up to the singer. He took it from her hand and wai'd her respectfully. She scampered back to her seat, giggling. Natti shot me a quick look. I smiled, pretending to be taking it all in good fun.

The band launched into another set while Chaiya downed another shot, dancing in her seat and singing along with Natti. When the song ended, Chaiya ordered a shot and brought it up to the singer. He graciously accepted it and drank it slowly while holding her hand, and her looking up at him longingly. Natti sat staring with her mouth open in disbelief. Then she slowly turned and looked at me. I shrugged and shook my head. I had already made up my mind in Vietnam and perhaps even the year before in Kuala Lumpur (although I hadn't fully realized it at the time), that this situation — I hesitate to call it a relationship — would not end well. Whatever feelings I had for her then had long since dissipated. I felt only a numb disappointment. But as I watched her flirting with the charismatic lead singer, that numb disappointment became feelings of disrespect and muted anger.

She probably would have sucked his cock right there at the front of the stage if he'd taken it out for her. My chest hurt from this betrayal. That hollow, sunken feeling in my solar plexus throbbed with a dull pain.

What did it matter? My flight to Phuket was in another two days. I wasn't sure if I could wait that long to get away from her. I just knew that I needed to get back to familiar stomping grounds — beautiful beaches and friendly bar girls. Life was too short and I was getting too old to deal with this ongoing psycho-drama. I was better off alone.

Chaiya returned to her seat, grinning widely and drunkenly contented. She had completely forgotten that I was there.

I sat quietly, brooding over my rum and Coke, my fifth or sixth one of the night, plus all the beers I'd been chasing them with. I was feeling a little tipsy myself.

Let her have her fun, I thought to myself. Why ruin it? If she wants to fuck that other guy, let her! We live in a free-will universe. We each possess the freedom of choice, and if Chaiya chose to go down that path, then fuck it, I'll help her!

It was near closing time, and the band played their final song for the night. As the singer thanked the thinning crowd, I waved my arms to get his attention and pointed to Chaiya.

"My friend wants to meet you!" I yelled. "She likes you!"

Chaiya laughed, shaking her head, "No, no, no...."

I leaned toward her and whispered into her ear, "Why don't you go with him if you want?"

She furrowed her eyebrows and frowned. "What? No!" she said, looking a little hurt.

The energy in the universe must be allowed to flow unhindered just as rivers must take their course and find their way out to sea, the charismatic lead singer slowly made his way to where we were sitting, his penis, now stirred to attention, pointing and probing, guiding him to Chaiya like a little plastic Boy Scout compass pointing due north.

But the myriad machinations in my drunken mind were for naught. The singer was a perfect gentleman and politely shook my hand as I introduced myself. I bought him a drink and offered him my seat next to Chaiya, but he declined and chose to remain standing. The bar was turning off the stage lights as they prepared to close for the evening. The singer looked like he wanted to get out of there and go home. Maybe he had a real job to get to in the morning.

Chaiya, demure and suddenly shy, kept her hands folded in her lap, while she and Natti exchanged pleasantries with the singer in their native Thai language. Chaiya had reverted to her distant, unemotional self, no longer smiling flirtatiously or batting her eyelashes. The bar, it seems, was not the only thing shutting down for the evening. The singer took Chaiya's icy demeanor as his cue to follow his bandmates out the door and bid us goodnight.

Back outside on the street, all was dark and quiet. Everything was closed — the shops, the food stalls. We said good-bye to Natti, who caught a Grab ride home. Chaiya and I walked back to our hotel in silence, our footsteps echoing across those old Hat Yai buildings. We didn't speak a word to each other as we crawled into bed and went to sleep.

—

I didn't sleep well and awoke a few short hours later from fitful dreams. I checked the time on my phone. 4AM.

When I booked my flight to Phuket a few days earlier, I remembered seeing a flight departing Hat Yai at eight in the morning. At the time, I thought that was too early. I'd have to leave the hotel by six. Check-in by seven. That meant I'd have to wake up at, what, five o'clock? Way too early.

But it was four o'clock now, and I was wide awake. Lying there in the dark next to Chaiya, who was quietly snoring. My face illuminated by the glow of my cell phone, I checked Expedia.com for available flights.

Sure enough, there was a flight leaving at eight that morning. $95 bucks, one way to Phuket. I went ahead and booked it. Now I had two flights going back to Phuket. I was just throwing money away. I didn't care. We had just remodeled our house, the wife and I, and I was flush with extra cash from the loan we had taken out. Before I left for Thailand, I gave the wife five grand for a trip she was planning to take back to Algeria to visit her family later that summer. (She never actually went.) I added her to my American Express Platinum account and ordered her a card with her name on it. In case she needed to pay for any big-ticket expenses while I was gone.

I was feeling like a millionaire. I could go anywhere and do anything. I never felt so free in my life.

I had a new consulting gig lined up when I got back to the States. Same company but different assignment. I didn't know it at the time, but I wouldn't last more than three months at the place. They would lay me off before summer. "Budget cuts," would be their explanation.

Would it have changed my behavior had I known it at the time? Probably not. The only thing I knew at that moment was that I had to get the hell away from Chaiya. I felt used, betrayed, like I was being cuckolded. Her negative energy was burning me out.

And she never spoke. About anything. She would never talk to me. She never had anything to say. Never had any opinions to express. No thoughts to share. Nothing. She was just this icy wall of silence. There must have been some kind of mental illness going on with her, and it had nothing to do with me. This much I determined.

Quietly, I slipped out of bed and began packing my things. My side of the bed didn't have a lamp, so I had to switch on the main room light to see what I was doing. It was one of those bright flourescent deals you'll often find in older Thai hotels, hanging from the ceiling in the center of the room. It was blindingly bright, like a headlamp on full blast.

The brightness of the light and my shuffling about roused Chaiya from her sleep. She saw what I was doing and got up to use the toilet. She was only wearing a pair of black lace panties. God, she looked sexy as hell, but I knew I had to get the hell out of there. Anyway, she'd mentioned the day before that she was starting her period.

While I continued to pack my things, I could see her watching me from the bathroom, pacing back and forth, like she was trying to figure out what was going on.

Then she came out. "What are you doing?"

"I have to go," I said, trying to avoid looking her in the eyes. "I have a flight to catch to Phuket."

"I thought your flight was tomorrow?"

"I bought another ticket for today. It's leaving this morning."

"Why? I thought you were going to stay until tomorrow. I don't understand. Why are you doing this?"

"I feel like I need to go," I said. "I feel like I need to get away from you."

Her face cracked and broke into a frown. She was on the verge of tears.

I don't know if it was the bright flourescent lighting casting strange shadows across the bewildered expression on her face, but she suddenly took on the appearance of a completely different person. It was as if she was finally allowing her true self to show through — it was the face of a severely desperate, frightened, and insecure individual. It was the face of someone still suffering from the effect of some deep-seated childhood trauma. In that single moment, all of her illusions, posturings, and affectations fell away, and I found myself sitting on that hotel bed next to someone whose face had somehow morphed into that of a haggard old witch. Wrinkles and creases appeared on her face, seemingly out of nowhere. The change was instantaneous and disturbing. It was like she'd aged a hundred years right before my eyes.

"I thought you wanted to go to the beach? I reserved a driver to take us tomorrow."

"Well, cancel it," I said, stuffing clothes into my suitcase.

"I already paid him a thousand baht."

I slipped a thousand-baht note from my wallet and handed it to her. "Here. Go ahead and cancel it. Or go by yourself if you want. Or with one of your friends."

She was openly weeping now, her face broken down in agony.

I was a little surprised and wasn't expecting this strong of an emotional response from her. I thought she didn't care. The entire time we were together, she acted as if she didn't. Regardless, it didn't change my resolve to get the hell out of there.

"I don't understand. What did I do wrong?" she pleaded. She was kneeling on the bed now, facing me. "Can you please tell me what I did wrong?"

"You didn't do anything wrong, Chaiya," I said. "It's just — we're not getting along, so I might as well go."

"Can you explain to me? What do you mean?"

"It's like I told you in Vietnam. I kept asking you — you don't talk to me. It's like you don't want me around. So fine. I will leave. I come all this way to see you, and you push me away."

"You say I pushing you away, but you the one who leaving. Why you have to go now? Why no wait till tomorrow?"

"I came here to see your mom. You kept asking me, and I kept saying, yes. I buy plane ticket. I come here, and then she cancel. I might as well go. No reason to be here."

Chaiya crept closer to me on the bed, her face looking more and more like that of an old witch. It was a face writhing in agony and pain.

"I told you already," she said, her voice growing louder. "My boy didn't want to come. We had a big fight. I was very angry with him. My mom didn't want to come if he didn't come."

"It doesn't matter, I guess," I said. "I have to leave for Phuket, anyway. Tomorrow or today. So I might as well go now."

She sobbed loudly, then punched me in the arm. Aside from the sex, this was the most physical and emotional I'd seen her.

I shrugged it off. "You don't have to get violent," I said. It was like being punched by a tiny kitten.

"As you know, I haven't been working. I don't have any money left."

Now I was beginning to understand the desperation and anxiety in her voice. She thought I was going to leave her high and dry. Abandon her without a dime. I had promised her earlier that I would give her some money to account for the time that she wasn't working while she accompanied me to Vietnam and Thailand. In her line of work, vacation pay was unheard of. Time off meant time not paid.

"Don't worry. I'm going to send you some money. I have to move some cash around, and it will take a few days for the funds to settle."

This seemed to calm her a little, and she retreated to her side of the bed and curled up in a ball underneath the ratty blanket.

I went over and tucked her in and gently kissed her on the head.

"You're going to be in my life for a long time," I whispered. "But now I have to go."

I'm not sure she understood what I meant. I wasn't even sure I understood what I meant. I slipped on my backpack, grabbed my roller bag, and rolled on out the door and to the musty elevator going down.

I got to the airport at just after 6am. The checkout counters were closed and wouldn't open for another hour and a half. I took a seat in a row of stiff plastic chairs and immediately fell asleep, exhausted and still a little drunk.

—

Back in Patong, I checked into the dubiously named Sleep With Me Hotel, which was far more upscale, cleaner, and more family-friendly than the name implied. In fact, it would become my favorite hotel in Patong, surpassing the other places I'd stayed at previously — the Hotel Clover, the Best Western, and the Baan Boa. You can't beat the location for the price. It's across the street from Bangla Road and right next door to the newly-remodeled Jungceylon Shopping Center. Smack dab in the middle of everything. There is a buzz of activity everywhere. You can almost feel the electricity.

I felt alive again. Like I'd been set free. Those last few weeks I'd spent with Chaiya had me feeling like I'd just come out of a failed marriage — the awkward conversations, the uncomfortableness of simply standing next to each other, the tiny everyday battles of arguing over where to eat or where to go. It was exhausting.

In Patong, I could be myself again. I could go to the beach without feeling guilty about leaving her back at the hotel room. And I no longer felt as lonely and isolated as I did when I was in her company. That vibe of negative energy dissipated after I left her in Hat Yai.

As soon as I checked into my room at the Sleep With Me Hotel, I slipped into a pair of swimming trunks and went to the beach.

At last, my vacation had begun.

—

I didn't even know Patong existed until a few weeks before I arrived there for the first time three years ago. I had been wanting to visit Thailand for nearly two decades, and after my 51st birthday, I finally had the opportunity.

My original itinerary called for flying into Bangkok, but after inspecting the region more closely on Google Maps, I realized it wasn't within walking distance of any beaches. And then I remembered a place called Phuket. It was all over the news when the Indian Ocean tsunami (also known as the Boxing Day tsunami) hit in 2004. I changed my itinerary and booked a flight for Phuket instead, which is how I found myself wandering around Patong's infamous Bangla Road in late November 2021 at the height of the Covid epidemic.

I didn't let that stop me. I announced big plans on social media and to anyone who would listen that I would "travel south down the Andaman Coast" to Karon and then "head further south to Rawai" if I had time. As if I were some jet-setting world explorer on assignment for National Geographic.

But I had only taken a cursory glance at the map that was included with my e-book copy of Lonely Planet's Thailand edition and had severely misjudged the distances between each town. I figured Karon and Kata to be an hour or two from Patong, and assumed Rawai was another three hours away. I was still in a Texas state of mind, thinking Dallas to Austin, and Austin to San Antone, where distances were vast, and you had to drive at least an hour to go anywhere worth getting to.

I explained my travel plans to Chaiya when we first met. We were laying in bed at the Hotel Clover. I told her I was thinking to spend a week in Kata and maybe another week in Rawai. She gave me a quizzical look.

"No need go for a week," she said. "Maybe just spend the day and come back, yeah?"

"No," I said, woefully ignorant yet confident. "That would be too much traveling."

She shrugged and went back to staring at her phone.

I learned soon enough that Karon and Kata were little more than a fifteen-minute tuk-tuk ride from Patong, and Rawai just a little further than that.

Fast-forward three years, and I'm in a tuk-tuk heading over the hill to Kata for a drink or three at Jintana's bar. I'd met her the year before when I happened upon her place along Kata's walking street. She operated one of the many pop-up bars running down the middle of the road between the regular brick-and-mortar bars and restaurants. I wasn't sure if her place was still open. Business was slow the previous year, and she worried that her shop wouldn't survive another lackluster tourist season.

It was a cool little area with a low-key vibe. Nothing like the madness and drunken shenanigans over on Bangla Road or Soi Cowboy. There were bar girls working here as well, but they were nowhere near as aggressive or scantily-clad as the girls working in those more notorious areas. And there wasn't music blasting from every doorway at ear-shattering decibels. You could have a normal conversation without having to yell at the top of your lungs.

I would have preferred to stay in Kata, but I couldn't find a room. Russia had recently invaded Ukraine, and the Russians trying to avoid the conflict had invaded this side of Phuket. Their numbers appeared to have increased since the last time I was here. Their blank stares and unsmiling faces could be seen filling every restaurant to capacity and crowding out the narrow and uneven sidewalks. Pale lumps of sun-burned flesh lined the beaches from end to end. It was safe to assume any white-skinned person here was Russian if and until you heard them speak in a language suggesting otherwise.

Jintana's bar was still there and open for business, and so was Jintana. I spotted her from a ways away. She had distinctive features and didn't look like the typical Thai woman. She looked more Vietnamese. Or mainland Chinese — sharp chin, sharp nose, deeply slanted eyes. She was thin and tiny, with porcelain white skin. She wore her long black hair tied in a ponytail high up on her head, Kabuki style. Although she owned the place, she shared a two-bedroom condo nearby with three other girls who also worked in her bar. The girls were freelancers and came and went with the ebb and flow of the high season.

"Sawadee," I said, taking a seat on one of the bar stools.

Jintana was behind the bar, wiping down the counter with a rag. "Hi," she said.

I ordered a Singha. "Remember me?" I said. "I was here last year."

She stopped her cleaning and gave me a long look. "Oh, hi....!" she said, "Long time. How you been?"

She didn't remember.

Then she barked something in Thai to a girl sitting at the other end of the bar. The girl came over and sat next to me. I ordered a drink for her as well, and she wai'd politely. Then I ordered a drink for Jintana. We all clinked our glasses and drank. Cheers! Salut!

At the other end of the bar, an old white guy had his face buried in the neck of a young Thai girl. He looked to be around 70 or 75 years old. The girl had a bored and slightly annoyed look on her face, like a house cat weary of being petted, while the old man pawed and groped her. Later that evening, the pair would hop onto the girl's scooter and disappear into the night. Back to his hotel room, I assumed. On subsequent nights, I noticed other bar girls doing the same. He was a regular, Jintana explained. He couldn't drive, and after an evening of buying drinks and groping the girls at her bar, he rarely had enough money to pay for a taxi back to Patong, where he was staying, so one of the girls would get the keys for the motor scooter and drive him home.

I played a few games of Connect Four with the girl sitting next to me, buying her and Jintana rounds of drinks as the night wore on. She was young, friendly, and attractive. It was all relatively innocent enough. Here's the thing — you've got to keep a close eye on the money you're spending whenever you're drinking in a place where bar girls are working. You might have only planned on stopping in for a drink or two, and the next thing you know, you're buying rounds of drinks and handing out thousand-baht tips. Then you open up your wallet a few drunken hours later and discover there's nothing left. The ten thousand baht you withdrew from the ATM earlier that evening is all gone. Gone like the girl you brought back to your room for a short-time romp.

Not that I was planning on doing anything of the sort this evening, or indeed for the remainder of my trip. I was perfectly content just sitting there, playing Connect Four with an attractive girl who spoke very little English. Even then, the money slips away. The two-week millionaire syndrome. Spending money like you've got millions in the bank.

This is not to say that the girls are padding the bill or otherwise trying to rip you off — I'm sure there's a fair amount of that going on as well. But the girls are there to make money. They're trying to earn a living. It only seems fair to buy them a drink or two and leave a decent tip, especially if you enjoyed their company.

What, did you think the girls were coming around because of your dashing good looks and charismatic personality? Many of them are single mothers with families to support and bills to pay. They've already been fucked — by life, by men, by their lowly socio-economic status. Allowing a drunk, smelly foreigner to grope and paw at them is simply a means to an end. I try to be a little more respectful than that.

—

The drinks are flowing. Everyone's having a good time. Handsome foreigners — "Handsome man! Handsome man!" Dumbfounded and eager tourists. Carefree bar girls who take their pleasures from sleeping with strangers. We all buy into the illusion. Next thing you know, it's been yet another ten-thousand baht night. How many more of these nights can you afford? When the girls find out you're broke, they will smile and wave politely before moving onto the next foreigner. Hope you'll understand. They have a toddler and an eight-year-old to feed and clothe. And the rent is due. And she needs to pay for her elderly father's medication. And the mango tree in the yard is dying. And the rainy season will soon be upon us. And we must visit the temple and give merit and pray for Lord Buddha to protect us and bless us with peace and love, and most importantly, with lots and lots of cash money.

—

After a few rounds of drinks, I was feeling pretty good. Had a cool little buzz going. The tenseness I'd been feeling in my shoulders the past few weeks was finally loosening up. It didn't hurt that my companion at the bar knew how to give a really good shoulder and neck massage.

Jintana came over, eyeing me slyly.

"You like her?" she asked, tilting her head discreetly toward the girl.

"Yes," I said. "She give very good massage. So relaxing."

Jintana leaned in closer to me and whispered, "You want to take her?" She tilted her head in the other direction, away from the bar.

The girl in question, my masseuse and new friend, pretended not to overhear our conversation and busied herself with arranging the checker pieces for another game of Connect Four.

"Not tonight," I said. "Maybe next time." Then I added, "I'm waiting for you."

"For me?"

"Yes," I said, grinning. "When you gonna come with me?"

Jintana laughed and retreated to the other side of the bar.

Knowing that I wouldn't be paying her bar fine for the night, my masseuse soon abandoned me for a geriatric gentleman who came in waving enthusiastically at her and smiling a very shiny, false toothed smile. He took a seat at the other end of the bar, staring at her with an eager look in his eyes. She wai'd me politely and thanked me for the drinks before joining the old man, who immediately wrapped his arms around the poor girl and began pawing and squeezing her.

I'm always a little surprised when I see these old guys come to Thailand and lose all sense of self-restraint. It's like a free-for-all to them. Just grab whatever you want. Have they been alone for so long that the slightest whiff of a woman is enough to drive them batshit insane? How long has it been since they sipped from the well of female companionship? Or maybe it's the little blue boner pills that drive them to acts of desperation and strange behavior? Maybe it's the frightening realization that time is running out. They're nearing the end of the road. They've only got a good five to ten years left to get it on. If that.

Whatever the reason, I'm sure the old geezer was going to get his money's worth tonight. He was smiling so widely, I half expected his teeth to come tumbling out of his mouth. He paid the girl's bar fine and disappeared with her down the alley before I'd even settled my tab. I told Jintana I'd see her tomorrow and caught a tuk-tuk back to Patong.

I timed my visit to Patong so I could celebrate this year's Songkran Festival with all the other drunken, water-fighting tourists. This was a decision that I would later come to regret.

Songkran wouldn't officially begin until tomorrow, and many shops had their water guns and water pistols up for sale on display racks near their entrances. There seemed to be more crowds of people than in previous years. The Patong I had encountered when I first visited three years ago at the height of the Covid epidemic, when everything was shut down and boarded up, when bars and nightclubs were forced to close at 11pm and everyone was forced to wear surgical masks in public. At the height of the insanity, hysteria, and fear-mongering, I decided to cram myself onto a crowded plane and fly halfway around the world to spend a month in a country that I'd never been to. But it appears things have turned around. Patong has regained much of its party town mojo.

With the 11pm curfew in the distant past, bars remained open into the wee hours of the early morning and packed with girls hoping to make up for lost time and money. In Patong, the Ground Zero of drunken hedonism is on Bangla Road. On any given night, sitting at any of the many bars lining the street, you can bear witness to roaming packs of bug-eyed Indian men staring dumbly at the half-dressed bar girls; Youtube influencers with GoPros in hand, trying to record the same and filling their channels with crappy, predictable content; Swedish families with young children in tow; Chinese tourists shuffling by with Hello Kitty backpacks and Louis Vuitton handbags. The Americans are easy to spot. Regardless of their ethnicity, it doesn't matter — Black, Hispanic, white, Asian — you can spot an American by their obesity, at least 30 or 40 pounds overweight, with pot bellies and thick ankle fat, often bearing tacky tribal tattoos. And they tend to waddle, off-balanced and clumsily, while dressed horribly as if they've gone shopping at Walmart. And to round off the list — worming their way through the crowds, often alone and walking with a determined, eager bounce in their step, are the horny old men with a pervy eye out for the girls or katois (ladyboys).

"Real" travelers, of course, hold their noses up at Patong. Only "tourists" go there. You're not seeing the "real" Thailand. It isn't an "authentic" experience.

There is some truth, however, to such snobbery. Patong is kind of a tourist shit hole, a cesspool of creepy farangs, a Disneyland-like playground for sexual deviants. (Only Pattaya is worse, I think, and beyond that, maybe the Philippines.)

But does that make it any less "authentically" Thai?

In Patong, like anything else in life, that's all you'll find — if that's all you're looking for. You could spend every night on Bangla Road and bring a different girl back to your room each night. In some perverted sense, you're helping the Thai economy by helping the girl and, by extension, her family who likely depend on the girl as their only source of financial support. Are those girls working in the clubs "fake" Thai women? Or real Thais? Is that an authentic ladyboy? Does he/she speak fluent Thai?

We must suspend judgment and set aside the hypocrisy that is Western moralizing. (It's mostly Western men doing all the whoring, isn't it? With Saudi and Indian men thrown in as well.) Their world is not our world, and the girls have already heard it from their cousins and mothers and gossiping neighbors back in their villages. They are scorned and looked down upon from all sides, and still they strive to provide for their families and do the best they can with what they've been given.

And what of the men, like me, who choose to vacation in Thailand alone?

I sit there minding my business, drinking my beers and my rum and Cokes. I bear witness to the grand illusion. I hopped a flight across an ocean to escape the stale ideologies of the American mindset. Freedom, motherhood, apple pie, democracy. I must regretfully inform you that the American people have been force-fed a steady diet of artificial bullshit for the past fifty years. After fifty-plus years, I have grown weary of my homeland.

"Oh, you spent your holiday in Thailand, did ya?" your co-workers will say with a wink and a nod.

And if you happen to mention that you enjoyed the company of a bar girl or two, the reply will almost always be, "You sure it wasn't a ladyboy?"

I've come to expect these kinds of lighthearted, if somewhat offensive, comments from friends, family and fellow Americans. If you know, you know. And if you don't, well — go and see for yourself. Learn to make up your own mind about stuff. Fact is, when it comes to sexuality, Western minds, like many in the U.S., are trapped in cycles of guilt and shame, perversion and gluttony. Swirling in toxic cycles of psycho-sexual duality and morbid obsession. Obsessed with labeling a thing and discussing its moral worth. Is it righteous? Is it wrong? Sex and sexuality can only be discussed in terms of Internet porn or Old Testament denunciation. God is a vengeful asshole and is about to strike you down in a fit of biblical rage. Thou shalt be judged! Cast thee into hell, thy sinner!

Everything must be labeled and stored in its proper category. Nice, clean labels that can be easily comprehended — man versus woman, gay versus straight, liberal versus conservative, good versus evil, black versus white. The American social and political landscape is blasted with high contrast distinctions, as blinding as the sun and easily discernible from ninety million miles away. Philosophical, moral, and spiritual shades of gray have been wiped from the communal color palette. It requires too much brain juice. Too much processing power. Takes up too much real estate in the brain, real estate that could otherwise be used for fighting wars, arguing with your neighbors or strangers on the Internet, or shopping at Walmart.

This is the American way of life, owned and operated by banks and corporations. Send 'em off to die! Fatten them up and bleed 'em dry! They don't want you wasting time talking about gonads and pie-holes. You got taxes to pay. The car insurance is due. The credit card bills are late. Forget about health insurance and retirement. You can't afford it. Get back to work, peon!

—

What the hell do I know? I'm in a tuk-tuk heading back to Patong. The hot, humid night does little to cool me down. Armpit sweat trickles down my sides. I'm not an expat. I'm no two-week millionaire. I'm unable to acclimate to this sweltering steam bath.

This being my fourth trip to the Land of Smiles in three years, my smile has bent into a smirk, and I begin to see things with a more cynical eye. It was too easy to be lulled into a stupor by the landscape and the seductive beauty of the women.

Sitting at the beach day after day beneath a languid sun does something to the mind. Your brain reverts to a primordial reptilian state. You would even moisten your own eyeballs with your tongue if you could.

Strange thoughts enter your mind. You find yourself entertaining ideas you would not have otherwise contemplated back home, back in the safety and confines of predictable routines. Thailand herself, in all her alien foreignness, can at times give the sensation of walking around in a hallucination. Your own private tropical fever dream. Indeed, returning to Thailand is like returning to an idyllic dream state. Instead of remaining trapped in a constant state of fight or flight, which is the norm for many people living in the U.S. — worrying about paying the rent, worrying about getting shot, losing jobs, losing their health insurance. The lizard brain in Thailand drifts into a state of acceptance and release. Let it go, let it go….sabai, sabai.

I am in this state of mind now, bouncing around in the back of that tuk-tuk in the semi-darkness, my mind idly wandering. Or maybe it was all the rum and Cokes I had at Jintana's place. A glass of the stuff with two cubes of ice has been my drink of choice on this trip. I sit back and enjoy the buzz while the tuk-tuk's motor whirrs and downshifts violently as it struggles to climb up and over the hill to Patong.

—

Bar girls constantly scan the front of the bar, like bored sailors on a ship at sea, scanning the horizon, keeping an eye out for customers or signs of a white whale — the mythical big spender with deep pockets, the guy who's going to buy her that new iPhone or pay her rent for the next six months. Typically an older guy in his forties or fifties, with paunches and graying hair atop a balding head. Usually, but not always. If it's too early for whaling season, the girls will settle for one of their regulars, which they are equally adept at spotting. The girls often know which customer belongs to which girl, and they'll call out to each other if one is spotted. "Kaaa! Kaaa!"

Various species frequent these waters. The white socks and sandals variety with cargo shorts and Aloha shirt. The flesh on these is pink, pale, and soft. You will sometimes find a tribal tattoo on their ankle or bicep. Mostly decorative. Something they did on a whim to appear edgy, to stand out from the crowd, feeling a little wild and crazy on vacation. There are millions of these guys — standing in line at the hotel buffet, carrying armloads of brand name shopping bags for their Thai girlfriends at Jungceylon mall, or standing in the entrance of go-go bars, dumbly taking a peek inside. They're mostly harmless. Or married. Obedient, tax-paying schleps. I could easily be grouped into this camp if I were forty pounds heavier and had a penchant for lame tattoos.

Then there are the heavily-muscled, heavily-tattooed guys with shaved heads and sculpted facial hair to match their chiseled physiques. They will usually have names that sound like cheap perfume — Armani, Fabian, Georgio, Dollar General, Fred. Hyper-masculine. Hyper-macho. You'll find them parading up and down Walking Street or along the beach walk. Amped up on anabolic steroids, cocaine, or both. Like pulsating penises, throbbing and fully erect. Chest and biceps pumped up and fully inflated. Clinging to one of their arms, latching on tightly, you will often find their Thai girlfriend, dark-skinned and feral looking with long, silky black hair and shark-like teeth. They are slowly moving in for the kill, and the guy's too high on his own testosterone to even notice. The girls will always leave them broke. You've heard the stories. You've watched the Youtube videos. Then, when the guy's brain is fried from too much coke, and immigration is banging on his hotel door because he overstayed his tourist visa, this is when he decides that now might be a good time to throw himself off that sixteenth floor hotel balcony. His demise might make it into the news the next day, and he will be forgotten after that. Down in the bars and clubs, it's all about fun and games, and new marks are arriving by the plane load every day. The show must go on.

As always, the girls remain perched atop barstools, scanning the horizon for new arrivals.

Just as they are situated now at Crystal Bar in OTOP Plaza.

One of the girls spots me a ways off and calls out to Ice, who's sitting with a customer on the other side of the bar. I hadn't seen her since the last time I was there a year ago. We texted each other nonstop on a daily basis right up until a few months after I'd returned home to the States. She'd let me know when she awoke each morning and when she got home each night after working at the club. She'd send selfies of her posing cute and smiling in her room or at a restaurant with her friends. She peppered each message with little heart emojis. Then the communications slowly petered off until she stopped texting completely, and I knew something had changed. I figured she'd met a new guy or something, which didn't bother me. We'd never been intimate or had genuine feelings for one another — well, maybe a little but nothing that would survive an overseas relationship. In any event, I texted her to let her know that I was back in Patong for a few days. I enjoyed her company, shooting pool and playing Connect Four. She was a Sagittarius and a gamer, like my wife. And also like my wife, she was hyper-competitive in a fun, teasing sort of way. Ice possessed that similar laid-back attitude with little need to take life so seriously. If you lose, you lose. Reset the pieces and play again. Sabai sabai.

Ice came up and gave me a hug, then led me to a table. I ordered drinks for the both of us, and for one of her friends, who appeared out of nowhere. Buying drinks for bar girls is like tossing bread crumbs on the ground. An entire horde of them will come crowding around your table. Before I knew it, I was buying drinks for another "sister. " Then the mamasan — a hulking bruiser of a katoi (ladyboy). Oh, and could I buy a drink for Ice's brother, too? He remembered me from before. He also worked there as a bartender.

I'd already spent a thousand baht, and I'd only been there ten minutes. Whatever. This is how the game works. They have to make money, even if it's just crumbs. Snatching one crumb at a time. Bird food for the birds.

I thought I'd get a few games of Connect Four in with Ice, or maybe shoot a few games of pool with her, but when our drinks arrived, she quickly toasted, took a sip. Then she sat her drink down and told me she'd be right back. She'd been sitting with another customer when I arrived, and she went back to sit with him. Blonde guy wearing a backwards baseball cap. Slight build but muscular. Arm tattoos. Your typical Patong farang. His countenance bore a slightly hardened look. Perhaps a stint in prison had been in his not-too-distant past. Perhaps he was struggling with an addiction or fighting off an infection.

He wrapped his arms around Ice, pulling her into him and burying his face in her hair. She nuzzled into him, standing between his knees, and sipped her drink, his hands casually draped around her hips. He was more than just a customer.

I downed my drink and ordered another. Rum and Coke on the rocks and a bottle of Singha. I had a cool buzz on and couldn't be bothered with a single thing in the world. It felt like things had been reset when I landed in Phuket. The slate was wiped clean. That awkward and uncomfortable time I spent in Vietnam with Chaiya was becoming a distant memory and quickly fading further and further into the background. I didn't know what I was expecting from her, but something definitely more than weeks of the silent treatment. Now I was alone but didn't feel as lonely as I did when I was with her. I was convinced she must have suffered some severe childhood trauma that now causes her to project those weird energetic vibes.

She always seemed perfectly normal whenever we were out drinking with one of her friends. It was a completely different story when we were alone together. It was like a switch was flipped that turned off her human side and instantly changed her back into an unfeeling, unemotional robot.

The bad energy between us felt so unnecessary. And so regrettable. I had no choice but to move on. I had a few weeks left on my vacation. Leaving her in Hat Yai and escaping to Phuket was the best move I could have made to keep from going insane.

—

My friendship with Ice never quite thawed to the level of flirtatiousness we were at a year ago. I was now just another customer. I still returned to Crystal Bar each night. She'd smile and wave, and I'd smile and wave back. Sometimes she'd come over and ask for a drink. Then she would return to sit with her other customers. I no longer held a monopoly on her attention.

The atmosphere of the place suited me. The girls weren't pressured to go with customers, and customers were not allowed to bar fine the girls. This policy, one that was strictly enforced by the hulking katoi of a mamasan, made for a more relaxed environment. The other bars in OTOP Plaza, while perhaps not having the same "no bar fine" policy, seemed to possess the same relaxed atmosphere. The girls weren't standing around half-dressed in lingerie or bikinis and shaking their asses in customers' faces. And while each bar played their own flavor of music, each refrained from blasting the music at such deafening levels that you could carry a conversation with the person sitting next to you without having to lean over and scream into their ear.

One night, I caught a tuk-tuk to OTOP Plaza — I must have been coming back from Jintana's bar in Kata — and the driver dropped me off in an area of the complex that I wasn't too familiar with. I got turned around and came in through one of the many side entrances. I passed a bar that appeared to be off by itself along the outer perimeter of the complex, out near the public restrooms where you have to slip a five-baht coin into the turnstile before it will let you pass.

The bar was bereft of the usual neon signage. If it wasn't for two geriatric gentlemen sitting at the counter, I would have figured the place to be closed. There were many such failed bars all over Patong and in Kata and Karon. They don't usually sit vacant for long. Too many optimistic farang with money to burn looking to open up shop. Maybe they're looking to start a new life. Maybe they're looking to move closer to their favorite bar girl. Maybe they're looking for the same thing I was looking for — a peaceful, simple existence.

I noticed a girl sitting at one of the high tables along the edge of the bar facing outward. She was resting her head in her hand and staring down at her phone. She looked out of place and appeared completely disinterested in her surroundings. She was beautiful. Smoky good looks, like a Thai Michelle Pfeiffer. The Michelle Pfeiffer from "Scarface." I passed in front of her, and she didn't even notice. I was headed for Crystal Bar but made a mental note to circle back later. It was still early in the evening, and I doubted she'd be around later. Some dude was bound to pick her up, but I'd promised the hulking katoi of a mamasan at Crystal Bar that I'd return to buy her another round of drinks.

Ice had her arms around the same guy from the previous night. I took a seat at the bar and she joined me for a drink, while her male friend eyed us very closely. Then she challenged me to a game of pool. There was no mention of all the lovey-dovey text messages we'd exchange the year before. There was no need. It was just one of billions of sparks that failed to ignite in the lonely campfire night. A slow fade into harmless flirtation.

She racked up the balls, and I broke. Then, grinning mischievously, she proceeded to run the table on me. I missed shot after shot. I was shocked. A year ago, I had to show her how to hold the pool cue while I explained that the white ball was used to hit the other balls into the pocket.

We played a few more games with her winning every one of them and rarely missing a shot. She had evolved into quite the hustler. No longer was she the naive country girl I had known the year before. Her makeup looked better — it wasn't just caked on like before. I noticed, too, that her style of dress had improved. The baggy jeans shorts were replaced with a slinky black skirt, and in place of the plain loose-fitting blouse, she now wore a low-cut top with a bra that amplified her modest cleavage. She didn't have much to work with but that to me was part of her charm.

I bought her a drink for each game she'd won and ordered myself another rum and Coke with a bottle of Singha.

She tilted her head. "Why you drink like that?"

"Like what?"

"You drink rum and beer together. Nobody else does that." She giggled, then downed her three shots like it was water.

I shrugged. "How's your boy?" I asked.

She had an eight-year-old son in Hua Hin that her mother was helping to raise. Many girls working the bars out here usually had a kid or a husband or a boyfriend back home waiting for the girls to send them money. A strange twist on the matriarchal society model.

"He doing good. He get all fours in school," she said, holding up four fingers.

I assumed getting all fours was the equivalent of getting straight A's.

After a while, she returned to her new boyfriend, who was frowning now and giving her the stink eye. I was left alone, content with sitting by myself and enjoying my drink, quietly watching everything going on around me.

It felt good to be back in Patong. It felt good to be by myself. It felt good to BE myself.

The first step in finding yourself is to get lost. Hopelessly, stupidly lost. Pick a spot on the map and buy a plane ticket for that destination. Every journey is a journey of self-discovery. Unless you're one of the bland personalities who prefer to visit Disneyland year after year, who choose to believe the infantile marketing ploy that it's the "happiest place on earth."

If Bangkok served as my base camp whenever I traveled to Southeast Asia, then Patong had become my own personal Disneyland. Maybe it was time to move on. Had I seen all there was to see in Patong? Was there anything more to it than sitting around on beaches, sitting around in restaurants, sitting around in bars? Was there anything more than just drinking and fuckin' around every night? Like Disneyland, as with anything else within the confines of this decaying three-dimensional time/space continuum, you begin to see through the illusion. The thin facade begins to peel away, and you discover once again that you are staring at yourself in a mirror. Self meeting self, as Edgar Cayce used to say.

—

A concern came suddenly into my mind which began to plague me: Where do all the turds go?

Thousands of gallons of raw sewage flushed through Patong's pipes every day. Fecal matter pinched out the bungholes of a hundred different nations. Human waste laced with toxins and chemicals — steroids, antibiotics, anti-fungal ointments, birth control, menstrual runoff. Green curry diarrhea from a billion Indian dudes. Pus-colored vomit of drunken Australian hard-ons and their sheilas. Various types of medication and myriad other kinds of prescription drugs. More and more fecal matter and human waste. This time leaking from the anuses of half a million Chinese tourists. They arrived in ten bus loads just the other day, dumped off along Patong Beach and left to forage for crabs and dried seaweed along the shore.

Where does it all go, there along this tiny little town along the Andaman Sea? They surely must have installed some kind of sewage treatment facility somewhere on the island? I couldn't imagine where. Patong sits at the bottom of a mountain on three sides. I cringe when I think of all that raw sewage being flushed directly into the ocean. Where else can it go? They're killing all the manatees. The bloated corpses are washing up along its shores with increasing frequency. What to do, what to do? It's either the sea cows or the millions of tourist dollars brought in by Instagram influencers, Youtube vloggers, and geriatric sex fiends.

Meanwhile, the bar girls still have kids to feed and boyfriends to take care of. The rent isn't going to pay itself.

—

Before heading back to my room, I swung by the bar I spotted earlier near the back of the plaza. There was the girl I'd seen earlier — still sitting in the same spot by herself, staring down at her phone, still oblivious to everything going on around her.

I took a seat at one of the bar stools directly opposite of her.

"Sawadee," I said. "I buy you drink?"

She looked up from her phone, surprised. She hesitated as if she didn't understand.

I made like I was holding an invisible bottle of beer and titled it toward my lips.

"Drink?" I said.

She nodded, then pointed to herself, questioning.

"Yes, drink for you, too," I said.

Despite the fact it was well after midnight, and the other bars nearby were getting a little loud and rowdy, this place was mostly empty except for the two elderly gentlemen who were still seated at the bar.

She returned with our drinks, and then we sat awkwardly for a few minutes trying to engage in conversation. She spoke very little English, and I spoke even less Thai. With the help of Google Translate, I learned that her name was Leni, and she arrived in Patong two weeks ago. Both lies, I assumed.

She was bored, she said. No customers. She wanted to go home and get some sleep.

"So go home," I said.

"Cannot. Have to wait until closing time."

"How much is your bar fine?" I asked.

She perked up at this. But she wasn't sure. She got up and went to speak to the mamasan. She returned a moment later and typed a number on her phone. She held it up for me to see: "$1,000."

"Okay," I said and slipped her a thousand-baht note.

She thanked me, wai'ing deeply. I got up to leave.

"I go home, too," I said, making a sleeping gesture with my head in my hands. "I very sleepy."

She looked surprised that I was leaving.

"Wait," she said, "I go with you."

"No, no. It's okay. I go home sleep."

As tempted as I was, I really just wanted to go back to my room and get some sleep. We exchanged numbers, and I told her I'd come back to see her tomorrow.

I walked back to my hotel, wondering why someone as attractive as her was working in that empty, hole-in-the-wall bar. If she worked at one of the busier spots, she'd have guys crawling all over her. Then she wouldn't be feeling so bored and sleepy, although she might be feeling a little sore in the morning.

My morning routine whenever I'm in Patong, or when I'm anywhere with a decent beach, is to go for a swim before the crowds of tourists arrive, which usually means getting to the beach at around eight or nine. I'll swim for an hour or so before getting something to eat at one of the food carts lined up along the beach or at one of the hotels across the street.

And so I begin each day in a relaxed and peaceful state of mind. There's something about swimming in the ocean that washes away the positive and negative charges leaving me in a state of complete neutrality. I care, and yet I don't care. I am a part of the world, yet completely detached from it. Floating on my back in the warm ocean, all emotion and anxiety are washed away by the gently lapping waves.

It took me many years, a number of failed relationships, and one failed marriage to realize how overly judgmental and opinionated I was. Maybe I was the product of growing up in an alcoholic household. Maybe it was the result of a constant exposure to Western media and 24/7 cable TV news and opinions. Or maybe I was simply an asshole. Some defect inherent in my nature. Nobody to blame but myself.

Whatever the reason, lazily bobbing around like a rotting corpse in the warm ocean beneath a glaring sun will eradicate whatever negative energy you've been holding onto. All your bitter thoughts, your petty jealousies, your pointless worrying about job titles and paychecks and credit card bills coming due. The sun-heated saltwater washes all of it away, wipes the slate clean. It's as if you'd been given a fresh new start, but really what you've been given is a fresh new perspective. You come staggering and stumbling out of the water, trudging through the wet sand (there's no graceful way to walk back to your beach towel), the late morning sun blinding you in the face, and you have nothing but complete, unconditional love for the world. You have glimpsed the true nature of reality and suddenly awaken to the fact that you no longer give a shit. About anyone. About anything.

When I got back to my room, I saw that I had a text message from Leni, the girl from the night before.

The water in her room wasn't working, and the manager said it would be a few days before it would be repaired. She asked if she could come to my room to use the shower.

This was a first for me. Here was an interesting opportunity. Or a giant red flag. This had to be a scam or some kind of set up.

She was texting me in Thai, and my responses were delayed as I copied and pasted her message into the Google Translate app and tried to figure out what she was saying. Then I had to type my response and translate that before cutting and pasting it into the messaging window and hitting send.

At first, I wasn't even sure how to respond. When a woman as attractive as Leni and oozing raw, animalistic sexuality asks if she can come over to use the shower, the obvious answer if you're a red-blooded straight male is to respond immediately with "YES!"

But there were other considerations to keep in mind. There's hooking up, and then there's hooking up in Thailand. There is a distinction, just as there is between "girlfriend" and "vacation girlfriend." Bar girls in Thailand possess a keen awareness of where they stand within that spectrum. Some will try to milk you for every baht you've got. Others, not so much.

In my own limited experience, however, Thai girls are nowhere near as ruthless or cutthroat as their Latin American counterparts in Mexico or Costa Rica. I suspect it has as much to do with religious and cultural influences as it does with global socio-economics and human trafficking. The languid concepts of Buddhist reincarnation and karma are much more forgiving to the sinful individual than, say, centuries of Azten bloodlust for human sacrifice and decades of vengeful and constantly warring drug cartels leaving decapitated heads along roadsides or hanging from freeway overpasses like so many milestone markers. This sort of shit will certainly have an impact on your cosmic outlook on life. It's an alien jungle in Latin America, and even the women smell a little....different down there.

But I'd been laid, and I was still feeling beat-up from the way things ended with Chaiya in Hat Yai. I wasn't ready for another entanglement with another Thai woman. Such a bizarre request from someone you'd just met the night before, to come use the shower.

I texted back and said that I had to meet a friend for lunch in Kata in a few hours, which was true — I had made plans with Jintana the night before to meet for lunch. She wanted to take me to a seafood place in Rawai.

Leni texted, "Do you have another woman?"

"No," I replied, "Just a friend. She owns a bar in Kata. I'll be back later this afternoon."

"Okay, I will wait. I'm very hot and sweaty, and I haven't bathed since yesterday."

I could appreciate how uncomfortable her situation must have been, assuming she was telling the truth and not setting me up for a scam. In Thailand, it's not uncommon to take two or three showers a day, especially during the hot season. But I wasn't about to drop everything and change my plans for a bar girl I'd only met the night before. Something didn't make sense.

———

I met up with Jintana and, not surprisingly, a few of her bar girl friends a short while later in front of her bar in the blinding white heat of a noonday sun. She'd recruited her bartender to be our driver for the day, and he picked us up in a late-model Toyota RAV 4. He looked like a Thai version of Brian May, the lead guitarist for Queen — tall and lanky, and with a head of frizzy permed hair that grew just past his shoulders. When he was working, busy mixing drinks, slicing lemons and limes, and stocking the freezer with beer, he kept mostly to himself and remained in the background, while the girls plied their trade with customers. Driving us in the car, it was a different story — he couldn't stop talking. He spoke near-perfect English, contrary to my earlier assumption. His Thai accent was barely noticeable. When I mentioned this to him, he said he owed it to having lived the past twenty-five years in Patong.

———

On our way to Rawai, we stopped at the Makro market to buy the ingredients for our lunch, including whatever fish and other seafood we planned to eat. Evidently, you bring the stuff to the restaurant, and they'll prepare it for you. Before today, I had no idea this was a thing. Jintana took the lead and picked out all the food. It was about ten pounds worth of fish and shellfish, which came to around $1,300 baht. The restaurant bill after everything was prepared came to around $2,000 baht. So $90 to $100USD for five people. Twenty bucks a person. Jintana says the restaurant gave us the locals' discount. I wonder how much it would have cost if we were a group of farangs?

—

The whole time we were out, Jintana made it clear to the other girls that I was with her. If we were walking somewhere, she'd rush up to my side and grab hold of my hand. When we were being seated at the restaurant, she motioned me to come sit next to her, instructing the other girls to scoot over. And when the food was brought out, and with each subsequent dish, she prepared my plate for me, making sure that I got the first serving. I was made to feel like a guest of honor. Or a king. I appreciated the gesture, but I felt a little awkward. I thought I was just meeting a friend for lunch, not attending some sort of pre-wedding ceremony.

When lunch was over, and her bartender dropped us off across the street from her bar, I got out with the other girls and was about to order a Grab ride back to my hotel, but Jintana told me to get back in the car. She and the bartender would drive me back to Patong.

"I want to see where you're staying," she said.

I took that to mean she wanted to come up to my room and spend a little time with me. But no — she literally just wanted to see what hotel I was staying at.

No problem.

We hugged and said good-bye. She had to rush home and get ready for work.

Leni texted me when I got back to my room. I had completely forgotten about her. The water at her hotel was still out, and she still wanted to use my shower. It was later afternoon, and she had to get ready for work.

Sure, I said. Not sure what I was getting into. This would interfere with my nap time.

She texted me a few minutes later from the lobby. I almost didn't recognize her, seeing that I'd only just met her the night before. She was wearing a pink baseball cap pulled down over her ears. It was a few sizes too large for her tiny head. Without makeup, she looked simultaneously older yet younger. She came shuffling toward me like a bag lady with her purse and small bag of clothes. She huddled close to me as we rode the elevator up to my room. Was she embarrassed? Humiliated?

"Sawadee," I smiled, wrapping an arm around her shoulder and giving her a little hug.

It was unfair to make any comparisons, but she didn't possess the same confidence and poise that Chaiya possessed, but perhaps this revealed more about Chaiya than Leni.

When Chaiya first stayed with me at the Hotel Clover, she seemed to know where everything was. She moved with familiar ease around the room, like someone who'd spent a fair amount of time in such places. Leni, by contrast, had difficulty working the little pocket sliding door to the bathroom. She managed to lock herself in when she went to shower, and I had to help her figure out the latching system.

I waited on the bed while she got herself ready. I wasn't about to make the first move. I wasn't going to try anything with her, except be a perfect gentleman. She wanted to use the shower, and I was only doing her that one favor. That was it. End of story. She didn't owe me anything. If she came out of that bathroom fully dressed with her purse dangling from her arm, then so be it. I'd walk her down to the lobby and bid her a good afternoon. Maybe I'd see her at the bar later that evening and buy her another drink.

When she finally emerged, she was wearing the hotel bathrobe, all soft and white.

"Feel better?" I asked.

She smiled and slipped under the covers, snuggling next to me. Slowly, she slid her leg across mine. I could feel the warmth of her pussy against my thigh, and I realized she was completely naked under that robe.

—

Traffic was a mess. I couldn't get anywhere. People were missing flights because they couldn't find a taxi to take them to the airport. Tuk-tuks, motor scooters, and minivans lined the main beach road, stuck in permanent gridlock. Nothing with an engine was moving. If you wanted to get anywhere, you had to walk.

I don't remember the Songkran Festivals from previous years being this bad. Officials announced that this year's festival would be a three-day celebration. We were in Day 2, and I had grown weary of buckets of ice water being dumped over my head and getting blasted in the face with water pistols. It was fun the first day. The water was a pleasant respite from the April heat. But now — going into Day 2 and stretching into Day 3 — enough already! I understood now why Chaiya wrinkled her nose when I asked her if she celebrated Songkran.

"It's for kids," she said. "And tourists."

But Leni was game. She had texted me saying she wanted to have lunch and partake in the water fights. I was near the end of my vacation and feeling a little lazy and burned out. Returning from the beach each morning, I would spend the remainder of the day lazing about my hotel room, watching Youtube videos on my phone and taking naps. I didn't really feel like going out or being part of a couple. I didn't feel like doing "couple" things. I wasn't looking for another vacation girlfriend, and I didn't want to be anyone's boyfriend.

One of the reasons I'd been returning to Thailand year after year was to conduct research and find a place to retire. Ostensibly. At least, that's what I'd been telling everyone.

My retirement plan was little more than a vague idea. A pipe dream. It was just something I blurted out whenever someone asked why I liked to spend so much time in Thailand. I had no plan. All I knew is that I would need to find a cheap place to rent, preferably within walking distance to a beach. And before I could do even that, I would need to have some kind of income stream established, preferably something of the passive variety, as the so-called experts advise. This passive income would need to be in the neighborhood of $2,000 to $3,000USD per month.

This was the extent of my "retirement planning." That, and watching a bunch of Youtube videos on the subject.

Of course, as soon as my flight touched down at Suvarnabhumi Airport, all of my so-called retirement planning went down that vacuum-flushed airplane toilet. I forgot all about retirement and went into wild-eyed tourist mode focused on living in the moment. Whatever thoughts I had about the future were thus confined to deciding what I was going to eat or drink and with whom later that evening. My energy went into spending money in real-time, in the Now. And then a month later, waves of guilt would come crashing over me as I realized that I had spent another four or five grand. Another month wasted.

Perhaps "wasted" is too strong a word. Maybe better to say another month spent in extreme leisure. Spending all of my money instead of saving it. No closer to retirement. I would have to fly back home and return to my office job. Make more money until the next time.

These thoughts floated through my mind while I waited for Leni in the plaza outside Jungceylon mall. Songkran celebrations were in full swing, and I stood off to the side as tourists and families with young children splashed each other with water guns on the dangerously slippery marble tile floor. How many people have slipped and cracked their heads open on those sharp tile steps over the years? I'd already seen a number of people slip on the wet pavement and land hard on their tailbones. Those cheap "Made in China" flip-flops with the hard plastic soles that they sell in all the touristy trinket shops offer very little traction on slippery ground.

Six months earlier, I slipped on a puddle of milk I'd spilled in the kitchen and tore a ligament in my right knee. The injury hadn't completely healed, and my doctor warned that it might never feel the same again. The discomfort came and went depending on how much walking I'd done on a given day. I developed the habit of being particularly mindful when walking across wet pavement, stepping carefully and walking flat-footed. Now when I see older people hobbling and limping around, struggling to get where they need to go on their own two feet, I understand their struggle.

Here I stand on the threshold gazing from middle-age into old age. In another year, I'll be fifty-five. Does Denny's still offer discounts for senior citizens? I didn't feel old. In my mind, I still identify with my 35-year-old self. Just a little grayer and about twenty pounds heavier.

Okay, maybe thirty pounds heavier.

Contrary to the popular notion that Thai women, like Thais in general, operate on "Thai time" and are almost always late to lunch or dinner dates, the few acquaintances with whom I made appointments to meet were without exception always punctual.

From May, who used military time when scheduling our trysts: "I will meet you at 20:00 ka."

To Chaiya, who texted her real-time locations while she was on her way to meet me at my hotel: "I'm leaving my room....I walking down Bangla [here, she attached a photo of a random bar]....I'm two minutes away....I'm downstairs."

Or when Ice texted me and asked if I was still interested in eating at a Thai restaurant I had mentioned to her the night before.

I responded, "Yes," and she responded a few minutes later, "I have arrived."

"Arrived?" I texted back. I thought she had meant later that evening. "You're at the restaurant?"

"Yes," she replied, "I am here now."

Leni was no exception. She texted me a "good morning" and a string of kissy-face emojis when she awoke. Then she texted she was going to shower and get ready. She was giving off strong girlfriend vibes. Like a true professional. Although, she was coming off a little clingy with her nonstop texting. I couldn't tell if this was part of her game. She appeared happy and cheerful whenever we met up. She brought with her a new kind of energy, a new love affair — but it felt to me like we were already near the end. Feeling burned out and running low on cash — I needed to be alone for a little while. Patong was the wrong place to be if you had any plans of retreating into isolation.

I would be flying back to Bangkok within a few days before continuing homeward, but here in Patong is where the party would come to an end, during the Songkran Festival. I appreciated the festive atmosphere — I just didn't feel a part of it.

Leni texted me promptly at one o'clock, our agreed upon meeting time.

"Where are you?" she asked. She was texting in Thai, and I had to use the Google Translate app on my phone to translate her message. Then I'd type my response in English and translate that into Thai, and then text it back to her. To think a decade ago, I would not have been able to have this conversation with her, much less any kind of relationship. (Can there be any real intimacy without clear and open communication?) There would be no way of communicating with Leni at all except through hand signals and rude gestures.

"I'm on the Bangla Road side," I replied. "Where are you?"

She responded with a photo of the bottom half of a random shop sign with the caption, "I'm here."

I had no idea where "here" was. This is what Chaiya used to do on our first few dates. We would agree to meet on Bangla Road. I'd ask her where she was, and she would respond with a one-second video clip of her feet and the ground immediately in front of her, "I'm here."

Were all Thai women like this? I wasn't born with a GPS receiver in my head. My brain did not have the ability to triangulate physical locations based on vague photos or one-second video clips.

Leni finally found me and we went upstairs for lunch at the Pizza Company, who probably make the best pepperoni pizza in all of Thailand. It was our second time eating there (my fifth time, personally), and it had sort of become "our" place. Again, with the new couple vibes. I was feeling even more numb and out of whack. But the pepperoni pizza remains one of the best I've eaten.

Afterward, Leni took my hand and pulled me toward Bangla Road, where we purchased colorful plastic pump-action water rifles from one of the many vendors that had set up shop along the already crowded sidewalks. The shop proprietor allowed us to load our guns free of charge in a barrel of ice water specifically for that purpose. Later on, it would cost us ten baht to reload at the ice water barrels in front of the other bars.

We waded into the dense crowd of Songkran celebrants, blasting away with our water guns. By the time we made it to the beach side of Bangla Road, we were both drenched. Along the beach, vendors had set up rows of food carts beneath large white canopies. We wandered around for a little while and worked our way to the far end where they were selling T-shirts and trinkets and Chinese knock-offs of brand name purses and sneakers.

Leni poked around but wasn't interested in any of it. She didn't seem to be much of a shopper, much to my relief. She tugged at my arm and indicated that she wanted to turn back.

"You want to eat?" I said.

She grunted, shaking her head, "No, no." She pointed back towards Bangla Road.

The language barrier had me feeling like I was trying to communicate with a deaf mute. Leni likely felt the same, the both of us grunting and making hand gestures at each other. It was too tedious to have to use the Google Translate app every time.

I let her lead me back into the water-fighting hordes. We went in blasting, but not before filling up at the nearest barrel of ice water and paying the ten-baht fee.

Leni was into it. Me, not so much. I was weary of the crowds and the water. She had taken on the role of wild-eyed tourist, and I had become the jaded and grumpy local. To be honest, it was refreshing to be with someone who was living in the moment and enjoying herself.

With the water-fighting, she gave as much as she was getting it. It was mostly men who were paying particular attention to her, I noticed, unsurprisingly — aiming for her nether regions or her chest area.

And there were school-age children running around, uncharacteristic for a street known for its nightlife and sex workers. Most of these kids belonged to the girls who worked in the clubs. "Bring Your Child to Work" day, Thai style. When one of the little runts popped up and shot us with water, Leni bent down and gently squirted them in the belly. She had three children of her own whom she'd left in the care of her elderly mother back in Chumphon.

Afterward, I took her shopping at Jungceylon mall. As I'd mentioned, she wasn't much of a shopper. She wandered aimlessly from store to store, seemingly uninterested in anything they had to offer. Finally, she settled on a department store and picked up a few things. One of the store clerks began following us around, guiding Leni toward the pricier items. When it became clear that Leni had had enough and was showing signs of mild annoyance, the cashier ushered her to the nearest register to ring her up.

The total for a pair of jean shorts, a baseball cap, and a few tops came to just over fifteen-thousand baht.

Leni gasped when she saw the amount flash on the cash register display. She shook her head violently and motioned to the clerk to put the stuff back.

The clerk smiled and calmly replied, trying to address Leni's concerns. I'm not sure exactly what they were saying — they were going back and forth in Thai. The clerk nodded toward me at one point as if to say, "Don't worry about the cost, sister. The farang will pay for it."

Leni was shaking her head, "No, no, no."

"What's going on?" I said.

Leni took out her phone and quickly typed something in the Google Translate app.

She held her phone up for me to see: "Too expensive. I'd rather have the cash to give to my children."

"It's okay," I said, waving her off, and handed my credit card to the cashier. "I give you more later."

Spoken like a true two-week millionaire, recklessly throwing himself thousands of dollars into credit card debt.

I had promised Jintana that I'd pay her another visit at her bar before flying back to Bangkok, but the Songkran Festival wouldn't let up. We were now in Day Three of what I didn't know at the time would morph into an unofficial four-day celebration. Thai officials had decided to literally shut the country down just so children and tourists could engage in water fights in the streets.

I couldn't get a taxi or tuk-tuk anywhere. Patong's main roads, all three of them, were stuck in perpetual gridlock since the celebration began. Most of the taxi and tuk-tuk drivers shook their heads and waved me off when I asked for a ride to Kata.

"There is no way."

"Cannot."

"Too much traffic."

"It will take two hours."

I approached a group of tuk-tuk drivers loitering at the curb and asked if one of them could take me to Kata. They all pretended to ignore me at first, and when I asked again, one of the guys scoffed and held up four fingers.

"Four thousand," he said, tilting his chin up like he was challenging me to a fight. Then he turned his back to me and resumed chatting with his friends. The usual rate was four hundred baht, one-way to Kata or Karon.

Meanwhile, Jintana was texting and asking if I was still planning to see her. It was nothing romantic, however much she liked to play it up. She had a business to run and had to work every angle. I'd spent a considerable amount of money at her bar buying drinks for her and the girls. I'd become a reliable income stream, like her other regulars, unlike the usual flotsam and jetsam tourists who came and went, never to be seen again.

But I couldn't find a way to get over the hill to her place. The roads were a sea of shining tail lights. Finally, I convinced an old tuk-tuk driver to give it a try, but only after I'd offer to pay him two thousand baht for his troubles, as if the extra bit of cash would magically make the traffic disappear. I hopped into the back of his vehicle and off we went.

We made little progress. After an hour of sitting in the back of that tuk-tuk and breathing exhaust fumes from all the other vehicles, we'd barely made it out of Patong and up the hill. I tapped on the rear window and motioned for the driver to turn back. He nodded, then signalled for me to come up and join him in the cab where he had the A/C blasting nice and cold.

Another hour later, I was back at OTOP Plaza. I stopped by the bar where Leni worked and found her with her head resting in her hand, staring at her phone and looking bored. The place was empty as usual except for the same two geriatric gentlemen sitting at the bar.

She smiled when she saw me and immediately got up to fetch me a beer. I told her to get one for herself and one for the mamasan, who had materialized out of nowhere in time for me to buy her a drink.

"Sawadee," said mamasan, smiling like a lizard.

My last evening in Patong was a quiet one. I paid Leni's bar fine, so she could leave a little early. The rule in her club, like with other clubs, was that regardless of bar fines, the girls had to remain in the club until midnight. Leni wanted me to wait for her, but I was tired and didn't feel like hanging around. She wanted to come back with me to my room and see me off at the airport the next day, but I lied and told her I had an early flight in the morning and wanted to call it an early night. She was comfortable and easy to be around, and we were cozy in bed together. I didn't have to work at it like I did with Chaiya, which felt a lot like chipping away at a twenty-ton block of ice. And sadly, there wasn't much point to getting any more involved with Leni than I already was. Nearing the end of my vacation, I doubted if I'd see her again.

Surely Leni, like other bar girls, has played this game before. They've seen plane loads of two-week millionaires come and go. They have the script perfected and share it amongst themselves, passing it down from girl to girl over the years, a kind of bar girl oral history. When it's time to play the end-game, there may or may not be feelings involved, but as with any true professional, their eyes are trained on the money. The request for financial assistance might not come on your day of departure, but it will come. Give it a few days. Maybe a week.

With Leni, it came a few days after I got home. She began sending me photos of storefronts with "For Lease" signs out front.

"I want to open shop," she texted.

"Okay," I said.

"It will cost $65,000THB, but I don't have. Can you help me please?"

I responded with a laughing emoji.

It wasn't really a scam, but it definitely was a hustle. As long as you recognize it for what it is — no harm, no foul.

With minimal education and scant job prospects, the girls are doing what they can to earn a living. Some get lucky and land a wealthy farang. Even luckier if the guy happens to be relatively decent looking and not more than sixty years old. Not many girls are looking to be nursemaids, and fewer still are willing to do diaper duty.

The fortunate ones will post photos of their latest catch all over social media.

She is happy. She is content. She has found love. Her financial future is secure.

For the others who are not so fortunate or attractive — well, they will continue working in the bars and buying lottery tickets from the old lady who comes by on her rusted old bicycle wielding a large wooden board with batches of tickets stuck to it until they themselves are the old lady's age, and then they'll start putting together a plan to open up a restaurant selling tom yum and pad kra pao to tourists who are yearning for that authentic Thai experience. All they need is a small investment — $30,000 baht, $50,000 baht. That should be enough to get them started.

You can't fault the girls for hitting up their farang boyfriends for cash. It's all part of the game, like a child who finds himself at a toy store — of course the kid is going to ask his parents to buy him something.

It was the dance in general that I had grown weary of. The back and forth exchange of pointless flirtation and pretend petty jealousies. I was tired of the Songkran crowds and endless hordes of tourists. No longer possessing the energy to converse with strangers with little more than a grunt or a nod, I fought the urge to retreat to my room and hide out those last remaining days.

Leni had been around, I could tell, but she was an overall decent person. I trusted her to the extent that I knew I could leave her alone in my room while I went for my morning swim and come back a few hours later and still find her there along with all of my belongings. Slowly, she would awaken purring and stretching, naked beneath the sheets. She was difficult to resist in that still-dreamy, sensuous, fuck-me-in-the-morning mood.

I was careful not to lead her on. When she had asked me who I was going to see in Kata, I told her about Jintana and her bar. Later, when she began showing signs of jealousy and asking me if I had other women, I told her that I was talking to a few, but nothing serious. I failed to mention that I was still married. In my mind, for all intents and purposes, I wasn't. Although my wife and I still lived under the same roof, we had been sleeping in separate rooms for nearly a decade. The gravity of health insurance coverage and maintaining mortgage payments, all of which were still in both of our names, just made it easier to remain in each other's orbit. I doubt many people would understand, and perhaps even a few might cast a skeptic's eye on our situation, but it was an arrangement that worked and with little effort. We both were happily content living together as roommates. If you don't believe me, feel free to ask my wife for her take on the matter. I'll leave it at that for now.

—

Even after I'd left her in that dingy hotel room in Hat Yai, Chaiya and I still kept in touch. She texted me every day, usually when she awoke in the morning and again before she went to bed.

Throughout her day, she'd send pics of what she was up to at her mom's place, some city in far southern Thailand whose name I can never remember, somewhere near the Malaysian border.

As I had promised her, I sent her money to help cover the time she took off from her nightclub job so she could come traveling with me through Vietnam. She had initially asked for $35,000 baht, but I gave her $60,000 (roughly $1,700USD). I didn't care. I was still flush with cash leftover from our home remodeling project. How often do you get to live like a king and spread around some of that temporary wealth? The money comes and goes in cycles, like the seasons. The next time around may not be so easy. Better enjoy it while you can.

Despite what happened between us, I didn't want to just leave her hanging. She was the sole provider for her son and elderly mother. She wasn't an evil person, and I don't think she had intentionally set out to hurt me. The chemistry between us just wasn't working. I'm not sure there was ever any chemistry to begin with. Maybe our entire relationship was just one prolonged hustle. More of a "working" relationship from her perspective. My emotions and judgment when I first met her three years ago might very well have been influenced from being in Thailand for the first time.

Here in the Land of Smiles, I had fallen under its spell. Everything was exciting and new. The people were friendly. The food was delicious. Everything was so goddamned affordable. I was bewitched and perplexed. This is the beauty of travel. You awake each day grinning stupidly, and you say to yourself, "What's next?" You cannot wait to see what lies ahead. What new things are there to do and see? Every step you take is literally a spot on the earth in that precise location that you are touching for the very first time. Every street is an unexplored street.

This fourth time around, however, I was seeing things with a clearer eye. My jaded, cynical self was beginning to peek around some of those street corners.

I can spot a come-on from bar girls before they can finish saying "Sawadee! You buy me drink?"

I detect the slightest smirk on a tuk-tuk driver's face when he asks if I came here alone. The presumption to that seemingly innocent question, of course, is that I came here to molest their women.

$1,000 Thai baht begins to feel like $1,000 Thai baht and not like $30USD. You can't go dropping it like $1 dollar tips at every restaurant or bar. Not unless you want to fly home wearing little more than trash bag overalls and Made in China flip-flops.

But where is home?

This once foreign land was no longer so foreign to me. With each subsequent visit it was beginning to feel more and more — like home.

— END —

about the author

Slacker. Tech burnout. Beach bum. Writer. Wanderer. Daydreamer. Taker of naps. Anthony Abelaye was born and raised in the San Francisco Bay Area and later relocated to the suburbs of Dallas, Texas, where he currently lives and writes.

He is the author of "Flea Market Weirdos and Other Stories."
For more information, visit: AnthonyAbelaye.com

Made in the USA
Coppell, TX
12 February 2025

45817606R00138